globalization

Naren Chitty, Editor

SOUTHBOUND
Penang

Published by
Southbound Sdn. Bhd.
Suite 20F, Northam House
55 Jalan Sultan Ahmad Shah
10050 Penang
Malaysia
Fax: 604-228 1758
E-mail: chin@south.pc.my
Internet: http://www.southbound.com.my

Typeset by Chin Kooi Hong
in Baskerville 9.5/11.5 points
Cover design by Adrian Cheah, C-Square Sdn. Bhd.
Pre-press services by Eefar Lithographic Sdn. Bhd., Penang, Malaysia
Printed by Jutaprint, Penang, Malaysia.

Perpustakaan Negara Malaysia Cataloguing-in-Publication Data

Mapping globalization / editor Naren Chitty
ISBN 983-9054-24-4
1. Information technology–Economic aspects.
2. Information technology–Social aspects.
3. International economic integration. I. Chitty, Naren.
338.064

Contents

Word worlds:
Editor's foreword

Naren Chitty

Ware, know-ware and war cultures

Streams of images flash across the screens of our lives, on computers, televisions, the newspapers, our very minds' eyes – depicting the 'real' world. These electronic, mechanical and bio-electric depictions of reality are real in themselves. Mechanically mass produced words and images flooded, in modern times, the world's semioscape, its symbolic reality. The electronic revolution has produced an e-scape which is inflating symbolic reality in an unprecedented way. E-scapes may be spaces where one can escape from other realities, but increasingly there is no escape from e-scape in the post-modem world. I like to give a more evocative name to the e-scape – 'Know-ware Land'. It is Know-ware Land because it is a space distinct from earth-bound geography, the kind of geography where terran gravity, territorial relationships and terrain have no significance. It is nowhere and everywhere. It is the natural habitat for knowledge as a commodity. States and corporations look toward Know-ware Land for new markets, for a new economy. States and non-governmental organizations see Know-ware Land, variously as a new forum for social regulation, policy negotiation and political influence. Like its parallel material Ware Land, grown out of the Industrial Age, Know-ware Land is a place where organizations and individuals exchange values, whether political, economic or cultural.

We inhabit mind-worlds of our own weaving, from threads of experience, experiment and sophistry.

> They are mind worlds because it is in our minds that we experience the world. But mind can be mined through communication and mind-wares can be produced industrially, bought and sold in the marketplace. The world is itself a mind-world because it is filled with mind-wares. Again, the world is a mind-world because mind-wares can also be projections of power and power projects (Chitty 1999, 5).

Know-ware Land is built of representations of reality (the stuff of constructivism) and artistic constructions. The words and images are grounded in post-industrial light and sound, the fabric of telematics.

Technologies for communicating olfactory images are currently under construction. There are resonances between constructivism at the level of the individual, social organizations, including states, non-state actors and international society. International society is an image of the symbolic interaction, within a shared environmental matrix, between states and non-state actors. The context of this political, economic and cultural interaction at the level of international society is what I call the P-matrix (Political-economic matrix). Know-ware Land reflects the P-matrix. Today it is but a reflection of the P-matrix. In the future our intelligence may inhabit Know-ware Land. Know-ware Land reflects the structure of our planetary society. The World Wide Web of interconnectivity and political economic relationships between computer users may be treated as a microcosm of the global political economic matrix, with all that is embedded within. The global political economic matrix, or P-matrix, is in my view the most comprehensive, unified and unifying social structure of contemporary planetary society. It cohabits a space with a physical environmental matrix (N-matrix).

In the contest between war cultures (domination for extraction) and ware cultures (consumption for gratification), the triumph of ware culture is to be applauded. The evolutionary trend toward know-ware culture is desirable.

> The military industrial complex is another legacy of World War II. The five-year mobilization transformed the relationship of government and the defense industry and created the symbiotic partnership that exists today. Before the wartime association there were few issues on which the two partners thought alike. Before the war most businessmen looked upon the military as boondoglers and practitioners of an absolute and barbaric art. Some of the most prominent businessmen, such as Andrew Carnegie and Henry Ford, were commercial pacifists who believed that the salvation of man lay in trade expansion. One day the whole world would become one great market. The choice of America, as they saw it, was between industrial progress and militarism, and the latter they equated with waste (Barnet 1985, 35).

The convergence of military, mercantile and policy elites around convergent technologies of war, ware and know-ware means, of course, that know-ware cultures, as much as ware cultures, can feed on war.

Lexicons of globalization

The first part of this book examines the political and cultural economic frameworks of knowledge society, with particular reference to education, the market and web technology. The matrix framework is discussed in 'Mapping know-ware land', the first chapter, which looks at the continuing need under globalization for employees with critical thinking skills. Sufficient to say here, that the P-matrix is viewed in the framework as imposing a functionalist regulatory order on international systems while also being constructed by human agency, through collective behaviour. In the present international system the regulatory logic is based on the policy goals of political and economic liberalization. At the same time we may note symbolic interactionist responses to policy images from the P-matrix, responses that cumulatively may transform P-matrix orders. The second part of this chapter discusses the dialectic between the roles of technologies of learning as media and as message.

If cybernetics is, in the Ampèrian sense, *the science of government,* is the cybernet government by science, positivist science? In 'Island in the stream', McKenzie Wark discusses the ontology of cyberspace and information technology's transformation of power relations in Australia. He notes the information proletarianization of those locked out of the new Brahman caste. Ware culture is pervasive.

As suggested by Weber, the Protestant ethic is no longer necessary after capitalist bureaucracies have taken root. Richard J. Barnet and others wrote about the military-industrial complex (Barnet, 35). In 'Hypertext, capitalism and military history', Belinda Barnet discusses the nexus between hypertext and *the machines of global capital and military science.*

Scott Shaner, in 'Webs of convergence', discusses how the Wild Web is being tamed by the webward expansion of commerce, through the kind of content structuration used in the larger media marketplace. A process of genrelization and portalization has commenced, making website form and location, respectively, more predictable.

The mind-world each of us inhabits continues to be constructed by overlapping mind-worlds projected by culture, religion, science, experience, media, government, corporations. In the cinematic fantasy, *The Matrix*, this multiple world is shown to be a shared computer-generated fantasy for battery-fed humans being readied for the robots' abbatoir and table. One might argue that the robots were infinitely more humane than we are in relation to our own battery-fed poultry. In 'Peter Weir's transnational aesthetic' Adam Knee describes the televisual fantasy of an individual's mind-world having been staged by a corporation.

International media and the crisis of identity

Part Two begins with 'Satellite television and new subjectivities', wherein Hart Cohen discusses the misfit between new communication technologies (NCT) and old ideas of sovereignty in an Indonesian context. NCTs are viewed as nodes around which new temporary subjectivities congeal. International media are wormholes through which P-matrix world constructions pour out into ethno-historical spaces (E-matrix) and into the fields of perception of individuals. Cohen argues that as new identities, ethnicities and media emerge, there needs to be a negotiation of global-local relations and media representation.

Addressing the formation of new subjectivities in India, Melissa Butcher examines the market and satellite generated youth culture in 'An imagined community of youth'. In addition to looking at the work of image-mongers, she looks at the impact of images on identity formation and the role of the audience, via the (reductionist?) voice of corporate research, in the construction of the media landscape.

In 'Globalization of film and television', Stephen McElhinney seeks to gain a true understanding of visual media consumption by Thai and Australian youth by investigating *both the systems and supports for supply and those which shape demand and consumption*. He examines the content preferences of 12 to 14 year olds in urban and rural sites in Australia and Thailand.

Yong Zhong undertakes an ethnographic study of 'Alternative uses of Chinese television and alternative passages to power', examining the response of viewers to programs broadcast by official Chinese television. He questions Stuart Hall's premise of readers as producers of meanings and Fiske's notion of preferred readings as tending to obscure a more prevalent *homogenizing logic of the financial economy of television*.

In 'Transnational communication', Anura Goonasekera examines the national and international policy consequences of new subjectivity-forming international media. In particular he is interested in the emerging WTO-driven trade-related transnational communication regime.

In 'Social distance in the different contexts: A Japanese case', Momoyo Shibuya unveils her study of the Japanese Press in Australia and Singapore. Here Japanese social distance (in particular, ethnic distance) is examined comparatively in two different administrative matrices (A-matrices), Singapore and Australia. Ethnic Japanese press in the two A-matrices are analysed comparatively for this purpose.

Reporting crises

In 'Migrant workers: Myth or reality?', Suda Ishida undertakes a case study of news narrative in selected Thai newspapers during the Asian economic crisis. Adopting a qualitative textual analysis of news and features, the study examines the coverage of migrant workers by two leading Thai newspapers, in an 18-month period beginning in January 1998. Here we are looking at P-matrix effects (migrant workers, Asian economic crisis, globalisation) on the Thai A-matrix, as well as Thai E-matrix effects as reflected in organs of the Thai A-matrix.

Jan Servaes and Patchanee Malikhao undertake a content analysis of 'Thailand in the *International Herald Tribune*'. In contrast with the Ishida chapter this one looks at the reflection, within a P-matrix organ, of the Thai A-matrix during much of the same period covered by Ishida.

In 'Thailand's economic crisis and its effects', Sripan Rattikalchalakorn looks at how local Thai opinion leaders, in the three functional areas of education, tourism and mass communication, viewed the crisis in terms of an opportunity for drawing on the Thai E-matrix in order to learn how not to repeat mistakes in the A-matrix on dealing with the P-matrix.

In a challenging bookend to this volume, "Covering the 'New World Order'", Bruce Allen examines recent internationally reported crises in order to identify shortcomings in reporting. He notes inadequacies in relation to provision of geographical, social, political and economic background information. A former broadcaster, Allen provides some useful suggestions to television broadcasters on mapping crises.

Papers by Allen, Barnett, Butcher, Cohen, Goonasekera, McElhinney, Shaner, Wark, Knee, and Zhong were first presented at an International Conference organized by the Macquarie University Centre for International Communication. This volume celebrates a decade of growth in the International Communication Program.

References

Barnet, Richard J. (1985) *Roots of war*. England: Penguin Books.

Chitty, Naren. (1999) 'Introduction' in *The Journal of International Communication*. 6:1 (June 1999), pp.5-6.

Part One

Lexicons of globalization

Mapping
Know-ware Land

Naren Chitty

As the market's influence on policy and as a shaper of knowledge wares grows, the role of universities as developers of thinking critical to the information revolution gains importance. There is a tendency to overlook important customers in the information marketplace. This chapter maps the information marketplace with respect to media and information technology (MIT) education and recommends an educational strategy for particular MIT education vendors, viz universities.

Mapping Know-ware Land

Framing the market

The information age has many characteristics. An important one is that the 'business of communication' has graduated in the business world from being merely 'communication of business' to occupying a central place as 'business of business' (Table 1). This is the simple fact behind the rise of an 'information marketplace'.

Table 1: Business of business

Non-central	Central
Communication of business as a business	Business of communication as the central concern of business
Advertising, financial reporting, marketing, public relations, research	Computer hardware & software production and distribution, Internet business, media shares, telecommunication shares

How has the 'business of communication' become the 'business of business'? We know that one of the contributory factors has been the convergence of technologies of communication. While this is an important convergence, I would like to remark that it is part of a wider convergence, a confluence of the technologies that allow elites to achieve and maintain their positions in society. The three elites or influentials identified by Harold Lasswell are the manipulators of symbols (information elites), of flows of instruments of violence (coercive elites) and of flows of goods and services (mercantile elites) (Lasswell, 1963). There is a striking parallel between Lasswell's typology and the political economy of the Indian caste system. The Hindu upper castes coincide with Lasswell's three types of influentials (see Table 2).

Table 2: Influentials

Hindu castes	Lasswell's influentials
Brahmans ('know-ware' elites)	Manipulators of symbols
Kshatriyas ('war' elites)	Manipulators of instruments of violence
Vaishyas ('ware' elites)	Manipulators of flows of goods and services
Sudras	Non-influential mass

If the commodification of information by business creates the information marketplace, the convergence of elite technologies widens and develops that marketplace. The broadened information marketplace displays educational and training wares, including MIT educational and training products that are part of the entry costs for individuals who wish to sell their skills therein. By MIT education I mean theoretical and practical courses which link media and information technology either within particular courses or within a programme of studies. These may be conducted by a variety of tertiary institutions, including the following:
1. secondary schools
2. training institutes
3. colleges
4. universities.
The information marketplace includes commodified MIT and other educational programmes.

Once a marketplace has come into being, new sellers and buyers will come into the market around new products. Sellers and buyers here refer to vendors and purchasers of MIT educational products and providers and consumers of MIT educational products. Training programmes and courses are likely to be influenced by potential demand amongst prospective employers for graduates. We should therefore reflect on different categories of employers and their needs. Without doubt MIT skills are needed in the corporate sector. However the corporate sector is not the only market for trained MIT personnel. The size of the corporate sector results in inadequate attention being given to demand from other sectors.

What are these other sectors? International society may be viewed as the transactional space of nation states, international organizations, transnational corporations as well as non-governmental organizations. The bulk of the corporate sector may be involved in the production and distribution for profit of goods and services. But there are ones which do not seek profit as well. And media, like other organizations, can be commercial or non-commercial, state or private owned. Where a particular media organization is located will have a bearing on the role it plays as a critical reporter of society.

Non-profit non-governmental organizations play an important role in representing non-commercial and non-governmental interests in influencing corporate and state policy outcomes in important international issue areas such as development, human rights and environment.

Domestically and internationally, there are four categories of potential employers of MIT graduates. These are: national and transnational profit-making corporations; governmental and intergovernmental profit-making organizations; governmental and intergovernmental non-profit-organizations; non-governmental non-profit organizations (Figure 1).

Figure 1: Typology of players in MIT employment market

Governmental and Intergovernmental Organizations **Non-profit STATE & INTER-STATE**	Non-governmental Organizations **Non-profit NON-STATE**
STATE & INTER-STATE Profit Governmental and intergovernmental organizations	**NON-STATE Profit** National and transnational corporations

What should be the relationship between MIT educational products and the larger information marketplace? What are the spaces within which agencies act in a globalized world? How can we place MIT education within a political economic theoretical framework? This paper seeks to map relationships in a globalized world using my matrix framework, which consists of Windows-type matrices, beginning with the environment (N-matrix), political economic (P-matrix), regional (R-matrix), administrative

(A-matrix), ethno-historical (E-matrix) and individual (I-matrix) matrices embedded successively in each other (see Table 3).

Table 3: Matrix framework of analysis

Matrix	Description
I-matrix	Individual's values, attitudes and beliefs embedded in E-matrix
E-matrix	Ethno-historical collectivities embedded in A-matrix
A-matrix	National administrative collectivities embedded in R-matrix
(R-matrix)	(Regional administrative collectivities)
P-matrix	International political economic system embedded in N-matrix
N-matrix	Environment (material conditions for human transactions)

Matrices are like folders in Windows 95/97. Each folder is a matrix within which other folders can be placed, each in turn a nest for further folders.[1] Individuals are matrices in which are embedded values, attitudes and beliefs. These may be conceived of as pixels, which together produce images of individuality or coloration. The self-portraits of individuality are viewed as arising from an interplay of George Mead's 'me' or socialised 'I', and the core of individuality, the 'I' (Mead, 1934).

E-matrix: Individuals are embedded in one or more ethno-historical matrices (E-matrices). E-matrices are systems with the goal of cultural preservation and reproduction. They may have begun as groups concerned with economic production and distribution, but because of shared historical and reproductive experience they evolve into ethno-historical matrices. A family 'space' is an example of an E-matrix in which even to this day some of both of these functions are performed. So is the 'space' of a nation. Larger E-matrices may incorporate smaller ones. E-matrices may overlap each other. Members of an E-matrix inhabit an ethno-historical space where a particular ethno-historical vocabulary has currency and primacy. Ethno-historical vocabularies are related to Benedict Anderson's 'sacred languages' (Anderson, 1990) and E-matrices are not unlike Marshall Singer's 'perceptual groups' (Singer, 1987). The primary motivation of an ethno-historical group is survival of cultural identity of the collectivity. Behaviour that defies the explanatory power of an individual self-interest-based political economic model can originate in an E-matrix. An example might be behaviour such as the voluntary self-immolation of Buddhist monks in Vietnam in protest against the United States.

---

1. The matrix model is developed in my chapter entitled 'A Matrix Model for Framing Newsmedia Reality' in Malek & Kavoori (eds), *The global dynamics of news*, USA: Ablex (at press).

A-matrix: When several E-matrices must share resources, either through domination of others by one E-matrix, or some other arrangement, they become embedded in an administrative matrix (A-matrix) of their creation. An administrative vocabulary arises, possibly strongly influenced by a dominant E-matrix. A-matrices are locations where state, business and media actors are to be found at national level. The rules of self-interest operate here in the conventional manner of individual interest maximization. A-matrix players must balance competing demands from E and P-matrices.

R-matrix: A-matrices may also group together in regional political economic matrices or R-matrices.

P-matrix: Several A-matrices, if they interact, will give rise to a global political-economic matrix (P-matrix) either based on the values and vocabulary of a dominant A-matrix or group of A-matrices (e.g. Western European state and non-state players) or through some other mixture of values and vocabularies. The A-matrices will be embedded in a P-matrix. Before Europe began to colonize the rest of the world, we might say there could have been a fragmented P-matrix. Today, as a bequest of world empires, there is but one overall P-matrix, the de-territorialized 'nowhere' space of the so-called world market, global culture and international system. The international vocabularies of this P-matrix include science, mathematics, western popular music, cinema and television, United Nations officials and journalism.

Table 4: Players in MIT employment market within each matrix

	State and inter-state		Non-state	
	Profit	Non-profit	Profit	Non-profit
E-Matrix			X	X
A-Matrix	X	X	X	X
R-Matrix	X	X	X	X
P-Matrix	X	X	X	X

The four categories of potential employers identified above are mostly actors within the P-matrix and E-matrices. Non-state profit and non-profit actors may belong to E-matrices.

Philosophical argument for promotion of critical thinking in MIT education

From a systems point of view, education and media may be viewed as processes having the function of 'social reproduction in socially preferred ways.' Additionally they may be viewed as having the cybernetic function of contributing to the provision of societal feedback. From being the responsibility of 'lesser' subsystems such as E-matrices, education has become the province of 'greater' subsystems such as A-matrices, which in practical terms may coincide with national governments. Material production and distribution has also moved from 'lesser' to 'greater' subsystems. Globalization demands that material production and distribution are addressed in a systemic way. Commodification of information by business and convergence of elite technologies have resulted in education and media being drawn into the P-matrix.

It is within the P-matrix that the convergence of elite technologies unfolds. As the political culture of market-driven and technologically determined policy universalizes, states' control over their steering mechanisms lessens. The market and therefore major players in the market take on a steering function for society. Corporate identities within the market contend to shape the market. We are all aware that the great 'imperial' visions of the waning twentieth century no longer belong to nation states. They belong to information age Brahmans such as Bill Gates and Rupert Murdoch, one seeking to vacuum life, commerce and art into his world of Windows, the other unleashing digital images over satellite footprints scattered across the surface of the world. The 'know-ware man' himself, Bill Gates, has a vision of the future, his own window on the world, that is treated as policy by governments the world over. Not only do governments treat Bill Gates as a head of state or government, inviting him to address parliaments and cabinets, many respond to the inexorable advance of Microsoft technology into states, firms, homes, bodies and minds by opening wide their policy windows to Microsoft-determinisms. The United States government (a conglomeration of sometimes conflicting agencies) has reminded itself that windows and gates are metaphors for bondage as well as freedom, expressing wariness of a possible Microsoft monopoly.

Universities have played roles in the steering process of social systems through the development of ideologies and technologies. Ideologies influenced political and economic cultures while technologies influenced political and economic practices. The promotion of technology as the driving force for policy in place of ideology has evolved into a powerful ideology in its own right. The corporate world and media have become mass-producers and distributors of technological and ideological knowledge wares. They are also responsible for the popularization of technology as ideology. Universities operate within enterprise cultures and begin to treat research and university education as commodities.

One can argue that what has evolved in post-modern societies are 'post-systems', where the steering mechanism is decentralized, as in the vegetable kingdom. A tree has some characteristics of a post-system. It has no central steering mechanism. However it continues to maintain its boundaries. A tree also has some characteristics of a system, having a hierarchy of system goals. A post-system could have competing goals.

The post-modern world is one where consumption-driven production and distribution of technology, or *technological transaction,* has become an ideology, one which has replaced political ideology as the steering culture. The evolution of technological transaction as ideology has historical origins in an educational culture based on critical thinking, of diversity of thought, within the competitive international military situation of the Cold War. The individuality of Mead's 'I' constantly fought against the 'me' or socialized 'I' to develop new initiatives (Mead, 1934). This takes place globally through an interaction between the endogenous cultural energy within E-matrices and their P-matrices (economized, technologized) forms. If the market ideology is so invasive that it mutes the 'I', creates a technologized 'me', the energy that produced the information revolution *may* course through our age taking us to a high technology cul-de-sac. The technologizing of 'I' and the E-matrices may limit the direction of individual, social and human development to one of markets and technologies. There may after all be other directions for human development.

Universities do not need to be the only institutions to perform cybernetic functions in society. Other institutions, commercial and non-profit, are involved with conducting MIT research and delivering MIT education and training. Universities do not have to be excluded from the market culture. There is merit in their selling educational and research products and skills in the market place. But the culture of technological transaction should not be allowed to blow out the flame of critical thinking. Universities have the responsibility, which other institutions may not, of helping students develop critical skills. Universities have a responsibility in providing a critical space within society, allowing for the critique of ideology and technology.

Addressing market demand for 'critical' MIT education

There is even a market logic for development of critical skills. The greatest demand for MIT personnel may very well be from corporate, state and inter-state institutions (including media, educational), worlds which are accepting of the logic of administrative communication, eschewing critical communication (Rosengren, 1983). These organizations occupy space within the P-matrix and A-matrices. However non-profit non-governmental organizations are also employers of media graduates with IT skills. Non-profit non-governmental organizations play important roles, politically or socially, linking individuals and communities with larger issues. Non-profit non-governmental organizations may occupy space within the P-matrix, A-matrices or E-matrices.

The business of education is not only 'education as business' and 'education for business,' though these are very important factors leading to the need to provide workplace skills. These skills are provided through programmes of study at secondary school, vocational school, training institutions and within wider university programmes. The business of education for universities is also to help students develop critical skills.

In practical terms the effect of technological transaction on MIT education has effects on educational policy and products as well as pedagogic style. The pressures on media education may be itemized as (1) student demand for courses, (2) the market's demand for graduates, and (3) educational values. The market's demand for graduates is the strongest force here, shaping student demand and educational values. The power of the market may be viewed as a useful force, as long as universities continue to provide students with environments in which they can develop critical skills.

I would prescribe two courses of action. First, MIT education within universities should follow the general trend in universities to globalize curriculum, student body and staff. Universities in the United States were among the first to globalize curriculum, student body and staff. Today it is important for university media and IT programmes to operate within organizational cultures which have accepted this trend, because we must all live and work within the P-matrix. Second, MIT education within universities should balance theoretical and practical courses within some courses and across the overall programme. Programmes should include theoretical courses that encourage the development of analytical and critical skills as well as practical courses in MIT and other areas which encourage development of practical workplace skills. The critical culture within which MIT education takes place should encourage the development of perspectives from E-matrices. In terms of theory this may involve the inclusion of broad political-economic perspectives as well as those from within areas of cultural inquiry.

Addressing educational wares

While the first half of this chapter dealt with the influence of the market on educational processes, the second focuses on the dialectic between the roles of technologies of learning as media and as message.

MIT or post-convergence communication technologies are the natural media for technologies of learning today. But we should recall that there always have been technologies of learning in human societies. For the purposes of describing complex and fluid historical processes in a simple model, we might distinguish between pre-modern, modern and post-modern technologies of learning. Lerner distinguished between media systems and oral systems, the former consonant with modern and the latter with traditional (Lerner 1958, 55). I prefer to use the terms pre-modern and modern because, after all, tradition may be incorporated into modernity. Pre-modern, modern and post-modern as used by me here refer to technologies of learning as media.

The table below builds on Lerner to relate characteristics, examples, audience, content and source with pre-modern, modern and post-modern forms.

Table 5: Characteristics of pre-modern, modern and post-modern media

	Pre-modern media	Modern media	Post-modern media
Characteristics of media	Interpersonal	Impersonal mediated	Interpersonal and mediated plus impersonal mediated
Examples of media	1. Classroom	1. National School System (NSS) 2. Classroom 3. Audiovisual support material 4. Broadcast media	1. NSS 2. Classroom 3. Multimedia 4. Internet
Audience	Individual/ groups	Mass	Individuals
Content	Prescriptive	Descriptive	Interactive Entertaining
Source	Hierarchical	Professional	Non-professionals Non-hierarchical

Popularization of education

National School Systems (NSSs) are important technologies of learning at the social level, which may be viewed as complex largely uni-directional communication systems. These have been quick to adopt new classroom and mediated technologies to learning situations. In the modern period, even if content in texts may have been descriptive, NSSs have been able to be prescriptive through reliance on libraries and textbooks. In the post-modern context the Internet is one's library and the distinction between legitimate scholarly knowledge and corporate information becomes blurred. Broadcast media already presented some challenges from the 30s to the 80s and resulted in new forms of audiovisual materials being used in teaching. Radio, TV, film and print had already in the 20th century contributed to the demand for technologies of learning to be entertaining as well as educational and for the exclusivity of theory to be replaced by a reliance on popular practical knowledge. Witness the success of *Popular Science, National Geography,* and numerous radio and TV programmes and films about anthropology, biology, chemistry, economics, geography, physic, and perhaps every other academic subject.

This process of popularizing knowledge has led to the commoditization of knowledge and information (know-ware) and has accompanied the development of the newly converged MITs. MIT is not the cause for the demand for infotainment and edutainment. That was nurtured by the cultural industries, particularly radio, TV, film, and print in the years after World War II. However, the newer convergent post-modern technologies of learning lend themselves to edutainment because of the interactivity and multimedia capacity.

While the desire to acquire knowledge, whether as entertainment or serious reading, can only be applauded, there can be such a thing as too much market influence. Uncontrolled market influence can blur the line between formal university-type education and formal training provided by various institutions and informal education and training provided by media. I think these distinctions, or some distinctions, are important because not everyone will be trained for the same kind of decision-making. There will be a difference in expectations of the student whose wish is to acquire MIT skills where her future decision-making will be within the framework of particular technologies, and the student whose wish is to be a policy-maker. And who is to say that the former should not end up one day as a policy maker? For this reason I believe strongly that university MIT programmes should empower in two ways:

1. First, and rather basically, they should provide students with MIT skills. This is becoming as important today as speaking an international language such as English.
2. Second, they should provide students with research, analytical, critical and communication skills, which will allow them to make those larger decisions in the future.

What does this mean for education providers?

There are serious questions related to the promotion of a purely market determinism in the development of technologies of learning as educational products, which I have addressed earlier. The questions are particularly difficult ones because commonly accepted values of capitalism and entertainment have been seen to loom large in the culture, information and education industries. Depending on one's point of view this could be viewed as beneficial exogenous change (modern uncritical outlook), problematic exogenous change (modern critical outlook) or selective endogenous displacement of particular values (post-modern outlook).

Table 6: Outlooks in relation to locus and nature of change

Modern outlook	*Uncritical outlook*		*Post-modern outlook*
	Beneficial exogenous change	Selective endogenous displacement	
	Problematic exogenous change		
	Critical outlook		

We should not proceed uncritically without recalling these various views of what is happening in the process of international communication. The Internet and what I have called Know-ware Land will not disappear. They are here to stay, here to grow, and these issues will remain with us in one form or another. While taking positions in relation to big picture political economic influences we must also recommend practical policies for states, national school systems and educational institutions to follow.

I think we cannot go wrong if we go back to Paulo Freire's idea of 'empowering' students (Freire, 1972). What will empower students in a contemporary context? I believe that students must be empowered by developing the following skills:

1. Ability to produce/distribute messages using MIT.
2. Ability to produce strategies of communication.
3. Ability to produce maps of society/social situations for themselves and employers.
4. Ability to examine maps of society/social situations critically.

These are different types of skills and not everyone needs all of them. The further up one goes (from 1 to 4) the more the skills become policy-related rather than purely practical. We need both the pure practitioner and the policy analyst.

I am not certain whether one can develop analytical skills through consumption of interactive audiovisual material with high entertainment values in quite the same way that one could develop those skills through the application of logic to the linguistic descriptions of situations. This is an area for linguistic inquiry. However I do believe that 'analysis' of situations which are represented in interactive media, using interactive media, should be possible.

With rising global population and the need for education to be delivered to larger numbers at a quicker pace, entertainment must surely be welcomed as a vehicle through which knowledge is delivered. The study of Latin and Greek is no longer considered a prerequisite for the development of logical thinking. Nor is English a prerequisite. Audiovisual media provide their own possibilities in relation to analytical processes.

However, this does not mean that we should not encourage those who have the resources to do so to follow traditional routes of knowledge acquisition. Nor does it mean that 100 percent of a program of study should be based on entertaining interactive media, on our *knowledge of desire*. We must continue to package knowledge as a judicious mix of that which attracts because it is entertaining and that which attracts because it is intriguing and challenging – addresses a *desire for knowledge*.

Conclusion

In the contest between war cultures (domination for extraction) and ware cultures (consumption for gratification), the triumph of ware culture is to be applauded. The culture of technological transaction should not be allowed to snuff out the flame of critical thinking. In a world where know-ware, ware and war technologies have converged we should have particular concerns about concentration of power. The critical faculty of society can make us aware of dangers presented by roller-coastering war and ware cultures. The evolutionary trend toward know-ware culture is desirable. However, educators need to respond creatively to the emerging new world so that this new world will also be responsive to the groves of academe. It would be a tragedy if the information age, born in the groves of academe, becomes the grave of academe.

References

Anderson, Benedict (1990) *Imagined communities*. London: Verso.

AMIC/Asia Foundation, *Communication education and the needs of the media: A collection of papers presented at a seminar held in Kuala Lumpur, Malaysia from 29 September to 1 October 1994*. Singapore: AMIC.

Chitty, Naren (1997) 'A tale of two cities: Contiguous moments of reported political and cultural reality in Sydney and Singapore'. Paper presented at the Political Economy session of the IAMCR conference held in Oaxaca, Mexico (July 4-7, 1997).

Chitty, Naren (1998) 'Mapping Know-ware Land'. Paper presented at AMIC Conference, Bangkok, 1998.

Chitty, Naren (2000) 'A matrix model for framing newsmedia reality' in Malek & Kavoori (eds) *The global dynamics of news*. USA: Ablex (at press).

Freire, Paulo (1972) *Pedagogy of the oppressed*. Harmondsworth: Penguin.

Lerner, Daniel (1964) *The passing of traditional society: Modernizing the Middle East*. New York: Free Press.

Lasswell, Harold (1963) *World politics and personal insecurity*. Glencoe, Il.: The Free Press.

Mead, George Herbert (1934) *Mind, self and society*. Chicago Il.: University of Chicago.

Rosengren, Karl Erik (1983) 'Communication research: One paradigm, or four?' *The Journal of Communication: Ferment in the Field* 33, 3, pp.185-207.

Singer, Marshall (1987) *Intercultural communication: A perceptual approach*. New Jersey: Prentice-Hall.

Island in the stream:
On being a small country in
the global village

McKenzie Wark

The millennial prophesies of the digital revolution never quite seem to have had the impact in Australia that they have had in the United States, which is surprising, given the very rapid rate at which most new media technologies are taken up in Australia.

Australians faced the actual, mundane millennium without too strong a sense of 2000 or 2001 as a turning point, either toward catastrophe, or toward transcendence. Perhaps, as Meaghan Morris once observed, this really is a 'relentless secular' culture, one in which religious eschatology, being weak in the first place, doesn't seek expression through other means. This may well be a good thing. I do not think it's the end of the world to be living in a practical, sceptical, pragmatic culture, one that defines the good life in something less than millennial terms.

There was of course one famous Australian millennial prophesy of recent years, although the sardonic form that it took is itself revealing of the weakness of the millennial genre. I am talking about the notorious reference, in the book Pauline Hanson sponsored, called *The truth*, to Australia's first President of the Republic. By the year 2050, Australia will have as its President Poona Li Hung, a lesbian of Indian and Chinese extraction. She is part machine, and her neuro-cybernetic circuits will have been engineered by a joint Korean, Indian and Chinese research team.

Hansonism is the herpes of the body politic. It is contracted through illicit contact with sorry old prejudices. It reappears, as an itch that can't be scratched, at times of stress. I am sure it will be back, which is why I want to take seriously this millennial prediction, which I think speaks about a certain kind of fear that the emerging information economy can generate in a culture which has otherwise not embraced all that much of the millennial vision associated with the information revolution.

There was one other famous Australian contribution to futurist discourse, and a more serious one, also by a political leader, but of a different stripe. I will come back to this alternative view of the future for Australia as an island in the data-stream presently.

From television to cyberspace

But first, a bit of backtracking through the prehistory of cyberspace. In Europe and the United States, the mass media was a topic that incited conflicting passions. Many modern intellectuals critiqued the banality of mass media. Canadian literary critic Marshall McLuhan became a celebrity by embracing it. He imagined print media as a sort of fall from grace, and new technology as transcending the limits of print culture and launching us into the collective consciousness of the 'global village' (McLuhan & Fiore, 1996). In the 1990s, the promise of cyberspace also incited a range of responses. New York critic Mark Dery's was caustic about the revival of McLuhanite 'theology of the ejector seat' (Dery, 1996). McLuhan's prophesies about the coming of the global village enjoyed a revival, largely sponsored by the Californian cyberculture magazine *Wired*.

Australian writers were rarely as evangelical in their embrace of new media technology. A more practical and sceptical dallying with it prevailed among writers such as Dale Spender (1995), Jon Casimir (1997), Daniel Petrie and David Harrington (1996). As if to (over) compensate, John Nieuwenhuizen ranted against cyberspace as 'cultural AIDS' (Nieuwenhuizen, 1997). Both Nieuwenhuizen and his opponents in this debate tended to overestimate the novelty of this particular 'information revolution', as if there had not been a whole series of information revolutions in the past century, each of which brought a unique set of changes in its wake.

It is simply not the case that cyberspace represents a unique and millennial break. Even before the federation of the colonies, Australia was caught up in a whole series of technological changes that generated new vectors for storing or distributing information. Communications historian K. T. Livingston lists telegraphy (1840s), rotary printing (1840s), the typewriter (1860s), transatlantic cable (1866), telephone (1876), motion pictures (1894), wireless telegraphy (1899), magnetic tape recording (1890s), radio (1806) and television (1923) as significant inventions that created new communication possibilities (Livingston, 1996).

Rather than see things in a technological determinist fashion, where these new vectors drive changes in everything else, I think it makes more sense to adopt a 'technological possibility' view. Livingston has an interesting take on the extent to which the possibility of telegraphy made it possible for the competing colonies on the Australian continent to think about cooperation. He points out that telegraphy was a significant topic of debate among political leaders in inter-colonial forums in the long, slow process of federating the colonies. New technologies make possible new vectors, along which information can travel more quickly, more reliably, more accurately or in greater quantity. These vectors create a matrix which makes it possible to generate new forms of political or cultural action. These forms of political and cultural action can in turn shape the way the next generation of vectors is implemented.

The relationship between telegraphy and federation is an interesting late 19th century instance of such a relation between a vector and the kinds of action it enables, and which in turn further the development of the vector. Telegraphy brought business and political elites into an emerging national space, while many ordinary people lived in a more local matrix of vectors. Television and the telephone extended the national space into ordinary people's lives, while business and political elites connected into a growing global network of communication.

In the 20th century, television makes it possible to generate vast publics, attuned simultaneously to the same message, the telephone makes it possible to coordinate personal connections, exchanging particular and self-generated messages (Innis, 1991). Through the television and the telephone, quite different kinds of culture coalesce: one based on normative and majoritarian messages; the other at least potentially enabling the formation of marginal and minority cultures. Through the television and telephone, quite different forms of political action can be generated. The election campaigns of the major parties use television to spray messages as widely as possible, trying to catch the transient attention of uncommitted voters. The telephone, on the other hand, is the weapon of choice of the machine politician, lobbying and persuading one on one. Television and telephone were much used vectors from the 1960s to the 1990s.

Communications historians Graeme Osborne and Glen Lewis argue that there have been three persistent themes in Australian debates about communication. The first is a technocratic concern with building infrastructure for national development. For a long time debate centred on which kinds of government institution ought to implement which kinds of technology, but the rise of an argument in favour of market led development in the 1980s was not unprecedented. A second theme is the view of communication as an agent of social control. The critical literature which decries the controlling influence of media that rose to prominence since the 1960s really just reverses the value of long held assumptions about the power of communication. Wartime propaganda managers of the 1940s saw control as a good thing, while journalists of the 1990s who had to work in the shadow of corporate media interests took the contrary view. The third theme is the concern over the role of communication in community and culture. Some saw commercial media as having a particularly poisonous effect on community; others, such as McGregor, adopted a more subtle view of the relationship between communication and culture.

Each of these three themes takes on a new inflection as mass media gives way to cyberspace. For Osborne and Lewis, the technological development of the vector, from the telegraph to the Internet, 'does not appear to have overcome the sense of social isolation or the existence of an inarticulate citizenship'. It is not enough, they argue, to improve the technology. There is also 'a fundamental sense in which the question of values needs to be addressed by students of communication if its role in community creation is to be better understood' (Osborne & Lewis, 1995). In my book, *Celebrities, culture and cyberspace,* my aim is limited to looking into the development of values within the communications matrix emerging at the end of the century.

I agree with writers such as K. T. Livingston, Graeme Osborne and Glen Lewis that the historical dimension to communication has been unjustly ignored, but I would add that it is also necessary to develop concepts out of that history. I am looking for concepts that not only grasp the past, but can articulate possible futures; concepts that not only grasp the technical and social aspects of communication, but the subjective and experiential side as well; concepts that might help articulate a debate about the good life on the cusp between the broadcast era of radio and television, and the post-broadcast era of cyberspace.

Conceptualizing cyberspace

'I belong to the first generation in Australia born into a world in which television already existed', writes Deakin University academic Scott McQuire (1998). I think he also belongs to the first generation of Australian media theorists using this lifetime of experience as a background for thinking about how media technologies transform both our conscious and unconscious lives in an ongoing way. For those of us raised by television, the so-called 'Generation X', it is clear that our perceptions are different to those who preceded us, who were weaned on cinema and radio. We are no better, no worse, just different. What is emerging in Australian media studies is a desire to confront the changes to media form since television on the basis of this experience of a prior transformation of which we are the product.

'Cyberspace is the defining figure for a sensibility produced by mediated cultures', writes Darren Tofts from Swinburne University, another of the TV generation of media theorists (Tofts, 1998). In his experience, 'cyberspace . . . invokes a tantalizing abstraction, the state of incorporeally, of disembodied immersion in a "space" that has no coordinates in actual space'. While it may appear to some that technologies like the Internet, multimedia, hypertext and so on created this space *ex nihil*, Tofts insists that 'cyberspace has its own sedimentary record, and accordingly requires an archaeology'. These are just the latest gadgets in a long process of technologizing the perceptions through which our bodies negotiate the world.

McQuire and Tofts go looking in different places for the conceptual prehistory of cyberspace. Tofts is interested in technologies of writing, from the clay tablet to the typewriter to the Internet. McQuire traces the effects of photography: 'The ability to witness things outside all previous limits of time and space highlights the fact that the camera doesn't only give us a new means to represent experience: it changes the nature of experience'. While he is shy of using the term, he sees in photography a cause for the 'anxious fascination with cyberspace.'

In my first book, *Virtual geography*, I tried to tackle a different aspect of the evolution of cyberspace (Wark, 1994). Ever since the telegraph, technologies have developed that permit the transmission of information that can move more quickly than people or things (Carey, 1989). The telegraph, telephone and television are steps in the development of telesthesia, or perception at a distance. Being able to perceive events elsewhere makes it possible to think and act on a scale far beyond the local but with the speed of the immediate. The Internet extends and refines these capacities.

While I take a different aspect of the past evolution of media form as the basis for thinking about the emergence and potential of cyberspace to Tofts and McQuire, I share a similar experience to these other two children of television. It is since television brought sound and pictures right into the living room that the degree to which media pervade and transform social space has really started to sink in, but it is only on the basis of being immersed in television that it is possible to think about the further potential for the transformation of culture by the development of these vectors.

Like Tofts and McQuire I am too old to experience the cyberhype about the Internet without some irony. For McLuhan, media was a potentially liberating force; for some people cyberspace was also meant to liberate us – from the tyranny of pop culture and its mass media vectors. The art of writing media theory in the 1990s, having experienced more than one wave of media change fire up the imagination, is to steer between the extremes of cyberhype and technofear. But this is not just a matter of muddling through to a middle of the road position. Those who stand in the middle of the road get run over. Its a question of examining what the real potentials are that lurk as yet undiscovered in the media's transformations of culture. The writers who gathered around the Melbourne-based *21C* magazine, including Darren Tofts, Mark Dery and myself, tried to articulate a historically and culturally sensitive reading of cyberculture that could be critical but not too negative, creative but not too naive (Crawford & Edgar, 1997).

Thirty years ago there was something of an unholy alliance of the new left and the old right 'intellectuals' against new forms of media-driven culture. This raised its head again in the 1990s. Senator Richard Alston, as Minister for Communications and the Arts, exerted influence to restrict our liberty to choose what we want to see on television, film and video. There would be no more 'electronic Sodom and Gomorrah', like the popular commercial TV sex and relationship show *Sex/Life*, if Alston had his way. As columnist Brian Toohey remarked, 'Sadly, a wrathful God has yet to turn *Sex/Life* viewers into pillars of salt' (Toohey, 1998). The deflationary secular irony in the face of millennial language is here quite instructive.

Meanwhile, the conservative pundit Robert Manne commanded support on both left and right for arguments in favour of censorship. He thought the screen versions of Jane Austen's novels that were popular in the 1990s were good models of family love. He seemed not to notice that they portrayed an era when women were barred from real jobs, and from public life, and could not even own and transmit property (Manne, 1996).

This kind of nostalgia for a nonexistent past is no less absurd than the McLuhanite millennial fervour for an impossibly utopian future. But alongside these tired themes of control and development, the third theme Osborne and Lewis identify, the theme of community and identity, has opened up into a much more productive debate. What I would call the virtual dimension of change, the creative potential to make things otherwise, has opened up within the space created by changing media vectors. Cyberspace contains within it many possible forms of community and culture that have yet to be actualized. What I call urbanity is the art, culture, and politics of trying to realize the virtuality the celebrities embody, the culture expresses, that cyberspace enables.

The future of Barry Jones

'Respected by all, feared by none', is how one journalist sums up the career of Barry Jones, who among many other things was Minister for Science for seven years under the Hawke government (Barker, 1998). If anyone had a vision of where Australia was headed, and how Labor culture was failing to anticipate the effect of the cascading changes of the 1980s and 1990s, it was Jones. I want finally to revisit his legacy to map out the space Jones anticipated Australia would find itself in.

It is fitting that Australia's first post-modern politician became a celebrity through his television appearances. In the 1960s, he appeared 208 times on Bob Dyer's quiz show *Pick a box*. If Jones is the only Labor politician of his generation who could safely be described as lovable, it is in part because his celebrity originated in these televised displays of his broad erudition. He was the acceptable face of that suburban oddity, the man who knew too much. He was the perfect go-between for urbane knowledge to the suburban public, and vice versa. With his rumpled suits scrunched over his shoulders, his salted beard, and a gaze that seemed to search out something on a high diagonal in the sky, Jones embodied an idea of what it's like to be a politician who is an ideas person.

'Am I interested in ideas? Yes. More than power? Yes.' It's a fatal admission, and a sign of what kept Jones away from real authority within the Labor Party or in government. Jones was the political celebrity of the lost idea. While he did get some additional funding out of Hawke for the sciences, his main legacy may well be his perception of the problem building up for Labor culture as it confronts an ever more complex cyberspace, and tries to turn its cultural values into power through public debate and the political process.

If the premise of democracy is the informed citizen, then the information revolution is a political revolution too. Jones understood more clearly than most that government is as much about information as it is about power, and that information technology transforms relations of power. This is one of the most remarkable themes he took up in his provocative book, *Sleepers wake!* While other institutions have modified themselves, often beyond recognition, in order to make the transition to cyberspace, Parliament has changed only incrementally.

In the century since federation, the number of members sitting in the House of Representatives went from 75 to 147, and the number of people they represented went from 3.7 million to 17.8 million. The number of people in the public service they had to oversee went from 11,000 to 350,000, but the number of hours members deliberated went down from 866 to 603 (Jones, 1995). The amount of public expenditure per person may have increased spectacularly, but the amount of it actually brought before the House for review in the annual budget papers declined. In short, more people and more public service, producing more information that is subject to less and less scrutiny by elected representatives of the people.

The consequence of this trend, for Jones, is disturbing: 'The democratic system may become increasingly irrelevant as a means of determining and implementing social goals, or allocating funds on the basis of community needs, if elected persons do not understand how to evaluate and relate segments of information in which each expert works.' Power has shifted from representative government to 'strategically placed minority groups occupying the commanding heights in particular areas of society – technocrats, public servants, corporations, unions'. As cyberspace accelerates, more vectors carry more information, and more information leads to an increased division of labour, as people specialize more and more to capture a specific part of the information flow and bring it under their authority.

One unexpected consequence of this shift in the balance of power is that it fed into the rise of Hansonite populism. Former Hanson minder John Pasquarelli insists that she simply refused to absorb his briefings. 'In response to my criticism of her slackness, Pauline, in a fit of pique, swept some of the briefing notes on the floor saying, "I can't retain, I can't retain".'(Pasquarelli, 1998). If this is true, it worked in her favour out on the fringes of suburbia – at least at the time of the Queensland state election. Having witnessed popular politicians such as Bob Hawke succumb to the specialist apparatus of the public service and elite academic policy specialists, part of the appeal of Pauline was the notion of the idea-proof politician.

The information proletariat

Jones identified early on that 'Australia is an information society in which more people are employed in collecting, storing, retrieving, amending, and disseminating data than are producing food, fibres and minerals, and manufacturing products'. This is the primary sense in which Australia can be called a 'post-industrial' nation. Changes to what the economy produces also changes its class structure. Jones identified the potential for the formation of an 'intellectual proletariat' composed of people locked out of the benefits of the information economy. Education is the main ticket into the urbane knowledge class who have the specialized skills to process information, and the urbane protect their knowledge assets closely, and try hard to make themselves a hereditary caste, passing on the culture of knowledge to their children.

Beneath this strata of comfortable and urbane information burghers is the information proletariat. A 'check-out chick' passing groceries over the scanner is doing the manual labour of cyberspace, producing the raw information on which, eventually, the supermarket's managers will base their business decisions. An unemployed machinist who cashes her dole cheque and gambles it on the nags is also, strangely enough, part of the information proletariat, as her bets contribute to the statistical matrix that is the cyberspace of the gambling industry. A couch potato lying on the sofa with a bag of chips zapping the remote is part of the information proletariat. The ratings figures, on which advertising rates for the commercials being zapped are based, is a statistical projection of the number of couch potatoes. Information proletariat is what the Kerrigans would be if *The castle* didn't end happily ever after.

The information proletariat gets little benefit from the information it generates, on which so much of the post-industrial economy depends. They are locked out of the education that might give them some leverage in this economy. They are assumed to be passive objects from which specialists of all kinds, in health, education, economics, welfare, marketing, extract information and project plans and decisions. But increasingly, they not only resent the way information is used as a power over and against them, they resist it. The unspeakable majority refuses, more and more, to be spoken to or for.

The radical proletariat Karl Marx imagined would be denied the material benefits of capitalism and would seek knowledge in order to overthrow this unjust order. But what arose in the late 1990s was a radical proletariat that had some minimal level of material benefits guaranteed by a Labor-sponsored welfare settlement, but was denied the virtual benefits of cyberspace, and resisted knowledge and the unjust social order that went with it. The lesson, or the moral, is that unless the fruits of the production of information are shared, cyberspace capitalism will be resisted, just as industrial capitalism was resisted until the labour movement won a share of the material benefits. The agenda for Labor in the next millennium is clear: it has to spread the cultural and economic benefits of cyberspace.

This was Labor's problem on the cusp of the year 2000: to make itself the power that might broker the interests of the information proletariat, the information poor. Blue-collar voters for Pauline Hanson's One Nation Ltd had to be persuaded that it was not really in their interests to resist the post-industrial order, but, to do so, Labor had to find benefits for those chunks of suburbia that had been shut off, or wanted to shut themselves off, from absorbing and applying new information. At the same time, it had to persuade the urbane beneficiaries of cyberspace that it is also in their interests to defuse such resistance.

'The community is the collective victim of profoundly unequal access to information', Barry Jones wrote in 1995. By 1996, I think it fair to say that whatever suburbia did not know, it knew that it was the victim of this new kind of inequality. Resentment of this kind of inequality took the form of what I would call bad information. Armed with the attack on 'political correctness' and 'post-modernism' sponsored by *Quadrant* and the *Australian*, amplified and simplified by talkback radio's 'emperors of air', resistance flourished as a deliberate flouting of the consensus values of cyberspace insiders.

Ironically, this might involve the use of the same vectors of cyberspace for the creation of just such a culture of resistance as are used for profitable and productive ends by others. The on-line newspaper the *New Australian*, with its front page links to both One Nation and the National Front, is a good example. Writing before Pauline Hanson put Ipswich on the map by winning the seat of Oxley in 1996, Barry Jones wrote that 'in Ipswich, a town with higher than average unemployment, nearly 70% of the homes with children have computers'. He uses Ipswich's local government sponsored Internet access programme as an example of the 'capacity of computers to enhance the learning experience'. Some adults may be learning how to resist the open information vectors of cyberspace by using those same vectors to create a cosy third nature that can repel new information, reading and writing for the *New Australian* and many other publications flourishing on the net.

As John Howard learned the hard way in 1996, playing with bad information is playing with fire. This populist resistance only *looked* thoroughly stupid. It was composed of people who no matter how humble their formal education had sophisticated and finely tuned bullshit detectors. These they fired up the instant they came across political celebrity, spreading itself about on television, radio, or the popular prints. Hard as it may be for the upper layers of suburbia to grasp, the lower layers who make up this populist revolt did not need their patronising attempts at enlightenment so much as a good reason to actually join the emerging public consensus on how to speak and act in post-industrial society.

Irrational resistance was a rational choice, and it worked. All the political parties, the urbane media and cultural elites, the suburban high moralists, everyone directed their attention to figuring out how to prevent the spread of populist culture and the bad information in which it revelled and on which it thrived. Much rhetoric was aimed at the resistance, but few good reasons were given for giving up resistance and joining the public consensus.

Part of the resistance was the National Party's problem. The Nats were clearly under pressure after they lost significant ground to One Nation at the Queensland election of 1998. But part of the resistance was Labor's problem, as blue-collar suburban culture was clearly a component of the resistance that Pauline Hanson's One Nation Ltd was able to co-opt. They are the symptom of a long term problem for Labor, and the title of Barry Jones's book *Sleepers wake!* might just as well be directed at the culture of the Labor Party. Poona Li Hung, it is worth remembering, was built by *skilled* workers – someplace else.

References

Barker, Geoffrey (1998) 'Respected by all, feared by none', *Australian Financial Review Magazine*, August, pp.12-17, at p.14.

Carey, James (1989) *Communication as culture: Essays on media and society*. Boston: Unwin Hyman.

Casimir, Jon (1997) *Postcards from the Net*. Sydney: Allen & Unwin.

Crawford, Ashley & Edgar, Ray (eds) (1997) *Transit lounge*. Sydney: Craftsman's House.

Dery, Mark (1996) *Escape velocity: Cyberculture at the end of the century*. New York: Grove Press, p.8.

Innis, Harold (1991) *The bias of communication*. Toronto: University of Toronto.

Jones, Barry (1995) *Sleepers wake!: Technology and the future of work,* 2nd edition. Melbourne: Oxford University Press, p.175.

Livingston, K. T. (1996) *The wired nation continent*. Melbourne: Oxford University Press, p.9.

Manne, Robert (1996) 'Strong women, stronger morality', *Australian,* 8th April.

McLuhan, Marshall & Fiore, Quentin (1996) *The medium is the massage,* San Francisco: Hardwired, p.67.

McQuire, Scott (1998) *Visions of modernity*. London: Sage, p.2, p.7 & p.85.

Nieuwenhuizen, John (1997) *Asleep at the wheel: Australia on the superhighway*. Sydney: ABC Books, p.180.

Osborne, Graeme & Lewis, Glen (1995) *Communication traditions in 20th century Australia*. Melbourne: Oxford University Press, pp.169-170.

Pasquarelli, John (1998) *The Pauline Hanson story*. Sydney: New Holland Publishers, p.112.

Petrie, Daniel & Harrington, David (1996) *The clever country? Australia's digital future*. Sydney: Lansdowne Publishing.

Spender, Dale (1995) *Nattering on the Net: Women, power and cyberspace*. North Melbourne: Spinifex Press.

Tofts, Darren (1998) *Memory trade: A prehistory of cyberculture*. Sydney: Gordon & Breach Arts International, p.15.

Toohey, Brian (1998) 'Naked truth on redheads', *Sun Herald*, 28th June.

Wark, McKenzie (1994) *Virtual geography: Living with global media events*. Bloomington: Indiana University Press.

Hypertext, capitalism and military history: How to take down a machine's particulars

Belinda Barnet

We should bear in mind that there is a machined essence that will incarnate itself in a technical machine, and equally in the social and cognitive environment connected to this machine . . . [t]echnical machines are founded at the crossroads of the most complex and the most heterogeneous denunciative components. (Guattari, 1995)

Section I

I do not mean to be a party pooper. Having worked with computers and hypertext for some time now, I am already convinced of the importance of new writing technologies, already convinced of the need to locate and open points for political intervention. It is just difficult to believe that hypertext will leap tall hierarchies in a blink of phosphor.

In the excited rush of theory over the last 10 years, explorations of the impact of global capitalism and the military history of the technology have been conspicuous only for their absence. The great body of work has been concerned with the post-modern, literary aspects of the networked text: a rhetoric of liberation. This work, although important for opening up dialogue about computing technology in the humanities, can seem a little myopic in a world of Microsoft and billion-dollar defence research projects. There are forces other than French theory directing this show.

I would like to trace the migration paths that ideas have taken between institutions and hypertext as a technology. In particular, how the connections between the military and the technology have unfolded, and the workings of capitalism in its conceptual development. I will be exploring the various machinic essences which have incarnated themselves in hypertext as a machine. I do not claim points for historical scholarship or for technical savvy: at most, I shall claim to unravel and complicate such approaches, and present some strategies for intervention. I would like to suggest that literary hypertext as a unified, liberating phenomenon is an optical effect.

Liberation claims pervade the field of hypertext theory. As Stuart Moulthrop (1997) has observed, common theoretical approaches tend to envision hypertext as embodying the iconoclastic radicalism of the post-structuralists. There is something both familiar and irresponsible about all this – we have been there already with the introduction of broadcast television and the liberation claims which accompanied that. Television did not make education more democratic and accessible, it did not increase our collective IQ. It became the midday drug of choice for the children of the baby boomers. Utopian thinking is a function of molarity, an overcoding which neglects pragmatism and the movement of parts: the gentle death of revolution, as Brian Massumi would say.

In order to build an alternative approach which views hypertext as a collection of conflicting forces (a 'machine'), I will first introduce the field of hypertext theory. For those of you who have encountered this material before, skip to Section II.

Hypertext as it is commonly defined is a means of organizing information in a 'non-linear' fashion, consisting of chunks of text ('lexias') connected by links to other lexias in a networked manner. The term refers to both the system and its contents. Theorists began exploring hypertext from a literary perspective in the late 1980s and early 1990s, claiming that the interactive nature of hypertext invites us to reconfigure our conceptions of 'text', 'narrative' and 'author' (Delaney & Landow, 1994, p.2) in a fashion more suited to the nature of the medium. Hypertext shifts the responsibility of construction partly to the authors who write the links and partly to the readers who activate them. It also encourages connection across disciplinary boundaries, abandons print-based conceptions of fixed beginnings and endings, and challenges narrative form based on linearity due to its dispersed, networked nature. Hypertext heralds a new form of writing: instead of the linear, passive narrative of the book and codex culture, we have the multi-linear universe of the networked system.

Post-structuralists, it seems, have been going on about this for decades, confined to the world of print. For Derrida, Foucault and Barthes, what was 'only figuratively true in print becomes literally true in the electronic medium' (Bolter, 1991, p.158). Landow, Bolter, Joyce and a handful of other hypertext theorists point out that the Barthesian text, a text which writes itself across the interface between the body and the unconscious as a living network, 'the blocks of signification of which reading grasps only the smooth surface, imperceptibly soldered by the movement of sentences' (Barthes 1974, p.13), is finally realized in the new medium. Similarly, Derrida seems to be yearning for silicon. He writes of a 'differential network, a fabric of traces referring endlessly to something other than itself, to other differential traces' (Derrida, cited in Landow, p.59). Hypertext and post-structuralism seem to be speaking the same polylogue. In fact, contemporary critical theory 'promises to theorise hypertext, and hypertext promises to embody and test aspects of [critical] theory' (Landow, p.40).

So far so convenient. A problem arises, however, when theorists attempt to extend the qualities of this semiotic view of communication and the hypertextual network out onto society and our subjectivities. From the networked text emerges the symbolic subject: hypertext theorists attempt to construct the reader, author and society as *themselves* heterogeneous, polysequential texts. For instance, hypertext as a Derridean network admits of an 'attenuated, depleted, eroding or even vanishing subject' (Landow, p. 75) who 'logs in' to a hypertextual matrix and exchanges informational patterns across the interface. For Bolter, hypertext even promises to realize a social network more suited to the way this fragmented consciousness works, to the process of subjectivation itself. As subjects in the 'late age of print', ours is now a floating consciousness, 'a network of signs, of which the computer is the embodiment' (p.208), and due to the influence of technology we are beginning to 'function in a hypertextual network of affiliations'. According to Bolter (1991, p.233), hypertext as a system 'has become the social ideal'. Something inside me feels a bit queasy as I read these words. A subject, a society . . . a whole universe emulating a system of links and lexias?

Perhaps this is where my feeling stems from. Claims such as these, investing themselves in 'propositional statements that ascribe agency to technology itself' (Grusin, cited in Snyder, 1996, p.122) and generalizing outwards to the subject, to society and politics, prescribe to a form of technological determinism. We 'seem to think the cyborg can lead our dance into liberation barefoot and alone' (Joyce, 1995, p.196). Technological determinism attaches a certain ideology – whether liberatory or Luddite – to the medium. Such claims seem ignorant of the fact that ideology is a human concept which is brought to bear upon technology, and, similarly, that the technology itself is literally and conceptually programmed by the subject, by the interlocking institutions of author/reader/text, by the limits and directives of the technology, by the immanent desires of capitalism.

I'll state my thesis explicitly. The current definition of hypertext relies on the structure of the networked system and its contents (i.e. hypertext as a thing-in-itself), and often envisions this system as the embodiment of radical post-structural theory. Consequently, it appears to be at war with the Line and Print Culture as we conceptualize them. This is the optical effect. This is the utopian dream we need to depart from. In some cases this perspective is then generalized outward, producing a society which is the specialized offspring of hypertext and post-structuralism, and a subject more concerned with extracting signals from the noise than it is with the apprehension and engaged desiring-production of itself and its environment.

I would like to note here that I am not arguing for the abandonment of literary perspectives: quite the contrary. The institutions of thought we have inherited have influenced the development and use of the technology. They are part of the assemblage, and thus an opportunity to rock the sedentary order from within. It is just that we need to stop playing 'snap' and 'perfect match' with post-structuralism and computers, to start using theory as a machine which can intervene in and, to some extent, produce the flows. If we encounter a perfect match, this means that we have done nothing to induce change and movement. We have just been playing with tracing paper, trying desperately to make old systems manifest as relevant and self-same. In a word, unthreatening.

Mutations. Movement. Let's meditate on this from a different perspective. If we are to view hypertext as a productive landscape without prescribing to a framework which fundamentally cedes control and revolutionary capacities to the system, if we are to open points for intervention by recognising the many contributory flows expressing themselves as this technology, we need to 're-embody reading as movement, as an action rather than a thing . . . [to find] a way of reading sensually' (Joyce, 1995, p.11). We need to recognize that the subject determines the shape of the technology as much as it determines her, and that this is not just a matter of counting links or hurling hosannas at some 'embodied multiplicity'.

The first place we might start is by redefining the term 'hypertext' as a thing which acts only in *relation to* other machines and view it in functional terms: that is, what it can produce. Viewing hypertext as a machine involves entirely rephrasing our question. Let us not ask: 'Is hypertext *like* this thing/that thing/ a Derridean network/a rhizome/liberatory/a Barthesian Text/a post-structural whatever'. Let us not over-code, play with cookie-cutters, make the edges neat. Better to ask, 'what else can I plug it into?' '(How) does it work?' and 'Which disparate elements are expressing themselves as this thing?'

Here is a periodic table of hypertext. As a machine, hypertext at once comprises and is in departure from previous generations of technologies, the demands of the workplace and educational settings, military research, the mass media, programmers and their pets, Microsoft and the corporate players, the perpetually mutating desires of the Web and its puppeteers, intellectual and artistic fashion, technological limits, the limits of capital. It arises from the connective synthesis of eye-to-screen, from the institutions of author/reader/text, from the behavioural grammar which emerges across the point'n'click interface, from the immanent desires of the machine of capital. It is an assemblage arising from the interrelations of a field of forces, these forces. It is inherently unstable and in a process of perpetual change. This is the ontology of hypertext. It is a system of directed flows. If we know where these flows and their intersections are, what they are emerging from, we can muddle them. I am going to begin my explorations from the periodic table listed above. Bit by byte. To read hypertext as a smooth, unified object with a liberal-democratic ideology says more about political composition of the critics concerned than it does about hypertext.

Section II

There is no universal capitalism, there is no capitalism-in-itself; capitalism is at the crossroads of all kinds of formations. (Deleuze & Guattari, 1987, p.20)

Capitalism. The limit of society, the limit of hypertext. It astounds me that so many writers in the field (including myself) have fostered such a romantic intellectual relationship with hypertext to the neglect of what seems so glaringly obvious: all technological developments are over-coded by the images of consumption and production. It sounds so simple, so pedestrian, almost trivially true. And that's just it. This is where we need to be conducting strategic interventions.

Capitalism has its own desires, and these desires are often coextensive with hypertext as it unfolds before us. Indeed, this *is* actually one of capitalism's desires: it wants to be immanent to everything we do, it wants to move our trigger-happy finger as it runs the mouse across those baubles and bright links. In this it is remarkably dexterous. We cannot locate it anywhere (it's Bill Gates, it's General Electric, it's . . .): it is a virtual body, a body without organs. It operates by locating and binding the dispersed flows of reality to its body, by constantly *redefining* the limits of this body and consequently the limits of society relative to the situation. It is supremely pragmatic, engaged, flexible. It operates by cultivating difference, cultivating the 'other', and then by *becoming-other,* by homogenizing difference, passing through it and redirecting it in the aid of the collective. So difference is tolerated, but it is then redirected in the service of capital. Schizophrenic flows 'are decoded and axiomatised by capitalism at the same time' (Deleuze & Guattari, 1983, p.246). We have to admire this dexterity, this dual operation, at the same time as exploring its operations, utilizing them and thinking strategically. It has two hands (or millions). Its remarkable capacity to reflexively snap up, slightly reconfigure and redirect the flows of life, this constant (re)circulation 'constitutes capital as a subjectivity commensurate with society in its entirety' (Deleuze & Guattari, 1987, p.452).

So, it is not a centralized thing. Its flows are schizophrenic, all over the shop. It is just that these flows are eventually flattened, axiomatized, bound to a desiring body. And this body is constantly changing form. We do not need to wheel out Derrida and press 'play' to demonstrate this. We just need to look out the window.

But before we begin to take down the particulars of capitalism, we need to address the widespread claims that hypertext is *opposed* to capitalism and the state due to its multi-linear nature. This is the 'rhetoric of liberation' which pervades critical work on hypertext. No matter their theoretical articulation, all liberation claims made for hypertext are fundamentally concerned with escaping the logocentric geometry of regulated time and space – the totalized, homogenized worldview which capitalism and the state are seen to promote. As we shall explore shortly, this is dangerously wrong on two counts. Firstly, capitalism is not a regulated thing from which we might escape. It is not so much *imposed* in the manner of state geometry as progressively immanent in our movements across it. It's a different kind of machine altogether, and warrants a different strategic approach. Secondly, as Stuart Moulthrop has elaborated in his 1997 paper, 'Hypertext itself is not a war machine, and is not opposed to the line and print culture as we know it'.

Recent explorations deploying the Deleuzian smooth/striated continuum make explicit the fact that the enemy in this literary 'war' has never been the Line or linearity *per se*, but 'the non-linear perspective of geometry; not the prison-house of time but the fiction of transcendence implied by the indifferent epistemological stance toward time' (Rosenberg, 1994, p.276). Although the rhizome, the war machine, the cyborg and the nomad differ in their particularities and composition, when theorists use them in relation to hypertext, they all explicitly play on the dislocated, time-irreversible processes of chaos theory, thermodynamics and associated 'liberatory' topological perspectives. The terms 'multi-linear', 'non-linear' and 'contingency' have been borrowed from physics to articulate hypertext's resistance to the dominant determinist episteme, a framework exemplified by the term 'dynamics', opposing it to the irreversible laws characteristic of statistical approximations that govern complex events, exemplified by the term 'thermodynamics'.

As Moulthrop has observed, the problem with this is that at a systemic level hypertext is unavoidably comprised of the geometries of Newtonian science: *linear or multi-linear, lines are still lines, logos and not nomos, even when they are embedded in a hypertextual matrix*. The author has been there before us, has laid down the lines and the possibilities. We can go this way or that way in the same way that we can choose this product or that product in the supermarket. There is a choice, but not a contingent or 'liberating' choice in this unfolding now. There is no 'becoming' on a purely systemic level. Hypertext is a machine, yes, but it's not a rhizome. This is too romantic a notion as well. Labelling it 'rhizomic' and shelving it in cultural studies won't do. We need to be able to adapt our theory and practice to the situation as readily as the machine of capital, and our strategies will need to come from outside the bounds of the state and from the fringe that capitalism has not yet detected: from rogue desires, from our bodies, from the 'unthought' of technology.

Even the semiotic hierarchy imposed by the institutional use of 'hypertext' or 'hyperfiction' undermines the supposed 'heterogeneity' of smooth space by imposing a predetermined grid articulating what matters and what doesn't. There can only be so many ideas linked to a particular node. We might also point out that the machine supporting the hypertext (drawing on both the Deleuzian and technological connotations of 'machine') is invested in hierarchical 'scripts or routines created by the author, the code that makes up the hypertext environment, the operating system on which all of this is running and the various layers of ROM or microcode that allow it to function' (Moulthrop, 1997, p.5).

Hypertext is thus invested (at least in part) in a framework of regularity, control and precise function. It is inextricably a part of State apparatus. The problem with this is that the War Machine, which best exemplifies the avant-garde's insurgency against sedentary culture must always be exterior to the state apparatus and its regulated grid at all times. 'If we acknowledge this line of critique (which I think we must), then we must seriously reconsider any claims about hypertext fiction as war machine, or indeed as anything en avant' (Moulthrop, 1997, p.5).

Although hypertext is not revolutionary, 'it would be the goal of any avant-garde use of hypertext to find a way to sustain the experience of dislocation that would indicate liberation from the hegemony of geometry: such approaches have yet to be accounted for' (Rosenberg, 1994, p.283). I would like to begin to sketch the possibility of 'contingent interaction' through the promising dislocations inherent to alternative interfaces later in this story. For the time being, however, we must reassess all our liberation claims. If linearity and multi-linearity are identical in terms of geometric relations to space-time, 'why should they be any different in terms of ideology?' asks Moulthrop (1994, p.310).

So hypertext is composed within the bounds of the state.[1] In plain terms, this means that hypertext is at least *a part of* what we have taken it to be fighting against: linearity, hierarchy, predetermined limits.

It would be wrong, however, to align capitalism with this hardwired episteme. And this is an important point, so we should go over it again. Capitalism is a different kind of machine altogether. It is not so much *imposed* in the manner of state geometry as progressively *immanent* to our movements across it. It is a virtual body, a body without organs, and its movements of capture are molecular and distributed rather than centralized. As previously observed, it is remarkably dexterous. This is where the danger lies. Unlike the determined grid of the state, it is difficult to locate capitalism due to its schizophrenic nature. And yet, it can also have an homogenizing effect on our movements across the interface. For although capitalism has turned quantum in its operations, it has done so in the service of quantity: 'consumption and accumulation are, have been, and always will be its reason for being' (Massumi, 1996, p.138). We require different strategies of intervention in this case.

The animal body, as it is progressively subsumed or spliced into the geometries of hypertext and its overarching desire for speed and efficiency (the retrieval of meaning), opens one possible space for strategic intervention. The different organs, the minds folded within the flesh, the embodied thoughts that smell like sweat and blood and shit and desire . . .

---

1. For a more extensive discussion of physics tropes in contemporary critical theory, see Martin Rosenberg's article in Landow (ed.) *Hyper/text/theory*, ch. 8.

Another utopian dream? Nay, another opening, an opportunity to resist homogenization, to encounter other universes of reference. A possible strategy. Like all other strategies, alternative interfaces are not an ideological overhaul enabled by the realm of techné, but a space for 'schizolupic break-out[s] from the bin' (Land, 1993, p.482). Bifurcations are enacted on the micro level by desiring-machines, across an interface which seeks to dislocate intentionality in conjunction with the marginalized sensory apparatus of the reader, drawing other minds, other organs into localized conversation with the technological machine, if only for a moment. These words are also a strategy. As each letter falls behind the cursor, I realize that they are open to being subsumed and redirected in the service of capital. This is how the whole thing operates. We need to perpetually open new spaces as the old ones are snapped up. To note the interrelations of the elements and how they operate across life, the interface and everything.

Section III

The limits of technology. This is another contributory flow, an element in our periodic table of hypertext. To my view, it is the major element. By 'limits' I do not mean just the limits of what Windows 98 can do, of the speed limits, the light barrier, the current hardware. I mean also the interactions of previous generations of technology upon this particular generation, of a flow which extends back to when we first picked up a stick in the jungle to help us get ants from an ant hill. Technology moves in generations of progressively more and more 'efficient' tools toward an ideal: control of the environment and the augmentation and eventual replacement of the *embodied* mind. How does this operate? Its current 'limits' shall also be defined, in part, by their former emplacement. The archeology of hypertext will give it a spin defining the arc of its vector. We might begin to explore this element by noting the institutional origins of the technology itself, the various organizations and agendas that it has invested itself in as it has formed as a technology and system of thought. There is a machinic essence which will incarnate itself in a technical machine, and equally in the social and cognitive environment connected to this machine (Guattari, 1995, p.39). Hypertext, like most technologies, has a long and illustrious history with the military and major corporations.

I shall be concerning myself here with the points at which conceptual and technological bodies have encountered the machines of global capital and military science in this century, the points at which the forces expressing themselves as hypertext have been and are domesticated into power relations. Why have certain concepts thrived?

First let us understand that the term 'military' can be misleading: the military is in fact not an entity but rather a group of services and bureaus that are often at odds with one another over issues of funding, research and strategy (Ceruzzi, 1998, p.7). Their influence has sometimes been contradictory and even inhibiting to the evolution of certain ideas. My focus will be on the US military, not because their story is any more important to what hypertext has come to mean than that of other countries, but because the development of computers, hypertext and military research in the years following World War II is particularly strong and complicated here. Similarly, although my study will be informed by a history of modern computing, I do not wish to suggest that hypertext might be defined by its attachment to a computer. Rather, I seek to highlight that in its formative stages it fostered a prolonged relationship with the universities and institutions surrounding their development, and that as a body it still retains traces of this emplacement.[2]

The war released an unprecedented sum of federal money into the engineering departments of several major universities across the United States, creating a climate of intense competition between universities in the development of new machines and the costly departments to house them, and disrupting the older institution of private philanthropy. The great problem with handling, producing and collecting information during the war translated into a focus in universities on developing information-handling machines. The US Defence Department became a *customer* to the universities (Ceruzzi, 1998, p.8), and engineering departments, during the Cold War more than ever, became economic institutions. The military *created* a market for the universities. This market was the climate in which some of the 'pioneers' of hypertext research, Vannevar Bush, and many years later, Doug Engelbart and Andries Van Dam, undertook their research.

---

2. Some readers will note that I have left Ted Nelson out of this story, which may seem a little odd. In 1965, Nelson actually coined the word 'hypertext' to describe 'non-sequential writing – text that branches and allows choices to the reader, best read at an interactive screen' (Nelson, 0/2), and he is often regarded as the founding father of the hypertext 'movement'. I have done this for two reasons; firstly, my concern here is mainly with the material history of the technology and its conceptual relation to the military and to institutions, and Nelson's work has neither eventuated in a hypertext product to speak of (or at least one remotely resembling Xanadu), nor sustained a lasting relationship with any one particular institution. Most importantly, however, his is a story which moves against the grain of many of the computing paradigms we have explored here, and a strategy of intervention in itself worthy of more extensive coverage than word count restrictions allow for in this work. As many writers have pointed out, the reason that Nelson's story is the greatest vaporware story ever told is probably because his ideas do not accord with those of capitalism or the military. His work has always been more poetic terrorism than marketable product. Theorists have trouble working out if Nelson is a gadfly or a genius. I think he is both. A good introductory chapter on Nelson's life can be found in Howard Rheingold's book, *Tools for thought*, 1995, pp.296-391.

Bush and the mind's machine

There is another revolution under way, and it is far more important and
significant than [the industrial revolution]. It might be called the mental
revolution. (Bush, 1991, p.165)

Documents on hypertext and information retrieval systems in general are
not known for their shelf-life. What, then, is it about the ideas behind
Bush's writings which have so influenced today's research agenda in
hypertext, multimedia, intelligent systems and networking? Linda C. Smith
undertook a comprehensive citation context analysis of literary, technical
and scientific articles produced after the 1945 publication of Bush's article
in the *Atlantic Monthly*, 'As we may think', a work which urges scientists to
turn to the task of making more accessible the growing store of knowledge
and proposes a prototypical machine for organizing and managing this:
the memex. She found that there is a conviction, without dissent, that modern
hypertext is traceable to this article. Indeed, the great body of American
authors writing from a historical perspective over the last 45 years which
treat of Bush maintain that it was the starting point of modern information
science (Smith, 1991, p.265). Given this, it is reasonable to view Bush's
memex as the creation myth of hypertext; it is one of the images of
potentiality which have guided subsequent design and development in the
field.

I would like to show that the memex was informed by the scientific
interest in mechanical-biological analogues at the time, and by the wartime
technological utopianism of which Bush and his 'revolutionary' memory
extender were a part.

During World War II, there was a concern that all aspects of human
function were open to failure and to the sorts of communication breakdowns
which ensued from emotion, fatigue, forgetfulness and hesitation. The war
machine was busy trying to write humans out of the command loop
altogether. Automatic weapons systems were a prime directive and millions
of dollars were funnelled into research. As historians on cybernetics – and,
more eloquently, film/video artist Manuel DeLanda in his recent book,
War in the age of intelligent machines – have observed, human thought was a
fatal flaw when it came to decisions concerning mass destruction.

Technical machines, with their clean lines and comprehensible analogue
operations, promised to write out the mess involved with embodied human
decision-making and bring the business of war under control. 'There can
be no doubt', observes Harold Hatt in his book on the birth of cybernetics,
that this concern for the automation of human activity in World War II
'was the impetus that gave birth to control theory' (p.14). Mess, noise,
information storms and hesitation were the biggest enemy. America in
particular had a long history of technological utopianism, and was distinctive
in its unprecedented dramatizations of mankind's ability to shape the future

technologically. The war served to focus and exacerbate this tendency. Technological utopianism was running rife, enthusiastically fed by the concerns of the war machine.

In all versions of the memex essay, Bush (1939, 1945, 1967) begins his thesis by explaining the dire problem we face in confronting the great mass of the human record, and our all-too-human inefficiencies in managing this. The body of scientific and engineering literature was growing exponentially, and this in particular concerned Bush; the institution he directed in World War II, the Office of Scientific Research and Development, had taken upon itself the task of translating the language of science from over 6,000 physicists and engineers (Rheingold, 1995, Chapter 9) into simple strategies for the warriors. Information and communication between institutions was approaching a critical threshold.

The interest and faith in biological-mechanical analogues as a solution to such problems was especially heightened at this time. Cybernetics and the idea that humans and their environment are mechanical systems which can be studied, improved, mimicked and controlled was growing, and later gave way to disciplines such as artificial life and artificial intelligence. The first step in cleaning up the mess was creating a reliable analogue to the natural order. The second step was eliminating the natural order and the breakdowns it was prone to.

The memex was a machine modelled on cognition and the 'intricate web of trails carried by the human brain' (Bush, 1945, p.106). This aspect of its design was important enough that it appeared verbatim in all of the memex essays. The memex was first and foremost an extension of human memory and the *associative movements* that the mind makes through information: a mechanical analogue to Bush's conception of 'memory'. Bush introduced this idea of associative indexing into information management. The memex was distinct from traditional forms of indexing not so much in its mechanism or content, but in the way it organized information based on transverse conceptual or linguistic linkages. In tune with the times, Bush believed that the real heart of our ineptitude at getting at the huge body of the human record was 'caused by the *artificiality* of systems of indexing' (Bush 1945, p.106) based on alphanumeric, binary and hierarchical structures. The brain was a much more suitable model than artificial hierarchies, and, most importantly, it could be improved upon mechanically through the magic of modern engineering.

With an item in consciousness, or before one, another allied item is suggested, and the brain or the memex instantly jumps to the second item, which suggests a third, and so on. Thus there are built up trails of association in the memory, of brain or machine (Bush, 1970, p.191).

The memex was originally proposed as a single-screen console equipped with levers and motors, a device providing access to information kept on microfilm in the user's desk, which was mechanized for retrieval 'so that it may be consulted with exceeding speed and flexibility' (Bush 1945, pp.106-

107). The memex introduced the concept of 'trails', a concept derived from work in neuronal storage-retrieval networks at the time, which was a method of connecting information by linking units together in a networked manner, similar to hypertext paths. The process of making trails was called 'trailblazing', and was based on a mechanical provision 'whereby any item may be caused at will to select immediately and automatically another' (Bush 1945, p.107), just as though these items were being 'gathered together from widely separated sources and bound together to form a new book' (Bush 1945, p.104). It was an electro-optical device which used spinning rolls of microfilm, abstract codes and a mechanical selection-head to find and create links between documents.

It is important to remember that the memex was never actually built. It was a *design* for a personal motor for the use of private individuals to manage their records. This flew in the face of the emerging paradigm of human-computer interaction that reached its peak in the late 50s and early 60s, which held computers to be rarefied calculating machines which were used only by qualified technicians in white lab coats in air-conditioned rooms at many degrees of separation from the 'user'.

> System programmes were developed by hand and then punched into paper cards. These cards are handed over to a special caste of technicians who are the only ones physically authorized to handle the machine. These operators feed the contents of the paper cards into the computer and, after a long wait, return the results to the programmer in the form of a printout. (DeLanda, 1994, p.219)

The military was interested in faster ways to interact with computers, but also wanted to 'maintain control over the quality and quantity of this interaction' (DeLanda, 1994, p.219), and *who* among the population could be permitted to do so. This meant maintaining a controlled distance between end users, technicians and the machines. Bush was suggesting that a symbiotic relationship was possible; indeed, the memex was none other than an enlarged, intimate supplement to memory.

Similarly, corporations like IBM were not interested in personal machines at the time. They built massive, expensive machines for large-volume data analysis and business, and from the late 40s onwards amassed their wealth and power by concentrating on the corporate market.

The memex was designed at a time when the dominant paradigm of human-computer interaction was 'so entrenched that the very idea of a free interaction between users and machines as envisioned by Bush was viewed with hostility by the academic community' (DeLanda, 1994, p.219). This was one reason that the memex remained vaporware (it also succumbed to technological obsolescence due to its analogue design). However, as indicated by the immense body of literature and reference surrounding it, it became an image of potentiality within the field. The technical side of the memex may have been outdated, but the idea of augmenting and *extending* human faculties migrated into future developments and helped to shift the paradigm of human-computer interaction out of rarefied numerical tasks and into the world of personal motors and human mind-amplifiers that Bush had imagined.

Doug Engelbart and the man-machine interface

Engelbart was a 'little navy boy' (Engelbart, 1988, p.235), an electronics technician for the war machine out in the Philippines, when he first picked up a reprint of Bush's article, 'As we may think', in *Life* magazine in the late 40s. In 1962, as his ideas about extending the human intellect were beginning to translate into reality, he reflected in a letter to Bush that:

> I was startled to realize how much I had aligned my sights along the vector you had described. I wouldn't be surprised at all if the reading of this article sixteen and a half years ago hadn't had a real influence upon the course of my thoughts and actions. (Engelbart, 'Letter to Vannevar Bush', p.236)

Due to his experience with radars during the war, Engelbart realized that the screen was the most important surface of contact between humans and digital machines. In a radar, the needs of complex informational problems had already brought tasks 'from the innards of computer hardware to the surface of the screen' (DeLanda, 1994, p.220), where it was rendered as a graphic, real-time picture which could be manipulated onscreen with a light pen. Although Engelbart was inspired by the graphic interactivity of the radar and the relative control, ease and speed which this afforded to the user, the idea that all computers might be transformed from million-dollar numerical devices into friendly workstations was difficult for the war machine to swallow at the time. It was also difficult for his university to swallow as a PhD thesis, being foreign to the institution of computer science at Berkeley, so he settled for 'something else' as a topic and then went to the Stanford Research Institute (SRI) to pursue his original ideas (Engelbart, 1988, p.190).

It was 1957, the year of Sputnik. SRI was interested in conducting military, high-end commercial and scientific research into computers. They humoured Engelbart's dreams of constructing a laboratory filled with psychologists and computer scientists to research the hybrid 'field' of intellectual augmentation for the first couple of years, until he got a grant from the Air Force Office of Scientific Research, which was beginning to incubate a concern to improve the way that intelligence operated machines.

The military began quietly listening to Engelbart's heretical dreams. He wrote a paper in 1962 called 'A conceptual framework for the augmentation of man's intellect' (CFA) on this research, and it met with much misunderstanding in the academic community and, even worse, angry silence from the computing community. He recalls that this was because the institution of computing science at the time kept trying to fit his ideas into the existing paradigm, claiming that if he was working on an 'information-retrieval' machine, why did he not just 'join their forefront problem pursuits and stop setting myself apart' with far-flung graphic interface concerns (Engelbart, 1988, p.190) and babble about the human side of things? Computers were still seen as hardwired mathematics.

'The hope is that, in not too many years, human brains and computing machines will be coupled together very tightly, and the resulting partnership will think as no human brain has ever thought', wrote J. C. R. Licklider in a paper he published in 1960 called 'Man-computer gymbiosis' (1960, p.131). When Licklider came from Cambridge to take over the Advanced Research Projects Agency's (ARPA) new Information Processing Techniques Office (IPTO) in 1962, he infected ARPA's main funding channel for experimental computing with a new paradigm. Licklider was not a military engineer like the vast majority of ARPA brass, but a civilian scientist, in fact, a psychologist with an interest in electronics. He had his own agendas for the future of computing, and, as his previous profession would indicate, these included a deep interest in the amplification of the human intellect by connecting computers to the 'human system' in a more intimate fashion, a concept also favoured by Engelbart.

When Engelbart approached IPTO for funding, 'there the poor fellow was, having advertised that man-computer symbiosis was the new direction. How could he in reasonable consistency turn this down'? (Engelbart, 1988, p.191). Stanford was told that IPTO would provide a million dollars to purchase a new time-sharing computer system for the project, and about half a million dollars a year to support the project. This was a substantial amount of money for a research project in 1963, and much more than the Air Force Office had provided earlier. SRI, which had previously regarded Engelbart's plans for a mind-extending laboratory with scepticism, sat up and took notice of their new million dollar man.

Meanwhile, the Air Force's needs to evaluate real-time radar and radio-transmitted data was growing and it nurtured other projects which were similarly engaged with human interface concerns, encouraged by the recent success of the 'flight simulator' project Whirlwind. Across the excitement, Bob Taylor, who was also an (initially civilian) psychologist working at NASA, offered more support to Engelbart. This was closely followed by funds from the Rome Air Force Development Center at Rome, New York. By 1967, writes Engelbart, 'it was recognized that the respective contributions from ARPA, NASA and RADC represented the significant parts of a coordinated programme' (Engelbart, 1988, p.192). The ARC and the augmentation paradigm it embodied was now officially endorsed and nurtured by the war machine.

The freshly outfitted laboratory, the Augmentation Research Center (ARC), began its work immediately. It started with a series of inventions which incarnated Engelbart's concept of a more hospitable man-machine interactive environment. Most of these focused on the way people connected with a computer across the interface. Central to amplifying the intellect was the speed and flexibility of the site of contact between the mind and the machine: to all people who denied that speed was significant to thought and choice, Engelbart provided a counter-example. He strapped a brick to a pencil and requested that people write with the assemblage. It did not take long to discover that 'our academic work, our books a great deal would change in our world if that's how hard it had been to write' (Engelbart, 1988, p.200). The technologies we interact with are not just tools to 'express' our thought, they actively define the *limits* of such thought. In a computer, the interface, peripherals and keyboard are central to such mutual production.

The project was called NLS, for oN-Line System (Ceruzzi, 1998, p.301), and FLS, for ofF-Line System, when the network of 'augmented individuals' was not active. A small army of programmers and computer technicians designed a system which could manipulate the smallest features of a chosen piece of information (character by character) to the largest features of its structure (the entire 'window' and what it is connected to). The screen could be divided into a number of windows, each of which could display either text or image, and the images themselves ranged from photographs to bar graphs. The information currently in view was sensitive to the movements of the mouse and keyboard; information could be reordered, linked, nested, juxtaposed, revised, deleted or chained window by window with a simple movement of the mouse or fingers. This was a prototype information-retrieval machine, but it was unlike any other which had come before it. The fundamental (and revolutionary) aspect of the system was its ability to allow a person to manipulate information in an intuitive fashion *as it was seen* across the interface, and to link, revise and window this in real time.

Incarnated in this way of navigating through such information 'spatially' was Engelbart's belief that the visual faculties were central to humankind's ability to grasp and control information, and also that we organized our thoughts in a visual, spatial manner. Hence, 'symbol-manipulation', which could speed up the selection process by condensing complex operational concepts into 'extremely sophisticated images' (CFA, p.21), was an important breakthrough. Symbol manipulation predicted the use of icons in graphic user interfaces. In emphasizing the human visual faculties as the most efficient information processors, he followed the ideas of many psychologists, psychiatrists and neurophysiologists at the time (with the exception of cognitive scientists and AI people), who believed that the best path to follow to understand consciousness was to 'understand visual perception' (Bennett, p.4).

At an ARPA principal investigators meeting in the spring of 1967, Bob Taylor and Larry Roberts announced that ARPA was going to make computer networks research and development a principal focus, and that the ARC research computers were going to be the ones connected by an experimental 'ARPA Network' (Engelbart, 1988, p.226). The ARC played an important role in the birthing process of 'ARPANET', as I shall explore later in this story.

NASA support ended by 1969, and, although RADC and ARPA continued their support until 1977, the project was crippled some by a lack of funds. At this stage, however, commercial interest was beginning to develop, and, although the team was keen to draw the project out of research and into the commercial market, the business of developing supporting applications and following 'targets organized by others' was far from Engelbart's original vector, he reflects with some regret (Engelbart, 1988, p.193). NLS, although it was designed to be *used* by a cross-section of professional workers, needed to be maintained as a networked system by a kind of knowledge elite who learned complex and difficult languages to operate it. Corporations who were interested in 'augmenting' did not wish to hire a small army of system operators, and were interested in but a few of NLS's functions. It needed to be trimmed down and tuned to the world of the post-war business boom.

ARPA support continued to dwindle, and in 1977 SRI sold the entire augmentation system to Tymshare Corporation. The system, named 'Augment', is now marketed as a package by Tymshare, and was adapted to a business environment through the 1980s.

> I'm going to terminate at this point, since after 1976 we really had no chance to continue pursuing this 'augmentation framework'. It seemed no longer to fit the pattern of research at ARPA, or with what SRI wanted to do. When we landed in the commercial world, we found that it wasn't what people wanted to do there, either. The Augment system stayed alive in a sort of funny, dumb way, often like taking a bulldozer in to help people work in their back yards. (Engelbart, 1988, p.229).

APRANET
In 1965, Bob Taylor worked out of his office in the Pentagon as director of IPTO, administering seemingly endless funds on behalf of the war machine to 'people who had a good chance of advancing the state of information processing technology by an order of magnitude' (Rheingold, 1995, p.207). After all, there was the USSR to compete with, who had stolen the attention of the world with Sputnik back in 1957. The US wanted to be at the forefront of military intelligence worldwide, and in an atmosphere of technological utopianism this translated into intelligent technology.

Communications across computer networks were originally designed to solve a military problem: information processing and control. Around the late 60s, while Engelbart was concerning himself with the great excess of information and efficient ways of augmenting humans to deal with this, the military were collating vital lessons concerning communications control. During World War II the Department of Defense had learnt that decisions concerning mass destruction were best done by machines. There was a need to write humans out of the loop, or, at best, to augment their faculties. As Engelbart had discovered, there was also an exponential rise in the mass of recorded information to deal with, especially scientific literature, and a concordant problem in finding and accessing this information across large distances. The military had discovered that in such an environment the independent will of the enemy often manifested itself as sabotage and interdiction – the destruction of vital parts of information networks. This fact made the survivability of a system once parts of it had been destroyed a major problem.

What if there were a nuclear attack? A centralized system could be taken out by a single strike, disabling the entire communications network.

> Paul Baran of the RAND Corporation undertook a series of investigations of this question, concluding that the strongest communication system would be a distributed network of computers having several properties: it would have sufficient redundancy so that the loss of subsets of links and nodes would not isolate any of the still-functioning nodes; there would be no central control . . . and each node would contain routing information and could automatically reconfigure this information in a short time after the loss of a link or node. (Denning, cited in DeLanda, 1994, p.120)

The creation of networks capable of surviving attack necessarily involved the *decentralization* of traffic control and the distribution of self-organizing capabilities to the components of the network. One of the benefits of such an arrangement was that processing power and specialist knowledge (i.e. scarce resources) could be shared in the absence of local resources or during a shortage or war. Also, if one node went down, important messages could reroute through a different path and still reach their destination. The risk, of course, was that control was decentralized and it was difficult to keep track of what was going on at every point in the network; given this, it is no wonder that the project was first trialled in universities and across civilian scientific centres.

In the fall of 1969, the first node of ARPANET was installed at UCLA. By 1973, there were 37 nodes operating, and today this network has evolved into a collection of (partitioned military and scientific) networks in the tens of thousands, and the wider public domain known as the Internet, whose networks number in the millions. The usefulness of computer networking demonstrated by ARPA and the Department of Defence was not lost on other communities and disciplines outside the war machine (Cerf, 1997). The birth of ARPANET is now widely held to be the creation myth of the modern Internet, and the platform through which the vast majority of people first come into contact with hypertext.

Andries Van Dam and the hypertext editing system

In 1967, around the same time that Bob Taylor was dreaming of an indestructible, distributed communications network for the Department of

Defense, Andries Van Dam built the world's first hypertext system at Brown University.

It ran on 128k of memory on a small IBM 360, the first general-purpose computer built by IBM. Van Dam, like many of the hypertext pioneers, was inspired by Bush's fears of a chaotic 'information explosion' and the 'various techniques and devices which could be used to cope with it' (Van Dam *et al*, 1967, p.294) modelled on the humble human brain. Like Engelbart, who was working on NLS at the same time at SRI, and like the numerous psychologists and psychiatrists exploring the connection between vision and consciousness, Van Dam wished to provide the user with 'unrestricted spatial options' (Van Dam *et al*, 1967, p.299) which would allow for more control due to the efficiency of the visual faculties, as could be seen in radar system displays.

The Hypertext Editing System had the basic hypertext functionality of linking and jumping between documents, basic browsing and search facilities and was later adjusted to accommodate multiple displays and windows. Writings were stored in a central computer pool, where they were accessed, viewed, changed and printed at will. It was designed to allow for the storage and management of a large body of information, scientific or academic. After the project was finished at Brown University, IBM sold it to the Houston Manned Spacecraft Center, where it was used to produce documentation for the Apollo missions (Nielson, 1995, p.40).

Section IV

These are some of the points at which conceptual and technological bodies have encountered the machines of capitalism and military science in this century, the points at which the forces expressing themselves as hypertext have developed. From this very brief survey, we can pick up a number of tendencies. Firstly, the early models of hypertext and their embodiments were not designed to 'democratize information' and liberate the average computer user from the confines of print, but to *control and manage* information explosions, and, especially in the case of Vannevar Bush and Doug Engelbart, to manage the scientific record and defend it against loss and decay in the face of this. Biological-mechanical analogues and a desire to augment, amplify or improve upon nature also seem to be recurrent: for Bush, Engelbart and Van Dam memex and hypertext were a way of augmenting the human mind to cope with a situation which seemed to be increasingly difficult to manage without technology. We might also note that the early Internet (ARPANET) was not designed to democratize information, but to survive nuclear attack, to distribute command and to manage information in novel situations.

So, to draw some things together. I am wanting to point out that in past incarnations the desires and tendencies of hypertext have not always had a liberal-democratic ideology. Similarly, the effects of capitalism on our movements across the interface have not always been about individual choice and autonomy. I am not, however, wanting to suggest that the military history of hypertext will direct its future. Capitalism will find its own uses for things. This chapter is a call for strategic criticism, for ontological anarchy, for poetic practice. For a recognition that *theory itself* is a machine which can be used to intervene in things, to disrupt the flow.

Hypertext is not a unified, liberating phenomenon. As a machine, it at once comprises and is in departure from previous generations of technologies, the demands of the workplace and educational settings, military research, the mass media, programmers and their pets, Microsoft and the corporate players, the perpetually mutating desires of the Web and its puppeteers, intellectual and artistic fashion, technological limits, the limits of capital. It is an assemblage arising from the interrelations of a field of forces, these forces. It is inherently unstable and in a process of perpetual change. This is the ontology of hypertext. It is a system of directed flows. If we know where these flows and their intersections are, what they are emerging from, we can muddle them.

References

Badiou, Alain (1994) 'Gilles Deleuze, The fold: Leibniz and the baroque' in Constantin Boundas & Dorothea Olkowski (eds) *Gilles Deleuze and the theater of philosophy*. London/ New York: Routledge.

Barnet, Belinda (1997) 'Storming the interface: Mindvirus, I/O/D and deceptive interaction' in Artlink: *Australian Contemporary Art Quarterly,* 17:4, December.

Barthes, Roland (1974) *S/Z*. Canada: Harper Collins.

Bolter, Jay David (1991) *Writing space: The computer, hypertext and the history of writing*. Hillsdale, New Jersey: Lawrence Erlbaum Associates.

Bush, Vannevar (1939) 'Mechanization and record', Vannevar Bush Papers, Library of Congress [Box 50, General correspondence file, Eric Hodgins].

Bush, Vannevar (1945) 'As we may think' in *The Altlantic Monthly*, Vol. 176, No.1, p.641-649.

Bush, Vannevar (1967) 'Science pauses' in *Science is not enough*. New York: William Morrow, pp.14-33.

Bush, Vannevar (1970) *Pieces of the action*. New York: William Morrow.

Cerf, Vincent (1997) 'Foreword' in Stefik, Mark (ed) *Internet dreams: Archetypes, myths and metaphors*. London & Cambridge: MIT Press.

Ceruzzi, Paul (1998) *A history of modern computing*. London and Cambridge: The MIT Press (see pp.36 and 37).

DeLanda, Manuel (1994) *War in the age of intelligent machines*. New York: Zone Books.

Delaney, Paul & George P. Landow. (eds) (1994) *Hypermedia and literary studies*. Cambridge, Massachusetts: MIT Press.

Deleuze, Gilles & Guattari, Felix (1983) *Anti-oedipus, capitalism and schizophrenia*. Minneapolis: University of Minnesota Press.

Deleuze, Gilles & Guattari, Felix (1987) *A thousand plateaus: Capitalism and schizophrenia*. Minneapolis: University of Minnesota Press.

Engelbart, Douglas (1988) 'The augmented knowledge workshop' in Goldberg, Adele (1988) (ed.) *A history of personal workstations*. New York, New York: ACM Press, Addison-Wesley Publishing Company, pp.185-249.

Engelbart, Douglas (1991) 'Letter to Vannevar Bush' in Nyce, James and Kahn, Paul (eds.) *From memex to hypertext: Vannevar Bush and the mind's machine*. London: Academic Press.

Grosz, Elizabeth (1994) *Volatile bodies: Toward a corporeal feminism*. St. Leonards: Allen & Unwin.

Grusin, Richard A. 'What is an electronic author? Theory and the technological fallacy', in *Configurations*, 3, pp.469-83.

Guattari, Felix (1995) *Chaosmosis: An ethico-aesthetic paradigm*. Sydney: Power Publications.

Hatt, Harold (1968) *Cybernetics and the image of man*. Nashville and New York: Abingdon Press.

Joyce, Michael (1995) *Of two minds: Hypertext, pedagogy and poetics*. Ann Arbor: The University of Michigan Press.

Land, Nick (1993) 'Machinic desire' in *Textual practice*. 7:3, winter 1993, pp. 471-82.

Landow, George P. (1993) *Hypertext: The convergence of contemporary critical theory and technology*. Baltimore: Johns Hopkins University Press.

Landow, George P. (ed.) (1994) *Hyper/text/theory*. Baltimore: Johns Hopkins University Press.

Licklider, J. C. R. (1960) 'Man-computer symbiosis' in *IRE Transactions on Human Factors in Electronics*, Vol. HFE-1, March 1960, pp.4-11.

Massumi, Brian (1996) *A user's guide to capitalism and schizophrenia*. London/Cambridge: The MIT Press.

Moulthrop, Stuart (1997) http://raven.ubalt.edu/staff/mouthrop/essays

Moulthrop, Stuart (1994) 'Rhizome and resistance: Hypertext and the dreams of a new culture' in Landow, George P. (ed.) *Hyper/text/theory*. Baltimore: Johns Hopkins University Press, pp.299-319.

Nelson, Ted (1965) 'A file structure for the complex, the changing and the indeterminate'. *Proceedings of the ACM 20th National Conferences*. ACM Press.

Nielson, Jakob (1995) *Multimedia and hypertext*. London/New York: Academic Press.

Rheingold, Howard (1995) *Tools for thought*. New York: Simon & Schuster.

Rosenberg, Martin E. (1994) 'Physics and hypertext: Liberation and complicity in art and pedagogy' in Landow, George (ed.) *Hyper/text/theory*. Baltimore: Johns Hopkins University Press, pp.268-298.

Smith, Linda C (1991) 'Memex as an image of potentiality revisited', in Nyce, J. & Kahn, P. (eds) *From memex to hypertext*. London/New York: Academic Press.

Snyder, Ilana (1996) *Hypertext: The electronic labyrinth*. Melbourne: Melbourne University Press.

Van Dam, Andries; Carmody, Steven; Gross, Walter; Nelson, Theodor H. & Rice, David (1967) *A hypertext editing system for the /360*, Brown University, Providence, Rhode Island: A report for the Center for Computer and Information Sciences.

References (websites)

Fuller, Matt & Simon Pope (1993) *Warning: This computer has multiple personality disorder.* http://www.altx.com/wordbombs/popefuller.html

Fuller, Matt & Simon, Pope (eds) (undated) *I/O/D2,* http://www.pHreak.co.uk/i_o_d/

Moulthrop, Stuart (1991) 'You say you want a revolution? Hypertext and the Laws of Media', in *Postmodern culture* 1:3, 1991. http://128.220.50.88/journals/ postmodern_culture/v001/1.3moulthrop.html

Moultrop, Stuart (1997) *No War Machine.* http://raven.ubalt.edu/staff/moulthrop/ essays/

Rosenberg, Martin (1993) 'Dynamic and thermodynamic tropes of the subject in Freud and Deleuze and Guattari', in *Postmodern culture,* 4:1, . http://128.220.50.88/journals/ postmodern_culture/v004/4.1rosenberg.html

Webs of convergence: Genre and flow on the World Wide Web

Scott Shaner

Over the latter part of this decade, the World Wide Web (Web) has become an increasingly important form of Internet communications. While access to the Internet remains limited by geographic, social and economic barriers, the rapid development of the Web has transformed the Internet into a popular new media form. Indeed, for many the Web has come to be synonymous with the Internet and its future possibilities.

Traditionally, the Internet has been celebrated as an anarchic, non-hierarchical, organic space, with no point of centralized control and the potential to destabilize social and political hierarchies. Much of this rhetoric stems from analyzes of computer-mediated communication which highlight the network technology[1] (e.g. packet switched data transmission which, from the perspective of the network, renders all nodes on the network equal to one another) or new emerging forms of textuality[2] (e.g. hypertext, which theoretically renders the processes of intertextuality more explicit and challenges traditional notions of authorship, creativity and meaning).

The emergence of the Web as a popular media form requires that we reassess our theoretical understanding of on-line communication. As the Web becomes increasingly commercial in character the communication it enables is increasingly similar to the type of communication characteristic of previous media technologies. Increasingly, the Web has become a means of realizing relationships in strategically represented computer-mediated contexts, often designed to construct, track and trade its audience as a commodity in a manner similar to television (Marshall, 1997).

---

1. For examples see Rushkoff, D. (1994) *Media virus! Hidden agendas in popular culture*, New York: Random House, and Gilder, G. (1994) *Life after television*, New York: Norton.

2. For example see Bolter, D. J. (1991) *Writing space: The computer, hypertext and the history of writing*, Hillsdale, New Jersey; L. Erlbaum and Lanham, R.A. (1993) *The electronic word: Democracy, technology, and the arts*, Chicago: University of Chicago Press. A more qualified version of this position is offered by Landow, G. (1997) *Hypertext 2.0*, Baltimore: Johns Hopkins University Press.

As a result, we are currently witnessing the emergence of traditional broadcasting industry configurations between the broader on-line industry, its texts and audiences (Cunningham & Finn, 1996). For example, research is beginning to show that a relatively small number of websites seem to account for a disproportionate amount of traffic on the Web (Adamic & Huberman, 1999). The on-line strategies of major media and Internet content providers favours producing sites which will act as our starting point, or portal, into the Web. Large media conglomerates, such as Disney, Microsoft, NBC, to name a few, are forming strategic relationships with on-line players to invoke familiar brand names for information on-line. These trends give rise to a hierarchy amongst different types of content on the Web, which in turn produces perceptions of genre and quality of information based on the type of relationship invoked by a webpage (Wilson, 1999).

To this extent, Web content is best understood via a comparison with the techniques associated with broadcasting. In contrast to the typical rhetoric surrounding the Internet mentioned above, I would like to assert the relevance of concepts from media and cultural studies, such as 'genre' and 'flow', to achieving a greater understanding of communication enabled by the Web. In short, I would like to develop how the concepts of genre and flow can be applied to the analysis of Web content.

Web genres

Adapted from the study of literature, genre analysis has been widely applied to the classification of film and television. However, as Feuer has pointed out, literary genres tend to be broader ahistorical classifications established with reference to a pre-existing theory of types of literature (e.g. tragedy, comedy (Feuer, 1987). In contrast, film and television genres are more historical and culturally specific manifestations of commercial and industrial logic derived from the observation of specific texts. As a result, the study of film and television has tended to employ genre categories similar to those in circulation within their industries in order to classify their texts (e.g. Western, soap opera).

Given the dazzling diversity of content and services available, one would have to be sceptical about deducing generic categories from a broader theoretical understanding of the Web in its totality. Web genres, like film and television genres, are probably best understood as historically specific and, in a manner similar to their film and television counterparts, tend to be defined by the on-line industry.

The analysis genre on the Web highlights a significant point of both theoretical and industrial convergence. Industrially, the recent appearance of regular types of Web content represents a form of industrial convergence as traditional media, mostly large transnational media enterprises, seek to optimize the structure of the Web in order to extract maximum profit from their on-line ventures. Theoretically, Web genres function in a similar manner to genres in other forms of media such as television. Genres are a common currency that inform and constrain industry practices, textual production and the expectations and interpretive capacities of audiences. As Neale has remarked with regards to film:

> Not only a set of economic practices or meaningful products, cinema is also a constantly fluctuating series of signifying processes, a 'machine' for the production of meanings and positions . . . Genres are components in this 'machine'. As systematized forms of the articulation of meaning and position they are a fundamental part of the cinema's 'mental machinery'. Approached in this way genres are not to be seen as forms of textual codifications but as systems of orientations, expectations and conventions that circulate between industry, text and subject. (Neale, 1980, p.19)

It is in this sense that the industrial context of production tends to promote certain genres over others within a single cultural form. In television, for example, economic constraints, introduced by the recently deregulated multi-channel environment in the United States and elsewhere, have led to the increased prominence of the talk show format. As Wilson has remarked: 'The talk show is paradigmatic within the medium's new financial priorities, displacing the continuous serial ("soap opera") as too expensive to produce' (Wilson, 1997). Similarly, government regulations, such as quotas for the transmission of children's programmes and domestically produced content in Australia, can be argued to have led to the prominence of certain formats, such as the compere-led programme where a local host merely introduces and accompanies foreign-sourced content.

The adoption of advertising-based business models and the public float of many Web-based Internet content providers, have produced a similar degree of 'systematized variety' and forces of homogeneity on the Web (Neale, 1980, p.26). The commercialization of the Web has produced a similar textual economy, making certain types of content and services paradigmatic. Competing portal sites such as *Yahoo!*, Disney's *Go Network*, and Microsoft's *The Microsoft Network* all provide their own versions of the same genres of Web content. Web genres, such as up-to-the-minute news and sports coverage, live events, on-line chat, interactive games, Web-based email and search engines facilities have all become elevated in the hierarchy of Web content.

World Wide Web as flow

In *Television: technology and cultural form,* Raymond Williams argued that to really understand the uniqueness of television as a communications technology one needs to analyze not only its content, but also the way different types of audiovisual content are presented in sequence or as a flow (Williams, 1974). Concepts like genre, borrowed from the analysis of film and literature, are able to deal with audiovisual content, but not the actual way that content is delivered via the medium. The concept of flow captures all the 'messiness' of television as a cultural form and as it is integrated into a set of practices known as broadcasting.

> In all developed broadcasting systems the characteristic organization, and therefore the characteristic experience, is one of sequence or flow. This phenomenon, of planned flow, is then perhaps the defining characteristic of broadcasting, simultaneously as a technology and as a cultural form.
> (Williams, 1974, p.86)

Williams was pointing to the fact that all previous forms of media were stand-alone entities or events. With television we are actually presented with various sequences of content, with each channel presenting its own alternative version as a broadcasting strategy. Williams' concept of flow in television applies to interaction on the Web as well. Rather than merely visiting a set of discrete content repositories, 'browsing' the Web is actually more like constructing a 'flow' from link to link and, most probably, site to site.

In fact, Web browsing is remarkably similar to the different types of flow set up by television. Jensen has argued that, rather than the single sense of flow described by Williams, the actual experience of television can be viewed to draw on three different types of flow. Firstly, there is the channel flow, or the flow as it is set up by an individual station (Jensen, 1995). Secondly, there exists a flow as it is constructed by the viewer. Although, the channel flow may in fact represent the programming strategies of broadcasters, viewers are of course free to switch channels or make other changes, which constructs another sense of flow based on an individual's actual experience. Lastly, all the possibilities from which a viewer flow can be constructed creates an overarching super flow, representing the sum total of possible sequences.

While the distributed hypertext environment of the Web may allow for greater choice from which to construct a flow than is the case with traditional broadcast media, the viewer flow in both forms of media can potentially be harnessed and organized to some extent. On commercial television, flow is dominated by programming strategies aimed at holding an audience over a day's viewing as well as clustering specific demographic groups around specific times for the benefit of advertisers (e.g. female viewers in the late morning and early afternoon, teenage viewers in the early evening. The concept of genre is a key factor in allowing broadcasters to manage and plan a successful sequence or flow by clustering specific types of viewer demographics around particular types of programming.

Likewise, if one looks to recent trends in Web publishing one can discern a number of strategies by which flow is managed. 'Portal sites', as they have been termed by the on-line industry, attempt to serve as a user's entry point to the Web, often by organizing or systematically rendering the Web into a single functional and useable resource. Portals attempt to maximize audience size and cultivate regular repeat visitors to the site in order to maximize profit from advertisers and other sources of revenue.[3] They do this by providing access to premium information content (as signified by brand), personalized content, Web-based email access, entertainment such as chat networks and games, search engine facilities, organized Internet events and other live Web content, amongst other features.

Portal sites represent a significant shift in the way the Web has come to be institutionalized as a cultural form by emulating the logic of broadcasting and moving away from the decentralized, anarchic and potentially egalitarian social space it was previously thought to be. The emergence of the imperative to maximize audience size has given rise to new strategies in the provision of on-line content via the Web. Firstly, the Web has become littered with familiar brand names for information drawing on our knowledge of traditional media sources.

Secondly, many 'brand' name sites have enacted strategies of vertical and horizontal integration, both industrially and in terms of content and service provision. The emergence of joint ventures between traditional media and Internet start-up companies, such as Infoseek, Inc. and the Disney's *Go Network*, joint ventures between television networks like the American NBC or, in Australia, PBL Ltd's *Channel Nine Network*, with *The Microsoft Network,* are three such examples. Horizontally, company takeovers have been slowly gathering speed, reducing the number of competing sites on the Web.[4] In terms of their impact on Web content, these alliances gather resources (e.g. content such as news wire services, email facilities, search engines, chat hubs,) at one single site in an effort to create a one-stop 'shop' for information and services on the Web.

In this sense, portal sites are to the Web what channels, or stations, are to television. They are the brokers who enact the strategies which structure and organize the possible flows of content within the medium.

In conclusion, I would reassert the importance of considering parallels between the Web and previous forms of media, such as television. As the Web continues to be shaped by similar political economic forces to those characteristic of broadcasting, we need to revisit traditional concepts from media and cultural studies, such as genre and flow, in order to better contextualize our understanding of the medium.

---

3. Indeed, advertising in the form of on-line banners may only be the tip of the iceberg. As the Web becomes more interactive and oriented toward e-commerce, brand name portal sites will be strategically positioned to attract large amounts of revenue from on-line sales and service provision.

4. America Online's 1998 takeover of Netscape Communications Inc is one example of lessening competition as Netscape's portal known as *Netcenter* came into the AOL fold.

References

Adamic, L. & Huberman, B. (1999) 'The nature of markets on the World Wide Web', Xerox Palo Alto Research Center, (http://www.parc.xerox.com/istl/groups/iea/www/webmarkets.html).

Cunningham, S. & Finn, M. (1996) 'Media theory and the Internet' in *Media International Australia*. No. 80, p.84-92.

Feuer, J. (1987) 'Genre study and television' in Allen, R. (ed.) (1987) *Channels of discourse: Television and contemporary criticism*. Chapel Hill: University of North Carolina Press.

Jensen, K. (1995) *The social semiotics of mass communication*. London: Sage.

Marshall, P. D. (1997) 'The commodity and the Internet: Interactivity and the generation of the audience commodity' in *Media International Australia*, No. 83, pp.51-62.

Neale, S. (1980) *Genre*. London: British Film Institute.

Williams, R. (1974) *Television: technology and cultural form*. London: Fontana.

Wilson, T. (1997) 'Narrowcasting and net narrativity: Talkshow as paradigmatic.' Paper presented at the Australian and New Zealand Communication Association Conference, Latrobe University, Melbourne.

Wilson, T. (1999) 'Researching and teaching cinema studies on the World Wide Web: A Malaysian instance.' Paper presented at the Australian and New Zealand Communication Association Conference, Sydney, Australia, July 1999.

Peter Weir's transnational aesthetic or 'What Truman Burbank can tell us about global communication'

Adam Knee

The Truman show, a satire about the potentially enormous power of United States based media industries, was one of the most critically well-received American films of 1998, but the chief creative figure behind the film was paradoxically not an American, but rather an Australian who has been working partially within Hollywood since the mid-1980s. Director Peter Weir's own professional existence has itself consistently felt the pull of America's media influence on a global level, and in this sense the themes of this 'American' text strongly register the transnational situation of its expatriate director. Weir has throughout his career sustained negotiations with American distributors and producers but has also generally tried to maintain some level of an Australian base for his films, even after achieving Hollywood success. This chapter will offer an analysis of the politics of *The Truman show*'s media critique in the light of recent debates about Hollywood hegemony and its relation to economic and cultural globalization. The tension between the 'global' and the 'local' which arises here will be highlighted both as it is articulated through the film text and as it has been played out over the course of Weir's career and through his larger cinematic oeuvre. The choices made by Weir – and by narrative protagonist Truman Burbank – will thereby be examined as possible responses to the problematics of individual expression in a post-national context.

Mediated boundaries

The clearest aspects of *The Truman show*'s media critique centre on the ubiquity, wide-ranging influence, and commercial motivations of mass media industries. In brief, the film shows how a media organization has no compunctions about tricking the main protagonist into living a lie. He is brought up in a world which, without his knowledge, has been completely staged by this corporation, so that he may be photographed at all times as the subject matter for a television show. The media giant is seen as all-powerful and all-pervasive, in its ability to pull off its cosmic ruse against

Truman, in the ubiquity of its hidden cameras, and in its infusion of Truman's 'fictional' world with product placements and other commercial plugs. Thus figured as the all-knowing source of creation, the media giant stands in as a post-modern substitute for divinity. One is clearly invited, moreover, to see Truman's home of Seahaven Island as an allegory for any media-influenced community of the 1990s – a reading made clearer when a friend dismisses Truman's growing paranoia about the world around him as a common fantasy of public media coverage, as well as in the numerous sequences showing 'real world' spectators in thrall to the programme and ready to purchase the items it presents; the 'reality' of Seahaven's commercial products extends to the spectatorial world.

The Truman show continually and pointedly plays on the confusion between differing levels of reality, conflating various registers of narration, various modes of discourse – evident in the fact that the title *The Truman show* refers to both the feature film and to the television show it takes as its subject. From the very opening of the film (which begins with what appears to be a promotional piece about the programme), we are never completely sure whether we are watching an excerpt from broadcast material, or out-takes from the surveillance cameras, or other material from the film's presumably omniscient narration. Regular shifts from more standard Hollywood camera setups to setups that imply the perspective of a surveillance camera, or to partially masked shots implying same, remind us that we can never be quite sure whether we are watching a television show, or a film of what occurs on the set of the show. The point, however, is that in effect there is no difference – at least not for Truman, and by implication, potentially, not for the rest of us. Commercial media influence, again, is seen to foster the blurring of boundaries between the 'real' or 'authentic' and the televisual or commercial. The film's clever use of sound adds to the sense of the media control and mixing of differing registers of reality; Truman's own day seems to be regulated by the banal talk and irritatingly light classical music broadcast on Seahaven's radio station, but it is precisely this music which constitutes the soundtrack for much of the film. The distinction between diegetic and non-diegetic music, like that between televisual and 'real' imagery, is largely effaced.

As the mass media here threatens to erase distinctions between reality and representation, so does it also appear to potentially alter the nature of the local and the global and to thereby blur the differences between them. There is very little to distinguish the locality of Seahaven (aside from its fictionality) – little distinctive in its people or 'culture' or architecture; all seems culturally and stylistically homogeneous. The homogeneity is, more specifically, that of a white, middle-class, middle-American media landscape, one rather perversely inspired by that media icon of small-town American community values, Frank Capra's *It's a wonderful life* (1946). The Capra film is alluded to in the geography of downtown Seahaven, as well as in Truman's favourite television programme, *Show me the way to go home*; that programme, according to a television announcer, teaches that 'No one is poor who has friends' – a line from the Capra film. We hear, moreover, that the broadcast of the programme follows that of yet another show emblematic of middle-class American domestic life of the postwar era: *I love Lucy*. Given that Truman's world has been wilfully constructed following the inspiration of such media models, it is little surprise that Seahaven is fairly bland and homogeneous, with markers of cultural, racial and class difference discretely effaced – witnessed in the fully assimilated token black family living across the street from the Burbanks and in the campaign to rid the streets of derelicts following the appearance of one (in fact a former cast member trying to contact Truman). The standardization of the local realm in accordance with the dictates of American commerce is also evidenced in the omnipresence of the aforementioned promoted products and advertisements for them – Mococoa cocoa (one wonders if Moccona was consulted), a boutique brewery beer, Kaiser Chicken, the Chef's Pal which Truman and his wife eventually wield against one another, and the Ford automobiles people drive (this last 'real' product in the fictional world marking yet another instance of the film's calculated ontological slippage). The sameness of the home architecture – a literally whitewashed post-modern amalgam of colonial and modern features – also reveals itself as rooted in a common commercial supplier, Carlton Colonial Homes. Also omnipresent is the town's predominant corporate entity, the aptly-named Omnicom.

The sense of the distinctiveness of Seahaven's locality is lost not only in its media-driven homogenization, but also in the promulgation of information about the most minute details of local existence on a global scale through the offices of *The Truman show*. The locality is thus primarily a virtual one, constructed through the discourse of the television show, yet consisting of no locally specific characteristics and disseminated beyond the physical boundaries of Seahaven Island. A sense of the literally global proportions of the broadcast corporation identified with the locality is made clear when we are told that the show's dome-shaped sound stage is (along with the Great Wall of China) one of only two man-made structures visible from space, that its employees are equivalent in number to the population of a small nation, and that its revenues exceed the GNP of such a nation. The programme's worldwide reach is highlighted through numerous cutaways to shots of viewers and consumers of *The Truman show* products, including a Japanese family with Japanese-language Truman paraphernalia on their walls, as well as through a montage sequence including newspaper headlines about the programme in various languages. Seahaven Island may be a virtual locality, but it is also a genuinely global village.

Yet while people around the world may share Truman's trials and tribulations, their passive televisual pleasure, it seems, comes at the cost of Truman's exploitation. The protagonist is an unwitting participant, the confines of the show increasingly interfering with his own desire for escape and personal growth. The villain of the piece is not so much this audience, however; while oblivious to the infringements of Truman's own personal rights and monetarily contributing to the corporation which oppresses him, it is nevertheless generally supportive of his goals. In the film's view, the blame can be more squarely laid with the production company, understood as actively orchestrating the commercial arrangements which dupe the audience and the textual arrangements which dupe Truman; by virtue of being all-seeing, all-knowing and all-powerful within the created universe of *The Truman show*, director Christof clearly develops a bit of a God complex, referring to himself at one point as 'the creator', and even believing he has the right to dictate the life or death of the man who serves as his protagonist. The clear primary target of this characterization is the Hollywood media industry, explicitly linked with the production house when we see the famous 'Hollywood' sign at the foot of the studio dome and again when we see one of the key technical staff members (perhaps wary of the longevity of his employment) reading the classified ad section of the *Los Angeles Times*. It is the arrogance of Hollywood, the film seems to suggest, its willingness to override the individual and local for the sake of US corporate benefit, which fosters American media hegemony.

Truman, Weir and Hollywood

At times the film may appear to underplay the global dimensions of its media critique – focusing, for example, much more heavily on the show's American audiences than its overseas ones – yet the forced dissemination of a certain 'Americanness' through the Hollywood media does indeed seem to be a central concern. While the protagonist may appear to be the archetypal all-American husband, the Americanness of him and his community is quite clearly revealed to be a media construction; adopted by the production company at birth, he has had his American identity thrust upon him, a notion highlighted in the over-determined Americanness of his name – his surname referring, appropriately enough, to a Los Angeles suburb known for television and film production, his first name bringing to mind the American president in office in the era of *It's a wonderful life* and *I love Lucy*, coincidentally also the era of a precipitous rise in America's global political and commercial influence. Truman, however, clearly chafes under the yoke of this identity, and the film's narrative progresses both as he begins to suspect its constructedness, its falseness, and as he determines to find ways to achieve personal freedom, a truer expression of self – in short, to more genuinely live up to the 'truth' implied in his first name.

This struggle with the forced imposition of 'Americanness' is one which clearly has multiple resonances in the film-making career of Peter Weir – and in ways which suggest Weir's own identifications would lie far more with Truman than with fellow director Christof. Weir saw his first feature film, *The cars that ate Paris* (1974), 'Americanized' by a US distributor in hopes of augmenting its commercial potential; his somewhat uneven and certainly unusual comedic and horrific tale of an insular community in the Australian outback thus became, by way of re-editing and dubbing, *The cars that eat people*. While not especially happy with that turn of events, Weir did continue to see the US market and the US film-making industry as potentially significant resources for him. The success abroad (although not, initially, in the US) of *Picnic at hanging rock* (1975) established the viability of an international market for Weir's (and other Australian) film, and a concern with this market can be seen in *The last wave*'s (1977) international casting of its distinctively Australian tale, as well as in partial funding by a US distributor. The positive US reception of *The last wave* led in turn to a (delayed) release of his earlier *Picnic stateside*[1] Weir's subsequent *Gallipoli* (1981), generally seen as a breakthrough to mainstream film-making for the director, was in line with this internationalization, planned in advance for a major international release by the US distributor Paramount. While Weir was somewhat disappointed in the distributor's evident lack of care with the film (which did not do exceptionally well in the States), it did give the director a still higher Hollywood profile, and his next feature, *The year of living dangerously* (1983), was financed by a major US studio and featured a major US star playing alongside *Gallipoli's* Mel Gibson.

Despite some less than satisfactory experiences with the Hollywood industry, then, Weir clearly saw involvement with that industry as something which could enrich his possibilities in film-making, something consonant with the intended course of his career. And from *Witness* (1985) on, he became, for many intents and purposes, a Hollywood director, overseeing US-financed, US-based productions, with largely American casts and crews. At the same time, however, Weir has very self-consciously developed strategies to resist a complete 'Hollywoodization', to retain a sense of local (Australian) identity in his film productions as well as in his own growing celebrity image. He has, for example, continued to work with a number of Australian production personnel and has also negotiated agreements allowing him to do his post-production work in Australia, where he maintains a part-year residence. Weir has also, on occasion, chosen to operate without US studio financing, as with the New York-set, Franco-Australian independent co-production *Greencard* (1990). Auteurist analyzes of the themes and stylistics of Weir's films also reveal significant continuities between his pre- and post-Hollywood works – most notably and pertinently a theme of communication, interaction, and negotiation between differing realms, cultures, nations.

---

1. Reported in David Stratton (1980) *The last new wave: The Australian film revival*, Sydney: Angus & Robertson, p.73.

Much like Weir, protagonist Truman, too, struggles with American cultural and economic hegemony, wants to break free and retain some autonomy, to achieve a greater sense of his own personal identity. This struggle for identity under the sign of Hollywood makes the text not only characteristic of Weir's work – but also, paradoxically, in some ways distinctively Australian. Most plainly, just as Seahaven Island is fully dominated by Hollywood, so has the Australian film industry, throughout its history, had to deal with US hegemony – both in the US domination of films released to theatres and in its siphoning off of local talent. We can also find distinctly Australian resonances in the particular forms taken by Truman's search for identity, his uncertainty over and interrogation of his origins. Truman is repeatedly and duplicitously 'orphaned' in the course of the film; the product of an unwanted pregnancy, he is adopted by the production company and given to fictional parents, one of whom is then taken from him in a staged boating accident, dictated by various narrative imperatives of the show. Truman begins to question his origins in earnest when he thinks he sees his supposedly drowned father alive – and has in fact seen the actor who played his father, who has surreptitiously entered the set as (the character of) a homeless man in order to make contact with Truman once more. We learn, in the context of Truman's questioning of what he thinks he has seen, that both he and his (fictional) father have been scripted as being only children – which is to say that the producers have worked to minimize any connection to a verifiable familial past, any concrete evidence of origins. The 'powers that be' eventually decide to solve the problem precipitated by the renegade actor's intervention by writing the father back into the script, on the premise that he suffered amnesia after being lost at sea. With Truman's eventual discovery of the lifelong ruse which has been played against him, however, the question of origins is once more opened in earnest.

Truman is hardly alone among Weir's protagonists in having lost his parents and in questioning his origins. Orphaned protagonists can for example be found in *The cars*, *Picnic* and *The last wave*, while the loss of a child protagonist's father occurs at the opening of *Witness* and the close of *The mosquito coast* (1986). Among these films, it is *The last wave* which most explicitly links the theme of being orphaned with interrogations of origins – and in particular of cultural and national heritage. In that film a white Australian's employment as the defense attorney for five Aborigines accused of murder serves as a catalyst for a personal crisis on the part of the attorney, involving a series of hallucinatory episodes and, eventually, a questioning of his values and frames of reference, an interrogation of his origins and their relationship to indigenous Australian culture. ('Where is your clan territory?' an Aborigine elder asks of the attorney, while scrutinizing an album of photos of his forebears.)

Coastal anxieties

Of course, it is partly in relation to the issue of past white-Aboriginal interaction, to a history involving the mixing of blood lines, forced assimilation, human rights abuses of various kinds, and the usurpation of native lands, that the issue of origins is such a resonant one in Australian culture. As Bob Hodge and Vijay Mishra argue, Australian cultural anxiety over origins and a related obsession over legitimacy point toward 'the occluded but central and problematic place of Aboriginal Australians in the contemporary Australian state and in the construction of the national identity' (Hodge and Mishra, 1991, p.24). For Australians of European descent, the preoccupation with origins has an additional source in the fact that ancestral lands are oceans distant and possibly obscured by unclear family history – a history in some cases involving convictism, another factor raising issues of legitimacy. The theme of being orphaned or abandoned by an uncaring parent has additionally been linked with perceptions of 'motherland', Britain's lack of adequate attention to Australia in times of difficulty.[2]

There are a number of ways the Australian specificity of such themes resonates in Truman's narrative. In pointing toward these resonances, I am not arguing that *The Truman show* is necessarily a conscious allegory for aspects of Australian culture and history. I do want to suggest, however, that the film evokes concerns and contradictions within the construction of Australian culture, that it operates on some levels as a vehicle for working through certain tensions within a (necessarily fragmented) Australian 'national psyche'. One example of the film's Australian resonance resides in the destruction of Truman's past, which, like that of the Aboriginal past, is dictated by the economic imperatives of others and is required for the (fictional) construction of the local identity of an island community. More pointedly, his removal at birth from his natural parents, with minimal chance of connecting with them again, so that he may assimilate into a 'foreign', constructed culture uneasily echoes the Australian policy of placing Aboriginal children with white families, to fit these children into the constructed Australian national narrative. The fact that the key trauma of Truman's childhood – a trauma centrally implicated in his questioning of his origins – takes place in an ocean off the coast of his present homeland at the same time echoes the traumatic moment in Euro-Australian history, that of separation from the past by an ocean. Specifically, Truman's trauma is the loss of his 'father' in a boating accident, staged by the programme in order to induce in Truman a fear of the water and to thereby diminish the likelihood of his leaving the island and the show.

---

2. See Malouf, David (1998) *A spirit of play: The making of Australian consciousness*, Sydney: ABC Books, Chapter 5 for a discussion of this theme in Australian culture.

The recurrent mention in the foregoing of the island nature of Truman's home, its proximity to the coast, is itself significant; what is possibly the strongest allegory of Australian identity in the film is that involving Truman's ambivalent relationship to his island locality. Seahaven, like Australia, is an island state, locally regulated and separated off from the rest of the world by seemingly difficult-to-traverse bodies of water – in the case of the film, difficult because of Truman's fears, in the case of Australia, difficult because of distance from other land masses. That the narrative of *The Truman show* is structured around the protagonist's uneasiness in defining his identity in relation to the island and its culture readily invites readings of the text with respect to Australian identity. Truman is regularly drawn to the coast, to the edge of his locality, during the course of the film. Even as a child, he expresses a desire to be a global explorer, an interest which teachers attempt to squelch. During a childhood visit to the beach, we see Truman attempt to wander off beyond the permitted boundaries of the controlled television sound stage, and his father is forced to carry him back. It is this nascent wanderlust which the show's producers attempt to counter in staging the father's oceanic demise.

The drowning incident succeeds in instilling in Truman a phobia of travelling over water, but it does not extinguish his attraction to the coast or his desire to travel. The film's dialogue quite explicitly links Truman's desire for travel and exploration with a desire to escape, to 'get out', as the protagonist tells his friend and confidant Marlon, 'Out of my job. Out of this city. Off this island.' When Truman proposes a round-the-world trip to his wife a short while later, however, she scoffs at the idea, noting the need to keep up mortgage and car payments, and suggesting that their plans to try for a baby should be 'enough of an adventure'. The sense of domestic entrapment evoked here becomes far more pointed as it becomes increasingly evident to Truman that his wife does not love him. Truman thus seems to want to flee his marriage, his humdrum existence as an insurance salesman, the financial obligations of participation in Seahaven's consumer economy, and, as his suspicions of a larger conspiracy against him grow, his seemingly duplicitous Seahaven acquaintances and their false friendship. Truman returns to the beach repeatedly throughout the film – in particular when this desire for flight is at its strongest, when he is feeling upset and fed up with his life in Seahaven and seeks to collect his thoughts. In this context, the coast comes to stand as a concrete defining edge of personal, domestic and local identity, a marker of confinement, repression and falsehood, yet paradoxically also a landscape eloquent of the possibility of escape, of elsewhere, of an ultimate self-actualization linked to a reclamation of origins and personal desires.

The coast, the beach, the ocean are of course all extremely fertile icons in the culture of the island Australia, with quite complex and sometimes contradictory significations. Yet while these icons immediately suggest a defining point in Australian national culture, historically and geographically, they have been given less attention in studies of Australian landscape iconography than one might expect. In particular, the coast as a symbolic border of national identity or as a site of interaction and exchange with other national or cultural traditions is seldom discussed. What has taken centre-stage, rather, is the bush, the outback, the wilderness in the construction of the Australian imagination, as well as the contrast of these natural landscapes with the city. The coast as the literal and figurative margin of Australian identity gets pushed to the margins.[3] One important recent exception to this tendency is David Malouf's 1998 Boyer Lectures, in which the author discusses how Australia's island nature has been central to both the country's history and its perception of itself.[4] Malouf notes, for example, how the island geography was linked in earlier times to a perception of national distinctiveness and wholeness – but how these perceptions have also given rise, at certain points in Australian history, to isolationist and conformist tendencies.[5]

A number of possible determinants of the presence of the structuring absence of the coast as border in critical literature suggest themselves, not least the aforementioned anxiety over Australian origins, the on-going disavowal of the oppression which was a component part of the forming of the nation. One could also cite white Australia's long-standing fear of an Asian invasion as a source of coastal anxiety – that is to say, a fear of 'counter-colonization', one which naturally intensified during World War II. A further 'coastal anxiety' can be seen to stem, in more recent years, from Australia's uncertainty over its global relationships and identity: is Australia now European, Asian, Australasian, or just plain Australian? How is the island to be defined in relation to the rest of the world and how do its policies in trade, immigration and military aid, for example, express this?

That Truman's own anxiety over the coast is itself a sign of some repression, an index of a deeper problem, is made explicit, as his response to the ocean is figured as a psychoanalytic symptom; his phobic reaction

---

3. For example, the chapter devoted to the beach in John Fiske, Bob Hodge and Graham Turner's (1987) *Myths of Oz*, Sydney: Allen & Unwin, illuminating though it may be, focuses on the beach not as a symbolic site of the articulation of the borders of national identity, but as an arena of a nationally specific negotiation between the natural and the urban. Another extended look at the beach in Australian arts and culture is offered in Geoffrey Dutton, *Sun, sea, surf and sand* – 'The myth of the beach', Melbourne: Oxford University Press.

4. Malouf, *A spirit of play*, see, especially, pp.7-12 and Chapter 5.

5. Malouf, *A spirit of play*, pp.10-11.

to water is in fact presented to us in all its irrationality even before we are informed about his childhood trauma. Nor is Truman the first of Weir's protagonists to have such an anxious relationship to the coast; Weir has dealt with the issue previously in much more explicitly Australian contexts. In *The last wave*, for example, the anxiousness and ambivalence of the attorney's relationship to Aboriginal culture is dramatized in part through the eruption of various chaotic natural forces and elements – storms and water chief among them – into his ordered modern existence; the film's interrelated clashes between European and Aboriginal, present and past, culture and nature, reach their apotheosis in a closing scene at a Sydney beach, where the attorney either witnesses or has a vision of an apocalyptic wave heading for Australia's shores. Still earlier, in Weir's *The cars*, we see another form of coastal anxiety at work in a tale of inland Australians who have formed their own closed, hidden community, following their own peculiar laws and customs, far from the difficulties and interferences of the shoreline cities. Their insular economy, we learn, is sustained through a kind of land-bound pirating, in which passing cars are lured to their doom.[6] A similar Australian scenario of inward movement presents itself in Gerald Murnane's surreal 1982 novella *The plains*, in which a would-be Australian filmmaker (a young Peter Weir perhaps?) travels inland to research the culture and environment of landowning families of the plains, an obsessively introspective people who have come to see themselves as politically and culturally separate from the corrupted coastal cities of 'Outer Australia'. We learn that among competing local political groups:

> The Brotherhood of the Endless Plain devoted themselves to an elaborate scheme for transforming Australia into a Union of States whose seat of government was far inland and whose culture welled up from its plains and spilled outwards. The coastal districts would then be seen as a mere borderland where truly Australian customs were debased by contact with the Old World. The League of Heartlanders wanted nothing less than a separate Republic of the Plains with manned frontier-posts on every road and railway-line that crossed the Great Dividing Range. (Murnane, 1982)

Breaking away

The Truman show in many ways recapitulates the narrative framework of *The cars that ate Paris*. The 1998 film again deals with an insular community which prefers to live by its own laws and through its own economy and to

---

6. Weir has himself explicitly linked the insularity of the film's community with the aforementioned Australian fear of Asian invasion. See Michael Dempsey (1980) 'Inexplicable feelings: An interview with Peter Weir', *Film Quarterly* 33, No. 4, p. 6.

restrict communication with the outside world and migration to or from that world. In both films as well, townspeople are dishonest to the protagonist as a matter of course and hinder his departure in part by exploiting his phobia over certain forms of transport, a phobia linked in turn to guilt arising from the his mistaken belief he has contributed to the death of a close relative, and in part by offering other familial ties to substitute for lost ones. The difference is that while in the earlier film the protagonist, once adopted by the community (after recovering from a car accident they have orchestrated), gradually begins to accept the insular life, in *The Truman show*, the protagonist wants nothing more than to flee. Again, this desire for escape from the Seahaven Island community is clearly linked with a need for freedom, and for selfhood, as well as for honesty, for real communication with others, the establishment of links beyond his own immediate realm.

As in many other Weir films, the protagonist's drive to reach beyond this realm, to interact with other worlds and other cultures, is also significantly linked with romantic desire. Truman's need to get away is in part a positive drive to regain the lost love of his life, a person/actress (Sylvia, cast as Lauren) who has appeared to communicate honestly and openly, if briefly, with him and who was whisked away by her fictional 'father', who claimed her family was moving to Fiji. 'It's fake . . . It's a set. It's a show', she shouts to Truman as she is led away, 'Get out of here. Come and find me.' Fiji – significantly, a popular travel destination for Australians – is thus what comes to dominate Truman's imagination of that which is elsewhere, the land of his dreams, the place where love, selfhood, open communication and realness will all be retrieved. It is for Truman the literal and figurative antipode of Seahaven, the place where 'You can't get any further away before you start coming back'. And Sylvia, in her seeming genuineness and honesty, is the antipode of Truman's wife, a notion concretized when we see Truman attempting to reconstruct Sylvia's likeness on the reverse side of a portrait photograph of his wife. Truman's first conversation with Lauren/Sylvia is also staged to emphasize her association with places distant: Truman spies her across a border of sorts, a hutch on his study desk at the college library. Several shots show Truman peering around the hutch, before he gets up the nerve to greet Lauren in Japanese, the language which she is supposedly studying and which further links her with the foreign. The two decide to escape the library together – and end up, naturally enough, at the beach, at the final border of elsewhere.

Truman eventually does make the positive decision to break away, to take his life (and, in effect, his programme, although he doesn't know it as yet) into his own hands, to connect to other worlds; he fools the surveillance technology and slips out of his home one night, and, evidently having come to grips with his coastal anxiety, he commandeers a boat to sail away from Seahaven. That boat he has stolen happens to be called the Santa Maria reminds us he is now fulfilling his youthful dreams of becoming an explorer, like Columbus sailing toward America in defiance of local experts who have claimed he will be unable to do so. The wrath of the creator, Christof, is visited upon him in the form of a computer-generated tempest, which produces a vast wave – one appearing very much like the last wave in the earlier film that bore its name. However, while that earlier wave, so infused with cultural contradiction and guilt, is too powerful to confront, bringing its 1977 narrative to an abrupt conclusion, Truman is able to survive the just as formidable looking wave of 1998; this wave is a studio-produced fake, after all, just like everything else in Seahaven. Truman continues on until he encounters exactly what Columbus did not: the end of the world. When the sail-boat smashes through the painted horizon, the creator decides it is finally time to address his unwitting agent down on earth. Christof admits the ruse, but tries to convince Truman that Seahaven is nevertheless the best place for him; however, the protagonist asserts his independence, noting, 'You never had a camera in my head'. After climbing a flight of stairs, he passes through a door to an unseen elsewhere, while, in mirroring shots set in an apartment somewhere in Los Angeles, Sylvia, having watched the unfolding of events on television, descends a flight of stairs and passes through her door.

This rite of passage – or rather passage of passage – across the ocean echoes a number of other moments of transcendence in Weir's earlier films, sequences which foreground a transit from one world into another, an exploration of new realms, realities, cultures. One can see parallels, for example, in the schoolgirls' eerie final ascent of Hanging Rock in *Picnic,* or in Frank and Archie's passage across the Australian desert in *Gallipoli,* or in the schoolboys' journey to their secret meeting place in *Dead Poets' Society* (1989) or in Jeff Bridges' vision of an ascent to heaven in *Fearless* (1993); in most instances such sequences seem to indicate generative acts of displacement, a movement beyond the self in order to expand one's horizons, to communicate with other realms. In *The Truman show,* likewise, the protagonist's passage marks the fulfilment of a lifelong desire to interact with worlds beyond his own, and it thus marks a truer expression of self and a movement toward maturity. Truman has been represented as distinctly boyish throughout the film (something clearly helped along by the casting of Jim Carrey), sporting oddly juvenile leisure attire and addressed diminutively by both his 'mother' and his wife, who offers him mugs of hot Mococoa Cocoa whenever the opportunity arises. Even in his most personal, private moments – his guilty delving into his basement trunk full of memorabilia and his surreptitious play-acting in front his bathroom mirror – his behaviour appears like that of a child. The bathroom sequences in particular seem ripe for psychoanalytic analysis: Truman, one might choose to argue, appears on one level still stuck at a 'mirror stage' of his development, still confusing his image with his actual self and not yet ready to comprehend his position in the social order. One could also note that this mirror which constitutes his undeveloped sense of self is quite literally a screen – a television screen to be precise – and that the scenarios he acts out are plainly indebted to the hackneyed plots of the juvenile television programmes he has been raised on. At the same time, the scenarios Truman acts out on the screen that frames his identity do show a progression toward maturity over the course of the film. Our first image of Truman has him acting out a scenario in which he is the heroic survivor of a mountain-climbing accident, offering his own body up as food for fellow survivors. 'Eat me', he insists, 'that is an order'. In his final 'performance', however, he is no longer passively offering himself up to be consumed by his audience; rather he is a space explorer actively declaring his new world for his own, naming it 'Trumania'. 'That one was for free', he adds at the end of this entertaining bathroom monologue, as though he has already grown to awareness that he is being watched, and that he has the potential to actively change the image of The Truman show.

Truman's oceanic voyage of exploration, then, indicates a movement from passive actor to active producer, as well as from an infantilizing, false marriage to a potentially more adult and genuine relationship with Sylvia. In the film's terms, this involves not only personal maturation, but political maturation as well, a greater understanding of the power of the mass media in the global scheme of things. Significantly, the new female object of Truman's desire is figured as the most self-consciously political of the film's characters, active in a movement to free Truman from his televisual shackles.

Part of what the film endorses, plainly, is the assertion of individualism in the face of strong media influences and the concomitant commercialization of mass culture. But while coming out on the side of selfhood and against artifice, the film does not, however, reject the mass media out of hand. The television show is what has allowed Truman (for the most part unbeknownst to him) to remain connected to the rest of the world; mass communication has rendered his local struggle a global one, has garnered him significant and potentially useful worldwide support. When Christof seems prepared to do Truman grievous harm with the weather machine, one of the producers warns him off with that 1960s activist watchword, 'The whole world is watching'. Thus the media, it is implied, can be a part of progressive political struggle. Truman does not ultimately accept what Hollywood feeds him, but rather chooses to positively take charge of the Hollywood text carrying his name, initially adjusting its signification, then causing its demise.

It needs be noted, however, that the progressive media activism presented here is being undertaken by one of the show's (albeit involuntary) personnel, rather than by the show's spectators. The mass audience – indeed even Sylvia – simply observes the events threatening the life of its hero without budging, transfixed by the programme; we are even shown a mother neglecting her crying baby because of her interest in the show. The whole world is watching, yes, but it is doing nothing more; the audience's media consciousness has evidently not been raised in the way that Truman's has. Most spectators are not ready to reach, like Truman, beyond their own worlds – a point reiterated in the film's final shot, in which a garage attendant, nonplussed by the sudden termination of his favourite show, immediately seeks a TV guide.

The responsibility for change, then, seems to be left here with the media-makers. Again, if we read the film as an allegory for Weir's career: Weir like Truman has broken away from a confined island environment to achieve a more genuinely global form of mass communication. Subsequently, Weir (like Truman) has worked within the Hollywood system but has taken active measures to ensure that his material is true to his aims, that it reaches beyond a parochial Hollywood perspective, is capable of communication beyond (and about) local borders. His is an attempt to take a position against local cultural insularity, but also against complete foreign control – that is to say, an effort to retain the traces of the local within the global.

The question that remains open, however, is whether Weir succeeds at this, either in *The Truman show*, or in the chosen course of his career as a whole. The film has to its credit focused much popular attention on problems of media dominance – though critics argue that many of its implied critiques are nothing new. And it does remain resolutely a Hollywood film, a component part of the system it questions, though such a contradiction is in itself characteristic of Weir's career, straddling the worlds of 'art cinema' and commercial cinema. It may be in part because of the involvement with Hollywood that many of the film's attacks are so muted, that it deals in such a whimsical way with the passivity of media audiences and that even the show's potentially murderous producers, though misguided, are not depicted as profoundly evil or intensely dislikable. In this softened view of exploitation, Columbus's journey of colonial acquisition can be rewritten as a voyage of escape and maturation, and even the state-sponsored assignation of indigenous babies to white parents can be symbolically reworked as a voluntary, all-white exchange of families. There may nevertheless be a real value in having an analysis of global media relationships disseminated in such a global and accessible, if necessarily sugar-coated, form.

References

Hodge, Bob & Vijay Mishra (1991) *Dark side of the dream: Australian literature and the postcolonial mind.* Sydney: Allen & Unwin, p.24.

Murnane, Gerald (1982) *The plains.* Carlton, Vic.: Norstrilia Press, pp.33-34.

Part Two

International media and the crisis of identity

Satellite television and new subjectivities: Media consumption and the dynamics of social and political change

Hart Cohen

New subjectivities: By way of a definition

In the assessment of a three-year study of global media in the Indonesian context, the insights into the consequences of global media expansion have necessarily become entangled with the economic and political crises current in that country. Unravelling the entangled web suggests the overview offered once by Bishop Belo, who in response to the question, 'What is wrong with Indonesia' answered, 'What is wrong with this country is . . . everything!' This assessment is reflected in the changes occurring on a massive scale and with unprecedented rapidity in Indonesian life: economic policies are set for a massive re-calibration, as is the entire political system under a reformed constitution with the potential for new political formations to contest the upcoming elections.

If Bishop Belo needed further evidence, he would not look further than the village of Liquisa and the recent events which appear to be overtaking East Timor at a rapid rate. Even as recent as July 1998, headlines were exclaiming: 'Jakarta crisis gives hope of freedom to East Timor'. Under this headline, Stephen Vines wrote: '. . . The Timorese have touching faith in the international community's ability to solve the situation and force the Indonesians into holding a referendum . . .' (Stephen, 1998). The Indonesians will hold a referendum, it seems, but not before the outcome can be guaranteed, and the 'touching faith in the international community' may now be increasingly questioned by the East Timorese.

As in the last major political crisis, the army's role may determine the kind of outcome possible. If army elites actively support the reform agenda without claiming formal power (as in Burma's current regime), the likelihood is for Indonesia to remain as a civilian-led government. Further complicating the situation are the strong and not so strong secessionist movements across the archipelago – for example the well-known Aceh, West Irian and East Timor movements; the lesser known Riau and West Sumatra pressure groups.

Recent ethnic conflict in the South Moluccas between Christians and Muslims is rehearsed and repeated in East Java, West Kalimantan and South Sulawesi. Even in the army's notorious Siliwangi Division, the appointment of a North Sulawesi Christian as its commander was rejected and followed by a failed coup outside the presidential palace on the night of 22 May 1998. The emergence of so-called ethnic rioting crosses contradictorily with the independence struggles of East Timor and Aceh, because they are themselves strongly identifiable within ethnic terms though still extremely diverse in terms of language and ethnicity (for example, there are 35 language groups in East Timor alone).

One of my arguments, then, is that the media of and about ethnicity has been overtaken by global media, and that ethnic media networks have participated in this transformation with mixed results. Against the controlled flows by governments and media corporations, individuals and ethnic groups have emerged to contest the field of meanings which both these dominant formations attempt to control.

(A long bracket is required here in reference to the current situation in Kosovo and the competing networks of diasporic communities so evident in the media to date. However it is too early to evaluate the consequences of this competition. Suffice to say that the media of diasporic ethnic communities mobilizes new subjectivities – which I define as a new kind of political identity in the context of global media.)

My research on the media consumption of satellite users in the Indonesian context suggested strongly that social and cultural change could be tracked as a congruent feature of the introduction of these technologies. Political change was always a repressed subtext prior to the fall of Suharto. It emerged in certain discussions in the qualitative accounts by media consumers of the much-valued though not uncontested news and information services of western media. In this respect, the momentous economic and political shifts in Indonesia were not precipitated by the new media environment, but, in a manner, they facilitated the channels along which the political subtexts could be expressed.

I recall a key moment of government-induced media censorship when the journals *Tempo, Detik* and *Editor* were banned. This occurred in 1992, well in advance of the May Riots of 1998 which precipitated the fall of Suharto. They were a damaging blow, however, not so much to the sense of media freedom which most realized did not exist under Suharto, but to the idea of modernity – that a rising middle class which saw itself as media literate enough to watch satellite television fare from all over the world, but not considered *modern* enough by its government to read the political commentary of mainstream journals like *Tempo*.

Further, these new subjectivities are often politically motivated in the context of crisis. Unlike the models of political development attributed to the modernity or post-modernity of global media, e.g. Habermas' Model of the Public Sphere, Mosco's idea of transnational citizenship or Murdoch's of a cosmopolitan democracy, these new subjectivities are the heritage of hybrid cultural formations. The Kosovar Albanians are a case in point, as are the Madurese of Kalimantan. These groupings have arisen where they have as a result of movement, migration – forced or otherwise – and it is this feature that makes these cultural formations 'diasporic'. How these movements have eventuated is a complex intersection of population, economic and labour policies characteristic of pressure exerted by global economies on national formations. If we use Greece as an example, the contradictions are clear. Greece used to be a net exporter of workers to Northern Europe and other similar destinations, but now itself hosts a large percentage of guest-workers in its population imported from neighbouring countries. What makes these subjectivities new is not the transnational identity itself, but the context of global culture and economy which must be negotiated by them . . . and therefore, unlike in an earlier period of colonisation, everyone in the world can now claim a transnational identity. That has been the mixed consequence of global communications.

In the context of Indonesia, then, how can we use this argument to understand the media environment and media communities which emerged to produce the massive social and political changes still underway in that country? First, an account of satellite television history may help set the scene.

The significance of satellites in the Asian context

In 1976 Indonesia decided to launch its own domestic satellite service, Palapa I, to provide a language programme designed to distribute Indonesian as the national language to an ethnically and linguistically diverse nation. The innovation was expected to relieve the Indonesian state of introducing an expensive terrestrial television system designed to achieve the same ends. The Indonesians grasped the spatially binding capacities of satellite television more quickly than other nations. This is because Indonesia, from its inception, has been preoccupied with achieving a unified political state. This moment can be interpreted as both a bureaucratic decision founded on technocratic and rational grounds and as a grand nationalist vision to create a singular and unified nation out of diversity. In retrospect, neither the bureaucratic decision nor the nationalist vision saw beyond the immediate desire to secure the nation. The unforeseen consequences of creating a radically new Indonesian mediascape, such as the spill-over of information, data and messages from foreign communicative sources and the exposure to Indonesian audiences of the emergent global media industry, initially escaped the attention of the Indonesian authorities. By seeking to create a singular state using new communication technologies the Indonesian authorities ignored the potential of the technology to create *new heterogeneities and subjectivities* and the resulting interaction of the local with the global. Though these contradictions are specific to the context of Indonesia's media history, they foreshadow subsequent problems of satellite communication throughout Asia. Foremost among these problems, faced in recent times by all Asian nation-states, is media policy formation – a critical intervention in the desire by governments to control mass media consumption within cultural formation. At stake is the issue of communication sovereignty – a concept increasingly vital to post-colonial political formations confronted by the constraints of global capitalism.

Satellites were introduced initially as a state initiative in the policy frameworks of development communication designed to introduce a modernizing economic and social agenda. Indeed entertainment was not perceived to be a legitimate function of television for these social engineering purposes. As such they were introduced for essentially domestic broadcast reasons but they opened up the potential for global broadcasting to become available to mass consumption throughout Asia, a fact not lost on international advertising corporations. The interplay between the local, national and the global in the television arena represents a set of problems and practices around the issue of national sovereignty that are paradigmatically displaced onto communication and information. These issue and problems are, then, most acute in the attempts to consolidate communication sovereignty.

The theory of 'new subjectivities'

I would like to begin with an email message I received from an acquaintance in Surabaya at the height of the current crisis in Indonesia. This message is not extraordinary in the story it tells nor does it suggest a heroic stance in comparison to the lives lost in fight for democracy – but only in the testimony it gives – in its struggle to communicate a desire to renegotiate the terms of social participation and agency in a changing and uncertain world. It is clear the current situation poses great threats to individuals but as well affords a rare opportunity to author one's political identification as citizen and subject. I reproduce the following message with no modification in language or expression:

> Hart, I'm sorry that I didn't send you e-mail on long-long time . . . :)
> You know that since November 1997 I to be social Worker at SAVVY AMIRA,
> Surabaya Women's Crisis Center, that is one of Non Goverment
> Organization (NGO) at Surabaya, and in the other hand I'm still teaching
> in my university and to do some research project.
>
> And in this situation (crowded situation in my country:(), I'm joint at
> Komite Perempuan Pro Demokrasi (KPPD), Surabaya (Surabaya Women's Pro
> Democracy Committee), this is a new organization that found by NGO,
> Society Organization, women's labour, career women, Student, and house
> wives too. We have the same Idea to concern for our country, and we have
> the first meeting on March '98, and on April, 21 '98, we had first
> 'demonstration' at Airlangga University.

Now, on weekly we have programme to discussion about this situation,
especially discus, thinking and try to found problem solving about
women's problem in this situation.
We have very bad economic condition, and women/house wives often feel
'stress' with this problem.
Some times I joint with student to demonstration too, maybe you read at
Airlangga University almost all of lecturer, and professor had joint with
their student too, they give their students's a spirit.
That's great, and we didn't know how 'must we do' except to do
demonstration. Demonstration is instruments for us to 'warning' our
goverment, because you know that our parlement is didn't 'healthy'
again . . . :(, out last election wasn't fair, too much falseness . . .
it's too nepotism at our parliament and our Government:(
It's too much coruption and colusion and our goverment. So we must
'warning' them.

Dear Hart, in this moment, sometimes I must forgeted my 'need' personal,
I thinking that I have to so something for my people . . .
Yeah . . . , maybe it's hear too idealism, but I hope I could still help my
people, especially for 'poor people' in my country.
wish me luck . . . :)

The message speaks for itself in the way it announces a form of participation
in the current crisis – a way of creating agency for oneself when there is no
longer any 'choice' in the sense that one must act in concert and individually
to effect change. However it raises issues which need to be explained within a
separate vocabulary in which a 'new subjectivity' can be said to be forged out
of a constellation of contexts and pressures currently featured within
contemporary societies.

The assertion that new communications technology has created *new
heterogeneities and subjectivities* is best grounded in a theory of the subject in
modernity and post-modernity. The question of 'new subjectivities' is best
interpreted as a practice of a politics of identity. In this regard the political
dimension to social life is privileged over the economic and ideological
dimensions because the subjectivist elements in identity construction are driven
by a quest for the realization of democratic social values. The politics of
identity, however, raise both individual and collectivist questions about this
process. This means that complex accounts of the relationship between
individual choice and desire must be contextualized within larger frames
involving ideas of community and lifestyle in a media-driven consumer culture.
Two conceptual tools aid substantially in the development of these accounts:
the post-modern and the post-colonial. The possibility of a civic pluralism in
which a situated knowledge within a complexity of politically negotiated
identities produces a self-styled counter-narrative. Though specific in the
manner these concepts frame the issues of identity, they both innovate models

or ideas on the historical moment of modernity. In the context of post-modernism, identity choice moves further than just reflexively balancing a plurality of social roles. It can involve a conscious experimentation with identity in which identity choice is a highly directed activity (see Lash & Friedman, 1992). In the context of post-colonialism, these identity choices entail great risks. Perhaps one manner of differentiating post-modernism from post-colonialism is the degree to which a post-colonial identity and related practices may involve risks that could extend to imprisonment or even death.

'Good-bye my love' or paradise in hell

The complexities of ethnicity, region, class and religion, and the demise of Suharto, suggest a national formation or deformation of multiple nations within nations, of a dysfunctional political system no longer able to sustain the 'national fictions' necessary for the 'imaginary community' of a unitary Indonesian state. The prospect of a 'Yugoslavia-style' Balkanization into warring enclaves has occurred to more than one professional commentator on the Indonesian situation. And with the current destabilization of the Balkans themselves, the metaphor 'Balkanization' becomes coterminous with the realities of both the Balkans and the Indonesian archipelago. The failure of the 'Yugoslavian' solution in the Balkans should inform the current crisis in Indonesia as a politico-ethnic crisis of huge proportions.

Driven by the emergence of a significant middle class in Indonesia (15-20 million who consumed US$4,000 per annum before the 1997 crash), interest by audience measurement companies and broadcast networks (including satellite TV) grew rapidly. The social and cultural changes emergent in this period across Southeast Asia were propelled by the explosion of communications industries and the primacy of media communication in the construction of political and cultural identities. This may be defined as a media context in which new subjectivities could be forged even if the 'older' subjectivities were themselves a consequence of the limitations of dubious social engineering and bland political management.

New subjectivities are expressed as a politics of identity negotiated in a media-driven consumerist culture laden with uncertainty and risk. The results are at best provisional and contingent with subjects intent on participating in social and political change while having to invent a new vocabulary in order to do so (as evidenced by the email message earlier). In this regard both the earlier development paradigm and the more recent participatory paradigm appear unable to cope with the paradoxes of the current situation, described aptly by the title of Biarjia Javant's essay, *Paradise in hell* (Javant, 1999), an attempt to understand the on-going contradictions in Indonesia without success – left by the final line of the essay to finally only to express remorse: 'Poor Indonesia'.

Tracking the fall of Suharto, however, is revealing to the extent that, if it is based in the historical moment of his ascendancy to power, the added complications of a global media in the 1990s and the consumerist culture intersecting with it can be better placed as to how they conspired to help effect change. (Though it may not be much help to explain the current chaos in Indonesia detailed in Biarjia's essay.)

The liminal zone

In the contemporary context of 'crisis' in Indonesia, the intersection of media, political resistance and social fragmentation illustrates graphically both the risks and opportunities afforded by the consequences of 'post-modern innovation'. It would appear that the post-modern media-techno sphere, through satellite and other innovations, both initiates and enhances a 'liminal' zone – a kind of 'in-between space' within which subjectivities, both individual and collective, can temporarily form. When the patterns of social and political activity are mobilized, this liminality may be extended to challenge the boundaries of authority and resistance. It is without doubt that the definition of this liminality is a specifically spatial one in the current Indonesian case. For example, Indonesian students initiated the challenge to regulatory authorities first on their campuses – a carefully designated liminal space – part of the fabric of the sociopolitical context but not fully of the social space represented by the street. When the students move off their campuses onto the streets, the liminal is radically extended. The non-student 'riots' and 'looting' which followed the killing of students by the armed forces extended the challenge to authority. This was both continuous *and* discontinuous with the space of liminality established. With the entry of the army (ABRI), the forces of rationalization and authority over the Jakarta streetscapes establish a counter-liminal definition of spatial control. The media also extends a parallel liminal space in the mediasphere. Subject to similar forces of authority and rationalization, this space is also modified in relation to the policing of the airwaves in the battle between the resistant and the conservatives in the current context.

I have argued earlier that the current crisis must be understood in the context of the 1965 coup during which Suharto gained ascendancy to power.

In theory, given the massive changes in mediaspheres and technospheres and the expansion of transnational media, should not the pattern and means of political change be radically different from what occurred in 1965? Yet we can recall the dominant images of the time (1965) in which the streets were also the battle zones for control over the hearts and minds of the Indonesian people, where the streets were also the point of contact between the controlling forces of the army and the establishment of the new regime. Indeed one could argue that the differences in historical terms are not that great, though we are at the beginning of the current crisis in terms of how the issue of ultimate political authority will be resolved.

I would argue, however, that the existence of the Internet and satellite television, to name two substantial new media technologies, has displaced an ideologically based and ideologically led conflict characteristic of the 1965 crisis. Today, the opposition is united in its desire to end the regime of the current supreme authority in the country. In other words, the transnational media mobilizes a post-nationalist politics – though not (contradictorily) devoid of the rhetoric of nationalist ideological content (hence my email correspondent's continuing articulation of 'doing something for my country'). This is, however, no longer characteristic of the anti-colonial, third worldist discourse characteristic of the struggle between Sukarnoist and Suhartoist forces across the Cold War divide of Marxist and anti-Marxist political values of the 1960s.

In post-colonial and post-communist world systems the targets are more immediate, and with the speed of global economic explosions the consequences of the reversal of economic fortune are extremely swift. The consequences: the main-streaming of a rebellion already in waiting – lubricated by the now more certain perceptions – of, as my correspondent puts it, government corruption, collusion and nepotism. (Barujia suggests that of the three terms in this contemporary rallying cry, collusion is not well understood . . . and he bemoans the importation of terms to describe indigenous problems.) I have suggested that this is a period in which new vocabularies are needed and sometimes this may mean importing terms that require time for meaningful exchanges to take place.

'Read banned books'

My entry into Indonesian research centred on an interest in the writer Pramoedya Ananta Toer, one of Indonesia's best-known writers. Through reading his tetralogy and then interviewing him along with his collaborators, a meta-narrative of Indonesia slowly emerged – one in which placed the New Order in stark relief to the emergent political culture in Indonesia throughout most of this century. Imprisoned by the Suharto regime and then placed under house arrest while his books were banned, he pointed strongly to the lack of political tolerance in Indonesian society. Not surprisingly, Pramoedya's harshest comments were reserved for Suharto, who he called nothing but a 'plant manager' – someone who had effectively reduced to zero any vestige of a political culture in Indonesia during his period in office. But the Indonesian intelligentsia of this period were also held responsible for being politically banal and subservient to the regime. As my work with Pramoedya wound up, I began working with students and staff of a Surabaya university on the developing mediascape, with special attention paid to satellite television. This work developed empirical and qualitative assessments of what consumers were doing with television and to some extent what they saw as its central values. Perhaps the strongest value to emerge was the greater choice afforded by global television in the area of news and current affairs, especially in relation to local news and information services, which were seen as controlled and hence less credible . . . censorship was also a key concern. Both these not entirely unexpected results recapitulated the Pramoedya work. As an author still respected in Indonesia, his books and pronouncements have moved public opinion, as Goenawan Mohamad once wrote anecdotally: 'A government official bemoaned the continuing banning of Pramoedya's books because it made them best sellers'. Indeed well before the 1997 crash and subsequent resignation of Suharto, the T-shirt emblazoned with *Read banned books* was not uncommon on Jakarta streets. Indeed the well organised student movement along with a worker's movement in the factories (highlighted by the PRD [People's Democratic Party] led by jailed student leader Budiman Sudjatmiko) has, in alignment with the ex-TAPOLS like Pramoedya, a view of the 1965 coup and banning of the PKI as foundational to the sustaining of Suharto – a regime in which the PKI was blamed for most things (while keeping its ageing leaders on death row) and which sustained a paranoia relating to the latter years of Sukarno's regime.

In effect, the current situation has buried in its fabric the events of 1965 and the subsequent extreme measures utilized by the New Order regime to retain power at the expense of all political opposition and a careful balance of military power. The audience studies relating to media reflected back the impoverishment of public political discourse (so underscored by the banning of Pramoedya's books and the huge political debates they unleashed when distributed underground), a hunger for information and the possibility that a large number of middle-class consumers would support a more liberal open-minded regime. In effect this has happened, but the movement has also unleashed the historically repressed ethnic struggles as well as the short-sighted policies like transmigration in which those transported became the fabricated 'new' ethnicities.

The bubble economy

The early 1990s saw an unfettered optimism emerging in the region as economic growth, fuelled by over-investment in the region's economies, presented a number of distortions. Not uncommon was the proposition that these previously undeveloped economies would, with the help of communication technologies, take a leap into a post-industrial or even post-Fordist age of capitalist globalization. Increased capital resulted in overproduction and speculation on a massive scale. When this turned inside out in the 1997 shake out, the payback for re-skilling, restructuring, uncertainty, lack of job security, etc, that went with the over-capitalization era appeared not to be forthcoming. Many Indonesians are now hard put to find the nine basic necessities – milk, rice, eggs, peanuts, sugar, wheat, cooking oil, detergent and soap – hardly a post-industrial leap. The crisis itself was pinned on currency speculators but Walden Bello (Bello, 1999) for one cites a global network of investors, journalists, investment analysts and academics who perpetuated the myth of a never-ending boom.

Whereas one could find a number of communications experts celebrating the role of communications and specifically of information as a currency for economic expansion, Bello cites the monopolization of communications in the region and the expansion of business news communications as a likely source of this puffery – a result of a collusion between editors and journalists to report positively on the expansion because they were themselves a part of it. I can recall an independent journalist after several years finally being able to place an op-ed article in the *Bangkok Post* critical of Thailand's financial sector. He showed the article to me in 1996. By 1997 Thailand's currency devaluation had triggered the crisis. Bello cites a contrasting example of commentary persisting with optimistic accounts at the same time without the consequences of final banishment for getting it completely wrong. Business journalists and investment analysts aside, Bello also cites a number of academic publications echoing the sentiments of the Asian miracle and states that, across both the left and right, few would tolerate a critique of the expansion economy, whether that referred to environmental decay, income disparities or growing technological dependencies.

The impact of the economic crisis on the media

If I may reverse the media-society determination thesis briefly, it is instructive to give an account of the impact the economic crisis has had on media production and consumption in Indonesia and the relationship to the ensuing role of the media in the political and social dimensions of the crisis.

Reference has already been made to the proliferation of the economic bubble by the apologists for expansionism. In the absence of national policies which can affect the global financial system, it is left to agencies like the IMF to clumsily prescribe the solutions. They effectively replaced national policy, not to mention the social and political wills and thoughts of a nation's people. This is the requirement of the new capitalism, and nowhere is the poverty of its solutions more apparent than in the role the IMF has played in Indonesia.

The Indonesian example demands some considerable remodelling of Amir's thesis. This is borne out to some extent by the impact of the crisis on the media. With currency devaluations around 400 percent, and the mass media dependent on foreign materials, advertising has declined by 50 percent. Programming has relied on reruns to fill gaps. Coverage is minimized as newspapers cut costs, with many closing down. Pages are reduced, contributions from columnists and readers cut back. Media companies even desire that their subscription lists be cut back because of failing to meet their usual demand.

The effect of globalization on media production will never be greater than in this situation. But the role of media in the current crisis has never been more critical – more important. And until the intervention of the government upon Suharto's return, the media had played a key role in relaying news of the street demonstrations to its constituency. Consistent with the earlier media analysis, the subjective features of local consumption appear to maintain a viable relationship despite the effects of globalization.

The effects of global capitalism predicted by Amir appear to be correct for the Indonesian situation. The major adjustment in his analysis is with respect to two issues: first, the economic history in which the Fordist economy coexists with a post-Fordist one in which the illusion of a post-Fordist world can be propagated when in fact the reality of Indonesia is that of a developing nation with mostly Fordist economic features. The so-called leap over the industrial development stage into the information stage was a far too simplistic projection of the early 1990s. Second, this illusion was built on very shaky political foundations – anti-democratic and authoritarian – and only now does the Asian values debate appear as impoverished as many claimed it was. Ironically the chaos which Amir predicts accompanies these latest contradictory demands of capitalism, may go to some lengths to have played a role in reconstructing a democratic impulse if not setting a very different course for the country as a whole.

Conclusion – the next stage

I would like to offer some comments relating to media profusion in the age of interculturalism, transnationalism and digitalization. The challenge it seems is clear. As we experience a increasingly complex world of hybrid identities and new ethnicities we can ask if the new media will respond in kind. Will the new media be able to reproduce the diversity of social, linguistic and cultural constructions reflective of the complex formations into which they will enter? The proliferation of channels in the digital media universe has not resulted in an equally prolific spate of new programming. A marked trend, however, in the localization of media production is evident from the adjustments made by Murdoch in his empiric expansion in India and China and in the expansion of cable networks concerned with proximity as a value in news, reversioning of popular programmes from sports to soaps. Despite this, opportunities for cultural and ethnic minorities for self-expression have shrunk when compared to the massive expansion of the television spectrum. In this respect the prospect of community or regionally based local television is still to be properly invented in which content, programming production and programme exchange all have a role to play, not in isolation from commercial and global television but in relation to it. If there is to be a move in this direction, the political construction of identity must negotiate the global – not 'retreat ahead of it' as Benjamin might say.

I leave the last word to Mattelart on this:

> When the 'local' is used to drive back the advances of the 'worldwide' or the 'international', one may find oneself excusing a movement that tends to diminish meaning and the capacity to act in concrete situations. The 'local' is of no real interest except where it allows a better grasp, by virtue of proximity, of the interaction between the abstract and the concrete, between experience and the universal, between the individual and the collective. (Mattelart, 1994)

References

Bello, Walden (1999) 'Fuelling the bubble economy', *The Nation,* 9 February 1999, p.5.

Javant, Biarjia (1999) 'Paradise in hell', in *Australian Review of Books*, Vol. 4, Issue 1, p.24.

Mattelart, Armand (1994) *Mapping world communication: War, progress, and culture.* Minnesota: University of Minnesota.

Stephen, Vines (1998) 'Jakarta crisis gives hope of freedom to East Timor', *The Independent,* Sunday, 26 July 1998, p.14.

An imagined community of youth: The formation of new subjectivities in India

Melissa Butcher

Introduction

The contemporary Indian media landscape reveals a syncretic layering of both western and Indian cultural products. Their meaning is further multiplied by the embedding of these products within an increased plurality of contexts of reception, as television and the plethora of post-liberalization media (including the Internet) stretch their reach into the countryside, the low-income suburbs, and into the market inalienable (such as religious iconography). The grammar of the visual vocabulary that is produced by this market-generated strategy of identity is distinctive and exemplary of notional constructions of a pan-Indian subjectivity – more particularly, a youthful pan-Indianness, as these syncretic images are aimed largely at a community which in itself feels halfway between two universalist identities, East and West. The selection and staging of visual vocabularies taps into this sentiment of ontological fusion. The new genres of cultural production that have resulted are implicated, as this chapter will argue, in the formation of a new subjectivity – an imagined community of youth.

An analysis of recent findings from India (1996-1999) will focus on the activity of the image brokers who produce and disseminate the imagery of this community, as well as the impact of its reception on identity formation amongst young people. The chapter will include an examination of audience research in the construction of market-generated subjectivity, as generous amounts of resources are now spent by transnational media corporations (including advertising, public relations, marketing and research wings) on determining exactly what it is that Indian audiences want. Ultimately, this will pose questions as to the efficacy of media education, that is, learning to critically read visual vocabularies.

Defining the field of production

The formation of a community of youth occurs within a configuration of culture, identity and the visual vocabularies of the media landscape. Culture in the sense it is used here is not only a 'whole way of life', but a distinctive 'signifying system' which is 'involved in *all* forms of social activity', including not only the traditional forms of artistic and intellectual pursuit, but also practices of popular culture such as journalism, advertising and fashion (Williams, 1981, p.13). Linking this definition of culture to identity, symbolic resources of societies are a tool which provides for the comprehension and management of the 'self'. Such resources are reproduced and disseminated as ways of understanding the meaning of human existence, and delimiting the 'correct' forms of selfhood, behaviour and authority (Kavolis, 1980). In other words they bound position and practice. The shared meaning of symbolic resources, synchronically and diachronically, is a marker of community.

For example, the shared understanding of particular market-generated cultural resources delineate a community of youth which can therefore appear as an identity construct (the sharing of meaning being a characteristic of identity), temporally and geographically locating the self within an intersection of cultural networks and relationships which can stretch from the individual, the subjective understanding that such a community exists, to a global community of youth.

A particular visual vocabulary is necessary to display this identity. Every community develops its own vocabulary, associated artefacts, means of staging, and specific codes to understand them, to create similarities and consensus or to differentiate itself against the codes of another community. Vocabularies are here used in a classificatory sense, to exclude rather than include members of differing communities, example to strengthen the notion of youth as being distinct from parents or the previous generation. A new social constellation therefore assembles through their identification with specific signs (Cohen, 1986) and their consumption of items of popular culture such as MTV, music and fashion (Sen, 1993, p. 214).

The visual vocabularies of the community of youth are embedded within the rhetorics of a wider media landscape, a text both informed by and informing flows that conceptualize India, and the global. The mediascape itself is situated within a larger field in which culture is translated, negotiated and continuously renewed and re-invented (Brosius & Butcher, 1999). Mediascapes (Appadurai, 1997) provide not only large and complex repertoires of images, the infrastructural capabilities of distribution and dissemination, and audience reception, but also include, I would add, two more characteristics – the administrative or ideological universe within which the media landscape is situated, which impacts upon its appearance and reception (for example, the development of television within a socialist clime or one of free market), and the ethnography of the producers, their own cultural networks which dominate their selections, their practices, and their perception of the images they produce or broker. This final point is of particular importance in examining the production of the symbolic resources of a community of youth.

The contemporary Indian media landscape[1]

I would like to suggest that the experience of economic liberalization in India is a generational one. That is, India has rediscovered her youth via transnational television and the extension of audiencehood to the largest sector of its population: 0-19 year olds (47 percent; 5-14 year olds are the single largest sector at 23.2 percent, while 15-19 are 10.8 percent). Young people not only understand how to use the new technology, they understand the new vocabulary of the media landscape, which is increasingly generated specifically for them.[2] They understand the new series of interconnecting grammatical codes forming in economic and social practices, constituting a shift in the cultural logics of consumption (Jameson, 1991) that has occurred since the liberalization of the economy in 1991. Young people are considered innovative by media corporations and related youth industries. Interviews with parents and grandparents found that it was young people that brought home new products (soap, toothpaste and brushes), or remembered the time their parent's television programme came on.

> Youth will accept newness better than [anyone] else. Youth by nature have their eyes open. (Shashanka Ghosh, executive producer and creative consultant with Channel [V], 1997)[3]

Marketing reports place the youth sector (generally a core audience of 15 to 24, but a target audience of 12 to 34) as the largest consumer segment in India (over 50 percent of the market share).[4] The media landscape has shifted accordingly, with entire channels now dedicated to this consumer market (Channel [V] and MTV India), and young 'modern' India taking centre stage in advertising and brand promotion.

To briefly explain the use of 'modernity' in this paper, it is recognized as an ideal construct, and I in no way would like to perpetuate its overarching universalizing precepts. The fluidity of social space challenges the defining of cultural change according to such polarities as modern/traditional, or global/local in theory. But in the context of everyday life, as elicited from the speech of research participants, these are still terms which are important points of orientation for people (see Mishra, 1999). Later I will note how the concept of modernity has been redefined by both audiences and the media landscape.

The image of virtual youth disseminated in the media is informed by an immense level of commercial research probing attitudes, values and tastes.

---

1. An analysis of the contemporary media landscape of India was carried out using qualitative document analysis and interview techniques over a three-year period (from 1996-1998).

2. It is understood that the use of 'young people' in this sense is extremely undifferentiated. As is noted later on, this landscape is predominantly urban and middle class.

3. Interviewed by the author 13 May 1997, Bombay.

4. 'What drives the Indian youth', *Brand equity – Economic Times*, 4-10 March 1998, p.1.

For example, Levi's jeans have set up a youth panel in Bangalore to look for the latest trends in youth culture. MTV conduct research not just on music preferences, but also youth attitudes to socioeconomic issues. Local retailing outlets conduct similar research. Transnational media corporations (TNMCs) and advertising agencies have also undertaken extensive research of the youth market in India and Asia. Consumer Insights, part of advertising agency McCann-Erikson Asia Pacific, runs 2,000 focus groups across all major Asian markets, including India, involving weekly discussion groups with teenagers.[5] The Cartoon Network, and advertising agency Ogilvy and Mather (O & M) have also conducted Asia-wide studies.

The studies produce typologies of 'youth' constructed via research tools such as DILOs ('Day in the Life Of' graphs where the weekday of the average 16 year old can be plotted) and MELTs (Major Element Lifestyle Themes). The typologies cut across all strata of urban, middle-class youth to create an average which is then reconstituted as Generation India, the Dissonance Generation, the Instability Era Generation, and of course, GeneratioNext and the MTV Generation. The nomenclature delineates the boundaries of a community of youth which is in the universe of urban middle and upper middle class. Of these it is not the 'mass' that is targeted but 'opinion leaders' and 'early adopters'. MTV's General Manager, Sunil Lulla, stated that 'We target modern India, cable and satellite homes that by definition is more modern'.[6] The actual ownership of the technology has then defined modernity. Channel [V] stated that their audience catchment extends to a SEC C and D[7] audience in mini-metro and provincial regions, but there are many other consuming classes in India, including the destitute.

---

5. Source from papers presented at the Youth Marketing Forum, 20 February 1998, Bombay, including a paper by Dave McCaughan, Consumer Insights Director, McCann-Erikson Asia Pacific.

6. Interview with the author, May 1997, Bombay. Tape recording.

7. The aim of market-generated identity strategies has been to reach a burgeoning middle class, post-liberalization of the Indian economy. The economic definition of middle class is generally given as an income of Rs2,500 (US$65) to Rs10,000 (US$250) per month. This does not, however, take into account undisclosed 'black' money. A recent National Council for Applied Economic Research (NCAER) study cited the middle class as having an annual income of Rs22,500 (US$640) to Rs70,000 (US$2,000) ('Small town, big money', *Outlook*, 11 May 1998, p.34). The rupee fluctuated between Rs35 to Rs40 to the US dollar. A more relevant definition of middle class perhaps is Socio-Economic Classifications (SEC), used extensively by TNMCS in India. These are based not only on income but also on the level of education and occupation of the chief income earner in a household. SEC A/B are generally considered the 'middle class'.

The generic descriptions of youth are widely used within a set of relationships that has become established between different agents of popular culture: the image brokers of transnational media, advertising, marketing, public relations and research corporations, music, clothing and entertainment companies, creative producers, technicians, brand managers, journalists and media planners that are incorporated into the media landscape, informing new genres of cultural production. The liberalized economy has allowed for new strategies of marketing, particularly fast-moving consumer goods. Pepsi can now place their international advertising on Channel [V] and MTV in English, and their local advertising in Hinglish and Hindi for the mass audience of ZEE TV or Door Darshan.

In an effort to reach the young consumer even more effectively, the terminology of 'culture' has been reappropriated by the image broker. Decisions, including those of a consumer, appear more likely to be made in social context, rather than in isolation, including global, regional, peer and family influences. Culturally proximate programming has proved to be far more popular than foreign imports (Singhal *et al*, 1998; Monteiro & Jayasankar, at press). It makes sense then that the notion of culture becomes an integral part of the marketing lexicon. Brands are increasingly immersed in the cultural context they will be seen in. The images resonate with familiar associations. In 1997, for example, the 50th Anniversary of India's Independence, 'freedom' was paramount, but redefined in the media landscape as 'Freedom to choose', concomitant with post-liberalization ideologies (see Pepsi's commercials at this time).

The result is that rather than an homogenizing layer of western cultural products over those nominally regarded as of Indian origin, a constructed discourse of fusion (of East meets West) is taking place. Rushdie has referred to this as a process of 'chutneyfication' (1997, p.89).[8]

> These chutneys, the new generation, are definitely the chutney generations.
> Yet this particular chutney is not one that you find anywhere other than in
> India. It may well have elements which come from the rest of the world but the
> particular flavour is entirely local.

What is problematic with Rushdie's observation is how 'local' can be defined in a global cultural space in which the local and the global are increasingly interconnected, to the point of Robertson's (1994) descriptive neologism, 'glocalization'. The media landscape reflects the selection of attributes of the familiar, but packaged within a western aesthetic. Where then

---

8. See also discussion of this phenomenon by Hannerz (1987) who refers to 'creolization', Gillespie (1995) who refers to 'hybridization' and 'cultural translation', and Appadurai (1997) who refers to the appropriation of cricket by India as 'vernacularization'.

does global stop and local start? Media forms, that is the aesthetics of particular genres such as advertising and television, are translocated and globalized, at times using the positive value attached to globalization (IBM's 'Its a small world', and 'Planet Reebok' advertising are good examples) (Sreberny-Mohammadi 1991, p.122). Ghosh, Channel [V]'s creative consultant, would take:

> ... campus humour, stuff that India never really saw, take a nice Indian [look] and do it influenced by *Pulp Fiction* or *Godard*. The content is incredibly India [including street scenes, or freedom fighters demanding dates with Madonna] but with completely pumped colours. *Familiar* but packaged. *Familiarity* is really important, [audiences] need to feel *comfortable*, that's how you can connect. Push something a bit further, too far and no one understands.

Comfortableness was also the defining marker of limits for many of the research participants – in dress, in social relationships (such as dating), in behaviour. Comfortableness marked the boundary that comes between social sanction and peer approval.

The comfort zone in the media landscape was created through the liberal application of the familiar, including the use of local language programming. Ratings consistently show that Hindi or southern language channels and programming is more popular than English. Only the Zee (Hindi) and Sun (Tamil) networks are profitable (at the time of writing). STAR network, despite its incredible brand presence (I would suggest due more to the presence of Rupert Murdoch than their programming), gathers only just over 10 percent of the market share (with five channels in the network; TAM ratings points, January 1999). STAR and other TNMCs have been forced to undergo a process of localization, incorporating dubbing and then local production into their programming schedules.

India's extensive film industry had, until 1991 and the advent of satellite and cable television, provided the main source of popular culture. It was, and still is, hugely popular (as 13 million a day are estimated to attend cinemas nationwide). With the rapid expansion of the television industry there was a need to fill new schedules and the film industry provided ready-made material (particulary programming based on the song and dance sequences). Recognizable heroes and heroines were transferred to the small screen. Transnational networks such as Sony began establishing their brand name by screening up to ten Hindi language films a week. The success of this early strategy may also be attributable to theories of context.

> Indians are not yet comfortable with Indians kissing. They are visually literate where Hindi films are concerned, they can decode the antics of Govinda (an actor) for example. But Mouthful of Sky [the first English language soap opera broadcast on the Government network, Door Darshan] didn't work because of this. The actors didn't seem comfortable with the language or situations.
> (S. Bajpai, media analyst, 1998)[9]

The use of film in the construction of television crossed over to MTV India. Their Chai Boy station identification featured a young chai boy (tea seller) dancing through the back streets of Bombay to a classic Hindi film song. The significance of the incorporation of such content is that when MTV began broadcasting again into India in 1996, on a dedicated India beam, they initially had stated they would maintain an 'international' look, and would not play Hindi film music. By this time, Channel [V], established in 1994 to replace MTV when the channel left the STAR platform, had created for itself an 'Indian' identity through broadcasting localized (Hindi, Hinglish, Hindi film and pop) programming content. Following research carried out toward the end of 1996 and early 1997, MTV also began a process of 'Indianization'. Now, according to William Roedy, President of MTV International, 'MTV India is the most localized, most indigenous product' they have in the MTV network of seven channels world wide.[10] In 1998, up to 70 percent of programming on MTV India was Hindi pop and film music.

This localization extended to advertising. The particularization of brands acquiesces to the idea that globalization does not have to equal homogenization, but localisation has itself become a globally homogenous strategy involving the creation of a standard, and the cultural softening up of the image.[11] Indications of the commodification of culture (the use of religious iconography for example) would suggest a transition in the boundaries of what is market inalienable as the skin of globalization is stretched over extant forms.[12]

The American and English jeans companies, Levi Strauss and Pepe, are two dissenters to the concept of localization of global products. Levi's utilizes pan-Asian advertising (in 1998 featuring a 1950s American school, and a theme of an affair between a student and a teacher) imbued with what they perceive as universal values of 'adventure and fun' (Marc de Mulder, Managing Director, Levi Strauss India).[13] Chetan Shah, Managing Director of Pepe, also took a similar approach towards his audience (the top bracketed SEC A, AI classes).

---

9. Interviewed by the author, 21 January 1998.

10. William Roedy, President of MTV International, from a speech presented at the MTV Youth Marketing Forum, 20 February 1998, Bombay.

11. For example, see 1997 print advertising for IBM featuring the 'Modern Indian woman' (short hair, dressed in jeans and T-shirt, but pushing a child in a pram, signifying 'traditional' Indian family values).

12. For example, a 1997 print advertisement for shopping precinct Snowhite Square featuring a man dressed in traditional dhoti (sarong) with three stripes on his forehead, symbolishing Hindivism, but wearing 'biker' boots.

> I take my audience today as global youth. Same values, same aspirations, more
> or less the same culture . . . Want to be out having a good time, eating out,
> dancing out, listening to music. I find it difficult to separate an Indian kid in my
> segment from a kid in the West . . . I don't see much difference except of course
> one is in a Third World environment, less economically developed. Aspirational,
> needs, attitudes are the same. (Shah, 1997)[14]

However, the overriding emphasis among marketing directors is to adopt brand localization. MTV has become the antithesis of its stereotype. 'No monolithic or culturally imperialist service would satisfy such a diverse and veracious appetite as that of the world's 18-24 year olds' (William Roedy). MTV's 'mission' is to create a haven in which culture and heritage is respected, but also one that expands cultural horizons built on a transnational audience which never existed as an entity before, which sounds like a good definition of an imagined community of youth.

An imagined community of youth

If young people form such a community a new set of rules and values applies which extends across local cultural lines. They can be placed within an historical context that is experiencing the same economic and social changes and the same memories at similar stages in their lives. The sense of continuity that this can engender is also a characteristic of identity. Such shared experiences include consumption patterns.

But identity becomes problematic when fusion predominates. What is foreign? What is local? The dilemma was itself reflected upon in the media landscape, in advertising and film in particular. The construct of the returning non-resident Indian (NRI), born and brought up in the United States or in Europe, faced with the dilemma of reconciling being 'Indian', that is possessing those values that are considered Indian (virtue, fidelity, family, duty over desire) along with their western worldliness, was a construct used in several popular Hindi films[15] and in advertising.[16]

---

13. From a presentation at the Youth Marketing Forum, 20 February 1998, Bombay.

14. Chetan Shah, Managing Director, Pepe Clothing India Ltd, interviewed by the author, 12 May 1997, Bombay.

15. For example, *Tere Mere Sapne* (1997), *Pardes* (1997), *Jeans* (1998).

16. For example, a local Pepsi product (mango drink) featured a young male returning from study in the USA. He has an American accent and 'poses'. He drinks some of the Pepsi Mango product and is transformed into a 'real' Indian again.

The result is, in effect, the reversioning of identity, like the foreign game show translated into Hindi. And the question that it poses is, if the external appearance remains the same, that of an 'international look' among urban SEC A-B youth, how are unseen values to be represented? A virulent strand of nationalism is therefore evident in the media landscape. The campaign for electronics company BPL is just one example, running from late 1996 up to 1997, both print and television commercials. Writers such as Ohm (1999) and Vachani (1999) regard these commercials as seminal markers of the transition to a post-liberalization media landscape. However, despite its nationalism, there is irony in the company's name: an anocrym that stands for *British Physical Laboratories*.

> I'd love to be an American. And enjoy the power my country holds. I'd love to be an Englishman, watching my language spreading through the world . . . I'd love to be proud of my country. I'd love to make people envious just by saying 'I'm Indian'. I'd love to make you believe it's possible. I'd love to make you believe in yourself. (BPL Press advertisement, Dhar and Hoon, 1996)

Such content is indicative of an increasing sense of trying to define what is Indianness in the face of globalization. And in defining India as such, the 'other', the West, is also delineated. The result was the second predominant feature of the media landscape – an othering of the West as morally inferior.[17] These sentiments were also displayed in the construction of the dichotomy between the NRI, who is somehow polluted by his contact with the West.

A third feature of the media landscape is the construction of India as not only young, but young with attitude, aspiration and ambition.[18] What is common to all these examples is the use of restaging of the familiar.

---

17. For example, see the Ruf & Tuf Jeans (1998) advertisement, featuring an American who 'abuses' an elderly Indian man for failing to understand English. He is reprimanded by the hero who states: 'We understand English and we also know how to respect our elders'.

18. Some examples again include Pepsi's 1999 Campaign, '*Yeh Dil Mange Mare*' (trans: This Heart Wants More), and the National Institute for Information Technology advertisement, 'Marketing Manager at 22, Vice President Marketing at 26, CEO at 30'.

19. Research took the form of focus groups with young people of 15-20 years old, in two distinct linguistic regions of India (Karnataka in the south and New Delhi and northern Uttar Pradesh in the north), in rural and urban areas, and using SEC A/B and D/E as further classification of urban participants.

Audience responses[19]

Youth in India are consistently marked out as a category vulnerable to the direct impact of the image.

> What we grew up believing, the younger generation don't believe in any more.
> (Seema Mustafa, Deputy Editor, *Asian Age*)[20]

However, the depiction of youth as a vulnerable category is something that is evident in public discourse regarding the impact of television since its inception in 1959 (from an overview of media landscapes of the 1940s and 1970s).

While it is another idealized dichotomy to state that post-liberalization is marked by a cultural shift from contentment and stability to striving to keep up with the neighbours, from protection of the weak (socialist) to survival of the fittest (Bijapurkar, 1998),[21] it is possible to suggest that extant authority (political, economic, social and religious) is challenged by an array of new possibilities within the field of economic liberalization. Adaptation seems to be the key to defining a new direction not only for the construction of images within the media landscape but also for the audience.

Young people appear capable of displaying both a continuity and disjunction of value sharing. It is, in Bijapurkar's words, an engineered, rather than an arranged marriage (1998). The western paradigm of modernity has been redefined in terms of 'independence', from family and gender roles in particular. While simultaneously belonging to many referent cultures, adopting multiple identities, which includes in some cases an international consciousness, some participants were capable of more fluid designations of themselves.

Dissonance between felt selves and social realities was reconciled by generating spaces for different behaviour, spaces of the new and the old, of Indian and western, conservative and contemporary.

> When we are at home we are like Indians, but outside home we are like
> westerners. (male, student, SEC B, Delhi)

Some participants were also capable of setting their own limits: on material and social aspirations, on mobility, and on 'freedom'. Given that 'freedom'

20. Speech given at a Media Advocacy Group Seminar, 23 August 1996, New Delhi.

21. Rama Bijapurkar, Strategic Marketing Consultant, from a presentation given at the MTV Youth Marketing Forum, 20 February 1998, Bombay.

was also an expressed desire of almost all the groups, this self-imposed limitation suggests Bell's (1973) antinomian dialectic of restraint and release as an active dynamic upon identity formation. The social context of participants played an important restraining role (in rural, urban, upper and lower income groups), although social censure towards suggestions of alterity was more evident in low-income and rural areas.

'Indianness' was bounded by the construction of the West as immoral, amoral at best, in compliance with the media landscape, with the family for SEC A-B groups, and the position of women for lower income and rural groups, as the point of demarcation. This boundary-drawing appeared as a notional display, however, tending toward a function of differentiation, particularly for SEC A groups who have already attained all the accoutrements of a global youth culture lifestyle (and some of whom came themselves from dysfunctional families).

Their stated abilities to deconstruct television texts tempered concerns regarding young people's vulnerability to cultural change. One determinate factor of alienation or association with particular software was the social context of the viewer. For example, one female participant from Bangalore (SEC A) found STAR Plus's English programming as 'nice serials based on our life and present situation'. For this group, a *Beverly Hills 90210* scenario is quite plausible.

6-a: It's good for watching, you can relate to Beverly Hills. There are good looking actresses.

6-d: The theme is the same, it doesn't matter if it's Indian or foreign.

6-e: Basically I think that if you too have some good Indian stuff that you can identify with that's fine. Till now there is not many Indian ones we can so it's basically the western stuff.

The response also indicates an opposition felt towards the programming that dominated the pre-1991 media landscape, that of Door Darshan, as being unable to fulfil their required symbolic universe.

However, the cries of degeneration created by programmes such as *Baywatch* are tempered by results that indicate that participants, even in the more cosmopolitan SEC A groups, found English programming at times 'very, very alien'. *Baywatch*, *The Bold and the Beautiful* and *Santa Barbara* were disliked because of their displays of 'sex', and because 'it is a very westernised way of presenting these programmes'. But occasionally local programming was also considered 'obscene', particularly film-based programmes (Hindi) as they are 'highly disgusting and monotonous'.

Where difference is measured in terms of comparison with local contexts, the resulting visual confusion and lose of referents is more stark in the lower income areas, resulting in the rejection of foreign programming. From a SEC D-E group, Delhi, female:

This can't be for us.

They don't wear sari or palau. We cannot find out whether they are married or not.

We wear sari and *lahenga* [long skirt] but they, both mother and daughter, wear trousers and shirt so we can't find out who is daughter and mother. Father talks to mother and daughter in the same manner. We Indians after marriage wear sari and cover our head. There we cannot find if a girl is married or not.

Some thoughts on the 'new' India

Research into participants' responses correlated so closely to aspects of the content analysis of the media landscape that it is difficult to know at what point they are informing each other. For example, marketing research presented in January 1998 discerned that establishing a sense of pride in cultural representations of India was a concern of targeted youth audiences. There is some evidence to suggest a greater acceptability of Indian popular culture, such as film music and Hindi pop, because of its repackaging within a global aesthetic. The lowbrow hybridized vernacular Hinglish, as a new form of language with its own encoded signification, has received a sense of legitimization through its use in such advertising campaigns as Pepsi (*yeh hi hai,* right choice baby; *yeh dil maange,* more). However, much of the corporate research I have accessed would have been carried out in 1997 (the 50th Anniversary of India's Independence) during an intense period of self-reflexivity within the public and political discourse of India. In terms of the production of television programming, producers are attempting, with finer and finer detail, to tailor make their products for audiences. MTV claims to base all its programming on research, while Channel [V] goes for a 'bit scientific, a bit gut feel'.

If it is accepted that the 'intense practice of identity' is at the heart of late 20th century politics, marked by a 'desperate negotiation of selfhood' (Friedman, 1994, p.102), the engineering of the Indian media landscape reflects this activity. The acknowledgment of the participant's own agency is tempered by a dilemma in this scenario of deciding what to accept, and what to reject of the meaning packages on offer. Among a generalized audience, research, both academic and commercial, points to a sense of dissonance created by a post-liberalization agenda in which familiar, familial values, and their concomitant ways of seeing, are no longer applicable. Those from higher socioeconomic segments can look for cues and different mixes from the global that come directly via international media, NRI relatives and travel. Others can choose from filtered processes, such as local media, which reassign, realign and assimilate global images.

Perhaps then, for the urban youth segment, SEC A and B, it was not so much the notion of challenging all that was 'traditional', but of finally feeling a symbolic resonance with the reality of their public life, that accounts for the construction of an imagined community of youth. Image brokers then play a psychological two-step with the boundaries of youth culture, sometimes leading, sometimes reflecting these trends. Emotive links are established through familiar associations which young people learn from the cradle, from their family and from school, and through key words such as familiarity, comfort, and the ubiquitous 'cool'. 'Cool', according to McCann-Erikson, is the ultimate legitimator, and 'belonging' the main motivation for teenage behaviour. The role of defining what is 'cool', and legitimating particular values, or consumption patterns, then becomes crucial.

Sunita Rajan, Director of Marketing, Channel [V], designated the channel as a 'trend':

> We are a trend. Quick, fast-paced. The imagery is heavily reflective of Indian culture. We are not about fantastically created montages of international stuff. We start from grass roots. Presented in cool, hip, fashion . . . Most viewers turn to Channel [V] because they have a certain aspirational level. If Channel [V] says it's cool, it's hip.

Collective consumption, be it a pair of sneakers or a television programme, reinforces the community of youth.

Conclusion

In conclusion, it is possible to suggest that a new subjectivity – a community of youth – is formed in the nexus of several interrelated facets of cultural production. Because of the prominence of the collective in determining patterns of consumption, reinforcing and adapting the familiar and the comfortable is the strategy of choice of TNMCs' production of a market-generated identity; and from this, a new collective has been formed with the extension of audiencehood to a community of youth, and the creation of specific genres of cultural production.

But the market-generated process of localization of a media landscape has not alleviated the rhetoric of imperialism, 'invasion from the skies', within India, possibly because its specious nature is evident. It is not for purposes of cultural reclamation or altruism that TNMCs and satellite television have constructed the genres of production they have, but rather as a logic of the staging of globalization and its underpinning logics of consumption. The localization of television content can be seen in the context of a stream of aesthetics, and production techniques, and organizational structures that have been developed predominantly in the United States. The distribution, access and manufacturing of hardware is still unequal (although this is one area where India has a good record, an indigenous satellite programme and hardware manufacturing base).

The strategies of TNMCs are in line with the need for expansion of the market, revealing preferred locations and areas of disinterest. Compare the intense focus on the South, and East Asia region, to Africa. Currently in India corporations including TNMCs, and subsequently advertising and marketing research companies, are attempting to expand their market further by creating associative representations with mini-metros and rural areas.

Even Robertson (1994), who developed the notion of glocalization, acknowledges that much of the construction of the local is done from above. While there are opportunities, local readings, negotiation, redefinitions (as seen in participant responses), the spaces within which this agency can occur are already circumscribed. Agency is tempered, not only by TNMCs for example, but by the extant social organization within which it must exist (the strength of social censure on the understanding of television texts was noted earlier). There are unequal spaces within the Indian social context where there is more possibility to reflect upon subjectivity and audience choice than in others. This has led to what the writer V. S. Naipaul describes as 'a million mutinies', small explosions that relieve the tension between the dialectic of release and restraint (liberalization and extant social context), but which on an individual front can be just as devastating as intense ruptures of the entire field of cultural production.

There appears to be a degree of fluidity and agency, of resistance to both extant social context and westernization, but it is contained and limited by the machinations of both social organization and regimes of accumulation. How then do we begin to proceed with finding a middle path?

From a media-centric point of view, if an audience approaches the television or the media landscape with a set of interpretative skills already in place, a sense of visual literacy begins to be engendered. There appears to be a need for these skills to be taught as much as reading and writing, not to be able to read a commercial in a more efficient manner but to be able to read it more critically, just as we are taught literary criticism and the structures of our patterns of writing and speaking.

To be visually literate is to be able to follow the non-linear grammar of the image, to trace its biography, which carries remnants of those who created it, and those sites where it has been staged within the media landscape, through a journey from producer to receiver. The audience becomes aware of their own additions to the story by viewing within the context of their own home, with different family contexts, and different values, all of which will impact on the image's final understanding. In the future, as technologies converge within even more flexible regimes of accumulation, as the TV becomes the Internet becomes a telephone or a personal computer, again the meaning of images will change.

If a programme of visual literacy (or media education) was introduced into the formal and non-formal education systems in India, or Australia for that matter, will this ground-up approach affect the creation and response to media landscapes? Is there a possibility that these shifts, these transitions in seeing, will impact on the entire field of cultural production, consisting as it does of an ecological field of interconnecting networks? Will it encourage participation, and assist in the erosion of television's unidirectional flow and hierarchical structures? In a revisioned future it is possible to envisage a country such as India with MTV and other TNMCs, with a rebolstered system of public broadcasting, with community television and radio, and a generation of image makers aware of the journey of images and the responsibility of their creation.

References

Appadurai, A. (1997) *Modernity at large: Cultural dimensions of globalization*. New Delhi: Oxford University Press.

Bell, D. (1973) *The coming of post-industrial society*. New York: Basic Books.

Brosius, C. & Butcher, M. (eds) (1999) *Image journeys: Audo-visual media and cultural change in India*. New Delhi: Sage.

Cohen, A. P. (ed.) (1986) *Symbolising boundaries: Identity and diversity in British cultures*. Manchester: Manchester University Press. pp.1-21.

Friedman, J. (1994) *Cultural identity and global process*. UK: Sage.

Gillespie, M. (1995) *Television, ethnicity and cultural change*. London/New York: Routledge.

Hannerz, U. (1987) 'The world in creolisation' in *Africa* 57 (4), pp.546-59.

Jameson, F. (1991) *Postmodernism, or the cultural logic of late capitalism*. Durham: Duke University Press.

Kavolis, V. (1980) 'The logics of selfhood and modes of order: Civilisational structures for individiual identities' in Robertson, R. & Holzner, B. (eds) *Identity and authority: explorations in the theory of society*. UK: Blackwell.

Mishra, S. (1999) 'Dish is life: Cable operators and the neighbourhood' in Brosius, C. & Butcher, M. (eds) (1999) *Image journeys: Audo-visual media and cultural change in India*. New Delhi: Sage.

Monteiro, A. & & Jayasankar, K. P. (forthcoming) 'Between the normal & the emergency: The spectator self, the other & satellite television in India' in I. Hapen & J. Waske (eds) *Consuming audiences*, USA: Hampton Press.

Ohm, B. (1999) 'Doordarshan: Representing the nation's state' in Brosius, C. & Butcher, M. (eds) *Image journeys: Audio-visual media and cultural change in India*. New Delhi: Sage.

Robertson, R. (1994) 'Globalization or glocalisation?' in *Journal of International Communication*, Vol. 1: 1 June, pp.33-52.

Rushdie, S. (1997) interviewed in *India today,* July 14, 1997, p.90.

Sen, A. (1993) 'The impact of American popular culture in the Third World', *Media Asia,* Vol. 20, No. 4, pp.208-223.

Sreberny-Mohammadi, A. (1991) 'The global and the local in international communications' in Curran, J. & Gurevitch, M. (eds) *Mass communication and society*. London: Edward Arnold.

Singhal, A., Svenkerud, P. J. & Rahoi-Gilchrist, R. L. (1998) 'Cultural transcendence as an alternative to cultural imperialism' in Melhote, S., Shrieb's, P. & Agaral, B. C. (eds) *International satellite broadcasting in South Asia*. Oxford, NY: University Press of America.

Vachani, L. (1999) 'Bachchanalias: The many faces of a film icon' in Brosius, C. & Butcher, M. (eds) *Image journeys: Audio-visual media and cultural change in India*. New Delhi: Sage.

Williams, R. (1981) *Culture*. UK: Fontana.

Globalization of film and television: A comparison of the preferences of adolescents in Australia and Thailand

Stephen McElhinney

Introduction

Establishment of trade links between countries and the opening of new national markets around the globe have supported the expansion of transnational trade conducted by media and information conglomerates across national territories. Similarly, establishment of a global market has been supported by communication and media technologies which enable the rapid dissemination of information and entertainment content across national boundaries and to communities throughout local territories. The possibilities of global communication have also permitted information to be transmitted in ways which erode the distance between event and audience – although locality, ethnicity and ethnohistorical difference have been awakened and reaffirmed at the same time. Furthermore, it is worthwhile to examine the impact of globalization of film and television on local audiences to investigate how the possibilities of communication and transmission of information and entertainment content are reflected in the preferences and access of communities separated by distance and ethnohistorical particularity.

Globalization is a concept that may be applied to the industrial practices of production, distribution and exhibition of film and television. However, whilst investigation of industry structures and content distribution provide a useful means to critique globalization within film and television, they are not particularly valid means to understand the actual state of consumption across national and linguistic boundaries. To gain a true understanding of the globalization of film and television it is necessary to investigate both the systems and supports for supply and those which shape demand and consumption. This study, therefore, is an attempt to ascertain the extent of globalization by examining the access and content preferences of adolescents aged 12-14 years living in urban, regional and rural centres in Australia and Thailand. These countries and locations were selected to provide a means to assess the globalization of film and television through a measurement of consumption.

Considerable attention has been given to issues encompassed by globalization within communications studies and related fields through works which have critically examined industrial, political, social and cultural issues related to the scope of production, nature of trade and consumption and impacts on information and control over the flow of ideas and perspectives. Recent works (Herman & McChesney, 1997; Lewis & Slade, 1994; Sussman, 1997; and Sussman & Lent, 1998) have identified a range of factors which are supporting the processes of globalization within communications and cultural sectors and industries such as film and television, including the formation of transnational corporations and practices which support large-scale and multiple businesses across the chain of production, distribution and exhibition. Alongside the global distribution and exhibition businesses of corporations – which have been described as 'collosal' due to the US$2b-$10b turnover they generate (see Herman & McChesney, 1997) – has been the development of niche businesses that control significant market share in particular communications or information products in country or regional areas.

The interaction between global industries, local companies and national governments is crucial to the globalization of film and television as it determines the production practices, distribution and exhibition of content. Here industries have sought to develop a global market for content, whilst national governments have responded to such forces in ways which include privatization and liberalization of local communications infrastructures, including broadcasting. Within cultural industries and some sectors of broadcasting, social, political and national economic imperatives influence the way in which the state regulates the market and the type of content and services which are made available. These factors affect the operation of film and television industries in both Australia and Thailand although the extent of regulation and purposes vary somewhat. In the main, both countries retain control over the sectors as a matter of national sovereignty and cultural expression. These factors, highlighted in ownership policies, cultural content standards and investment regulations, mean that global corporations with interests in film, television, publishing, news and information are often required to address local concerns or establish joint-ventures with local companies to supply services or distribute products such as films or programming. Local companies, with an inherent understanding of national market particularities and standing with governments, therefore act as an important link to supply of content produced for wide global distribution into national systems while also addressing the need for particular cultural expression.

The difficulties inherent in developing national approaches to the distribution of films and television programmes have assisted national operators to build particular businesses in regional markets. Lewis and Slade (1994) and Lewis (1996) have described the role of Thai corporations in building regional markets in Southeast Asia for culturally particular content.

Corporations with interests in telecommunications and broadcasting have been prominent in building a regional market using satellites and information technologies for services particularized to suit the needs of local audiences. Furthermore, Australian corporations have also been active in building businesses outside the country, in activities such as cinema distribution. Companies such as Hoyts and Village-Roadshow operate thousands of screens in Europe, Asia, North and South America (Carr, 1998; Masojada & Meichelboeck, 1997).

Australia and Thailand both provide examples of local media entrepreneurs forming joint ventures with major global companies to exploit expanding middle-class consumer markets. In Thailand, a shopping mall developer formed a partnership with the United Kingdom-based investment company Pearson Plc to build a baht 1 billion (A$5.2m) Disneyland or Universal-Studios-style theme park to be called *Sahariviya City,* which is expected to draw 12 million people per annum. The developer, SVCT, also held preliminary talks with US- and Japanese-based entertainment companies, including MCA (Universal Studios), Paramount and Warner Brothers (Suchontan, 1996). Similarly, Channel Nine, which is the television broadcasting arm of Australia's largest media company, Publishing & Broadcasting Limited (PBL), formed a joint venture with Microsoft to provide content for an on-line information and entertainment service that is likely to ultimately be provided via digital television (Crowe, 1998, p.28). These examples illustrate the importance of local entrepreneurs and companies in supporting the establishment of a global market for cultural content and activities that are primarily supplied or determined by transnational corporations.

Globalization of film

Film is an industry where the majority of material traded globally is supplied by transnational corporations, although they often rely on independent studios and joint venture arrangements for production. Such global trade has also come to include material that has been developed for audiences outside traditional English-language markets and particularized to suit local tastes through use of appropriate language or even produced with a specific audience in mind. Global trade also makes classification of the national origins of film and television content problematic, especially as this is one of the key markers for discerning 'local' or cultural expression. Film and television production for both the US and global market have moved offshore to seek lower cost structures, which ultimately benefit the profitability of transnational companies (see Lent, 1998). However, this type of spatial diffusion of activities also makes identification of the source of films and television programming more difficult, and renders classifications of what comprises the output of national industries difficult. An illustration of this point is illustrated by the fact that the Australian Film Institute (AFI) classified a film about colonial life in New Zealand, *The piano,* as a local film whilst rejecting *Romeo and Juliet,* despite the fact the majority of the creative and technical personnel on the latter film being Australian citizens. Table 1 illustrates this point:

Table 1: Globalization of film production: Identifying Australian content

	Romeo and Juliet	*The piano*
Director	Australian	New Zealander
Script writer(s)	Australian	Australian
Producers	Australian/American	Australian
Lead actors	American	American
Developed in	Australia	Australia
Financed in	USA	France
Shot in	Mexico	New Zealand
Post-production	Australia	Australia
AFI definition	Foreign	Australian

Adapted from Anon (1997, p.4)

It can be argued that, whilst the overall global trade in film is dominated by material which is distributed by transnational corporations into national markets, there are often local industries which seek to provide culturally particular content for audiences; however, such production is often a small part of the overall trade. O'Regan (1993) has made a similar point in discussion of the global trade in television programming. He suggests that the ubiquity of material sourced from the United States in broadcast schedules in many countries around the world can obscure recognition that there is significant trade in content apart from in the English-language. While this may be the case for television, evidence from Australia and Thailand would tend to indicate that imported content is both widely released and popular with local audiences. Table 2 illustrates the point that even when a national industry such as Australia's receives considerable government support its output is a relatively small proportion of releases.

Table 2: Theatrical releases in Australia 1990-1995

Year	Australia & NZ	US	UK	Canada	France	Rest of Europe	Asia	Other	Total
1990	25	153	20	6	27	14	7	1	253
1991	23	149	21	3	16	16	8	4	240
1992	32	135	26	6	9	15	5	1	227
1993	25	172	13	5	14	17	8	5	259
1994	28	153	22	6	17	13	12	1	252
1995	14	171	23	3	17	13	6	5	252

Source: Australian Film Commission (1996)

Furthermore, the ability of local industries to provide films which compete with imported films in the distribution and exhibition schedules of commercial operators is reduced when there is ready acceptance of foreign content, and shared language and similar cultural values are reflected within imported content. For example, Table 3, showing box office figures collated by the Motion Pictures Distributors Association of Australia (MPDAA), lists the highest grossing films up to 1995:

Table 3: Top 10 films at the Australian box office to 1995

Position	Title	Origin	Box office (est.) $ millions
1	Crocodile Dundee (1986)	Australia	47.7
2	Jurassic Park (1993)	USA	33
3	E.T. (1982)	USA	32.6
4	Forrest Gump (1994)	USA	30.5
5	The lion king (1994)	USA	27
6	Mrs Doubtfire (1993)	USA	26.2
7	Pretty woman (1990)	USA	26.1
8	Crocodile Dundee II (1988)	Australia	24.9
9	Strictly ballroom (1992)	Australia	21.7
10	Four weddings and a funeral (1994)	UK	21.4

Source: MPDAA (1996)

In Thailand, however, differences in cultural and linguistic conditions hinder the direct transferral of films produced for western and English-speaking markets to the local audience. Furthermore, language and cultural differences in Thailand have traditionally split the audience into two distinct markets. Locally produced low-budget films in the *Nam Nao* tradition, farces and comedies are popular among Thai people in rural and regional areas. On the other hand, western content has traditionally been more readily distributed in Bangkok, where the audience is more cosmopolitan.

The relative costs to obtain the rights to screen a western film released by a major distributor and those of Chinese and Thai origin is an important factor determining the territory in which they exhibited. The higher costs associated with the rights for a western film act to reduce the territories over which they are distributed globally and within countries such as Thailand, where low audience demand and capacity to pay for admission exist outside Bangkok. In such circumstances western films are poor economic prospects for exhibitors, especially as people in rural communities prefer Thai and Chinese folk tales and martial arts material (Punya Ubon, 1994).

Thus, cultural differences and poor market prospects have acted to limit the ready distribution of western-language feature films beyond major urban centres in countries where language and cultural particularity act to inhibit demand. In addition, the increased sophistication of film making in Thailand has meant culturally and linguistically relevant material is more readily available. Hence, larger-budget Thai films are increasingly capturing public attention and competing with western films for box office takings, especially in Bangkok and other centres. Some caution should be exercized in using box office takings alone as a marker of popularity, especially in countries such as Thailand where a differential exists between the price of admission in Bangkok and to movie screenings upcountry. In 1995 cinema admission in Bangkok could be up to 50 baht, while for some screenings in regional Thailand admission to the same film could be as low as 10 baht. The result of this situation is that box office earnings are skewed toward films popular with city audiences. However, Table 4 demonstrates the success of local productions in capturing audiences in Thailand.

This table also illustrates the impact of western films at the Thai box office in terms of earnings. This is a strong indication that the global trade in feature films includes countries outside the English-language market and the ready acceptance of the audience to pay to see such films.

Television

Television comes more directly under the ambit of state control and regulation and therefore displays different characteristics to film. In Australia and Thailand, operation of broadcasting services is largely restricted to national companies although exceptions have been made as technological change and

Table 4: Top 10 grossing films of all time in Thailand

Position	Title	Origin	Box office (est.) million baht
1	Jurassic Park (1993)	USA	74.3
2	Speed (1994)	USA	60.5
3	Die hard with a vengeance (1995)	USA	60.5
4	This world is only for you (1995)	Thailand	55
5	Sia-Dai [Wasted youths] (1995)	Thailand	52
6	Cuckoos at Bang-Phleng (1994)	Thailand	45
7	Batman forever (1995)	USA	44.6
8	Sunset at Chao-Phraya (1995)	Thailand	44
9	Waterworld (1995)	USA	42.4
10 (equal)	To be reborn with you (1995)	Thailand	40
	The mask	USA	

Anon. (1996)

industrial conditions have required foreign investment. Unlike film, which operates with less state intervention, television is regulated in terms of service areas and in relation to content, including the requirement to screen local content. Nonetheless imported content is present on local screens due to the cost advantages of purchasing proven programming wherever it is feasible and attracts significant audiences. However, language and cultural particularity presents a barrier to importation, as commercial operation is largely predicated on audience numbers. The development and increasing sophistication of the Thai broadcasting industry following liberalization and privatization of the sector, provides an example of the proposition provided by Lent (1993) that local content has increasingly replaced imported programming from the United States in many countries in Asia. In this case it may be argued that the ability of local programme makers to provide culturally particular material in local languages has reduced the need to fill schedules with imported programming that was subsequently dubbed or subtitled.

In terms of distribution, the nature of television services in Australia and Thailand also act to ensure that communities in urban and rural communities largely receive the same programming. Government policy in both countries has ensured that television services are networked and provided to as many people as possible. This has meant that most rural communities receive services which are typically provided for capital city audiences, with very little content that reflects local or particular conditions. Thus, unlike film distribution and exhibition which operate primarily as market-driven industries, television has been given a greater role in 'nation-building' by governments, either through historical operation or licence agreements with private providers.

Globalization and the youth market

Recognition that the audience is fragmented and has particular tastes and capacities to pay for access, has led media companies to develop specialist products and services for market 'niches'. This development has led to 'youth' becoming a recognized global market although even this broad grouping is segmented by advertising and marketing industries (Kline, 1995). Addressing youth (aged 12-24 years) as a global market has been driven by limited prospects for growth in countries such as the United States, where competition is strong for audiences, and by a recognition that many countries readily accept English-language content. Also, market research has encouraged media companies to vie for the US$55 billion per annum (including US$4 billion in Australia) that people this age are believed to spend on cultural activities and entertainment (Tulich, 1994). Furthermore, a global market is being sought by TNCs and other major suppliers of information and entertainment products designed for the youth market in response to market saturation in the United States and the readiness of young audiences to consume film and television products. Interest in distributing content in Asian countries and entering joint ventures to promote local product is also being encouraged by the high proportion of populations aged under 25 years. People aged under 25 years are considered to be the peak market for sales of cultural and entertainment products (Masojada & Meichelboeck, 1997).

Furthermore, in terms of globalization and the production of content for this market, a number of scholars (e.g. Bell, 1993, pp.165-168; Hamilton, 1992a; Hamilton, 1992b; Kline, 1993; Kline, 1995) and sources such as UNESCO (1995) have noted the spread of a global youth culture that is carried by means such as films, television, advertising and recorded music:

> The worldwide pressures of popular culture . . . to penetrate other cultures are
> powerful, and often accepted and even welcomed by people from different
> cultures with alacrity and enthusiasm. (UNESCO 1995, p.27)

Certainly much has been made of the apparent adoption of western-originated youth culture throughout the world during the last few decades. This apparent trend followed the globalization of product distribution by primarily US- and European-based entertainment corporations, which dominate a great deal of the trade in cultural commodities (see Herman & McChesney, 1997). Recognition that the audience is fragmented along lines of ethnicity, gender, class and so on has prompted industry to react by developing specialized practices and processes, characterized as post-Fordism, which permit a far wider range of material to be provided than was the case (see Cunningham & Jacka, 1996). Post-Fordist industrial practices have allowed development and distribution of content to niche audiences, including youth, which is itself segmented and fragmented along numerous lines globally and locally. Here the results gathered from Australia and Thailand can be used to provide empirical evidence to test these issues and build a better model of the globalization of film and television. By comparing Australia and Thailand it is possible to discern if the programming and films supplied by the global trade are readily accepted by adolescents in these countries, and to identify if there is any cross-cultural similarities between the preferences selected by the adolescents both between countries and the city and countryside.

Methodology

Three locations in both Australia and Thailand were selected as sites for investigation of the preferences of adolescents aged 12-14 years. In Australia, the state capital of New South Wales, Sydney, the regional centre of Tamworth, and the rural community of Manila were chosen. Comparable sites were selected in Thailand, including Bangkok, the town of Si Saket and an adjacent community in Si Saket province. Students at local schools were surveyed between January 1994 and February 1995 via questionnaires administered during classes, to ascertain preferences and access to film and television. Students at six schools were canvassed in each country. Although a variety of research methodologies could have been applied to gather data on preferences, Lonner and Berry (1986) note that questionnaires are a valid and useful means to elicit information in cross-cultural circumstances as long as appropriate care is taken to ensure that translation is effective.

This research, as it involved both assessment of the industrial nature of film and television industries and the preferences of adolescents aged about 12 years in Australia and Thailand, draws heavily on ethnographic approaches to mass communications research in recognition that arguments, whether they be on theoretical, economic or cultural grounds, may be strengthened through reliance on ethnographical evidence. This need to sustain critical theoretical argument through assessment and comparison of empirical evidence gathered from the students, the community and the industry, has been readily adopted within political economy as researchers recognize the value of ethnographic approaches that provide evidence on the relationship between the audience and the films and television programmes they view and the ways they interpret this content (Pendakur, 1993).

Results

Television preferences in Australia

There were 77 programmes mentioned by the students in Australia as being within their favourite three television shows. In general there was considerable overlap between the locations in terms of the programmes the students nominated, with 31 of the 77 programmes mentioned by the adolescents in both Sydney and Tamworth/Manila. Overall, the 163 adolescents surveyed in Australia made 2.66 selections per questionnaire. The most popular programmes are listed in the Table 5 below and are categorized in terms of location and number of adolescents who mentioned them.

Table 5: Top eight most nominated television programmes in Australia

Programme/Origin	Sydney	Tamworth/Manila	Total
1. *The Simpsons* (US)	45	38	87 (53%)
2. *Home and away* (Australia)	19	28	47 (29%)
3. *Roseanne* (US)	13	6	19 (12%)
4. *Home improvement* (US)	12	3	15 (9%)
5. 'Cartoons' (various)	8	6	14 (8%)
6. *Hanging with Mr. Cooper* (US)	10	2	12 (7%)
7. *Ren & Stimpy* (Canada)	8	3	11 (7%)
8. *SeaQuest DSV* (US)	2	9	11 (7%)

The large number of programmes named by the students in Australia demonstrated that they had varied tastes as far as the programming present on Australian television allowed. The figures in the above table demonstrate that animation (*The Simpsons,* 'Cartoons' and *Ren & Stimpy*) holds the greatest overall appeal to the students of both Sydney and Tamworth/Manila, with three positions in the top eight shows. In terms of the source of programming it is apparent that programmes made originally for broadcast in the United States also appealed to the students. The only Australian programme in the top eight was the soap opera *Home and away.* The other seven programmes are imports, although the category 'Cartoons' could include animations from both Australia and overseas. In general terms, analysis of the source of the 77 programmes mentioned by the students also supports the argument that English-language imports are more attractive to this audience than locally produced material: only 27 Australian productions were present in the full range identified from the questionnaires. In terms of the total preferences expressed by the students, only about 28 percent were for locally produced programmes. These preferences covered a wide range of content types, including soap opera, news, current affairs, games shows, sports and children's programming.

Analysis of the figures contained in the above table also demonstrates that only a few programmess captured the majority of preferences expressed by the children in both centres, with the animated comedy series *The Simpsons* being the most popular show, being mentioned by more than 50 percent of the respondents. The second most popular programme, *Home and away,* was mentioned by almost a third of the respondents, while the remainder of

Table 6: Top eight most nominated television programmes in Thailand

Programme	Bangkok	Si Saket	Total	
1. *Chingcha Chali* (drama series)	41	5	46	(22%)
2. *Khun Ying Chom Kaen* (drama series)	16	16	32	(15%)
3. 'Cartoons'	19	12	31	(14%)
4. *Twilight show* (variety)	9	13	22	(10%)
5. *Mai Long Mai Ru* (documentary/drama)	4	18	22	(10%)
6. *Yam Mua Lom Pat Huan* (series)	20	-	20	(9%)
7. *Si Thum Sakrai* (variety)	19	1 (2%)	20	(9%)
8. *Yutthakan Khayap Nguak* (comedy)	15	4	19	(9%)

programmes that received significant mention attracted much smaller proportions of the combined preferences, although were still clearly quite popular.

Television preferences in Thailand

The predominance of locally produced content in Thailand and its apparent appeal to the audience is demonstrated in the answers provided by the students in Bangkok and Si Saket. Unlike the Australian results which, displayed the fact that imported programming was popular with the students, the data from Thailand displayed a greater preference for local programming, although several Chinese-series were named in the overall listings. These results show that a variety of programme types also appealed to the students and that 'Cartoons' once again figured highly in the preferences expressed. Unlike other forms of television content, it is likely that the cartoons mentioned by the students were imported, as animation easily lends itself to particularization through dubbing of dialogue into local languages. Whilst Chinese series figured in the preferences there were no programmes from the United States or the United Kingdom, although these had figured prominently in the Australian sample. Several explanations are possible for this finding. Firstly, from an industrial and economic perspective it is likely that programming from western countries is more costly to screen than local productions. Secondly, that Thai broadcasters prefer to rely on local producers for content to ensure that the audience receives culturally appropriate material. Thirdly, that the Thai audience prefers local productions to those from western sources in general or Chinese programmes because they have greater relevance to their lives and expectations.

Film preferences in Australia (Sydney & Tamworth/Manila)

A total of 114 films were named by the students canvassed in Australia. Of these films 91 titles were nominated by the students in Sydney and 69 in Tamworth/Manila. The students nominated an average of about 2.5 films per questionnaire in Sydney as against 2.1 in the country sample. Analysis of the origins of the 114 films nominated in Australia demonstrates the fact that imported films predominated in the selections generated by the students, and local productions held a marginal position in comparison with imported films. Of the 114 films nominated only six were produced in Australia and none of these films received enough nominations to figure in the top eight films named by the students. No Australian film registered in the top five nominations in Sydney or Tamworth/Manila. All of the top eight films were mentioned by nine or more of the students. Table 7 lists the films registered most in preferences from both Sydney and Tamworth/Manila. This table provides a breakdown of the respondents, gives a percentage of the students who list the film and shows the origin of each film.

Table 7: Top eight films named in Australia

Film/Origin	Sydney	Tamworth/Manila	Total
1. *Speed* (US)	19	6	25 (15%)
2. *Aladdin* (US)	17	2	19 (11%)
3. *The lion king* (US)	1	14	15 (9%)
4. *Jurassic Park* (US)	8	4	12 (7%)
5. *Cool runnings* (US)	8	4	12 (7%)
6. *Home alone* (US)	8	3	11 (7%)
7. *The mask* (US)	–	11	11 (7%)
8. *My girl* (US)	7	2	9 (5%)
Forrest Gump (US)	–	9	9 (5%)

From this table the popularity of films produced and distributed by major entertainment companies is readily apparent. Of the nine films that featured most in the preferences, eight; *Jurassic Park, Forrest Gump, The lion king, The mask, Aladdin, Speed, Home alone* and *Cool runnings* figure in the top 50 films of all time at the Australian box office (MPDAA, 1996). It is also worth noting that *The mask* made the list on the strength of support from the students in Tamworth/Manila as it was released after the data had been collected in Sydney in June/July 1994. It may be argued that the strength of support for these nine films, which accounted for a third of the 376 preferences provided by the students in Australia, could be based upon the fact that they had all been produced and heavily promoted to the adolescent audience.

Film preferences in Thailand (Bangkok & Si Saket)

A total of 86 films were named in Thailand, 57 in Bangkok and 45 in Si Saket. The films may be categorized by place of origin and nomination into three groups: Thai (29); Chinese (27); and western (30). In total, the students in Thailand named an average of about 1.41 films each, which was about 1.5 films less than their counterparts in Sydney. Table 8 illustrates the number of preferences registered for categories based on the origins of the films.

Table 8: Comparison of the origins of the films nominated in Thailand

Origin & total number	Bangkok	Si Saket
Thai (29)	13	20
Chinese (27)	14	21
western (30)	30	4

Table 8 demonstrates the differences in the origins of the films named in Bangkok and Si Saket. Clearly more Thai and Chinese films were named in Si Saket than in Bangkok, and more western films were nominated by the students in the city than either Thai or Chinese productions. This provides evidence that the students in Bangkok readily accepted western material and supports the argument that the market for these cultural commodities includes areas of Thailand, particularly Bangkok. The figures also show that the students in Bangkok have ready access to films from a range of sources yet have chosen more western films than both Thai and Chinese productions as being within their three preferences. Further analysis shows that the students in Si Saket nominated the bulk of the Thai and Chinese titles. Whilst these figures show that western material is primarily concentrated in the preferences of the students in Bangkok, Table 9 on the next page demonstrates the level of popularity of these films compared to Thai and Chinese material in terms of the number of times they were mentioned in the questionnaires.

Furthermore, the figures also show that much of the support for western films can be attributed to students in Bangkok nominating the films *Demolition man, Terminator, Aladdin* and *Total recall* in numbers whilst support for Thai and Chinese films was overwhelmingly due to the preferences generated in Si Saket.

Table 9: Top eight films named in Thailand

Film/Origin	Bangkok	Si Saket	Total students	
1. *Jurassic Park* (US)	37	1	38	(18%)
2. *Ban Phi Pop* (Thai)	3	23	26	(13%)
3. *Phu Ying Ka Khrai* (Chinese)	2	11	13	(6%)
4. *Total recall* (US)	12	–	12	(5%)
5. *Terminator* (US)	11	–	11	(5%)
6. *Aladdin* (US)	10	–	10	(4%)
7. *Demolition man* (US)	6	1	7	(3%)
8. *Khabuankan Su Phi Mai Mi Thoi* (Chinese)	3	4	7	(3%)

Discussion

The development of transnational media and communications corporations has been noted as a factor in the integration of national territories, including those without shared linguistic traditions, into a global marketplace for films, television programmes and other cultural products. Global trade has been facilitated by a range of factors, including the establishment of technological infrastructure that permits widespread distribution of content, the liberalization of media systems to allow increased imported content on local screens, and the commercialization of services which require popular and audience drawing content to support income. Furthermore, whilst global distribution is dominated by cultural products developed and distributed by transnational corporations, national industries have a role in carrying content to local communities. In the main such local distribution is carried out by cinema exhibitors and television stations which have knowledge of audience particularities in terms of tastes, expectations and economic potential. The relationship between globalized supply and localized consumption is therefore predicated on the trade links between transnational producers and distributors and exhibitors operating in local markets. However, whilst this global supply appears to be dominated by films and television programmes produced largely for western and English-language audiences there appears to be significant local production in both Australia and Thailand. Thus audiences in Australia and Thailand are largely able to select between imported and local content which are both available at cinemas and on television.

The effect of this is illustrated through the preferences of the adolescents in Australia and Thailand. In terms of both film and television it is evident from the Australian sample that imported and primarily US-sourced content has been favoured whilst the situation appears to be significantly different in

Thailand. The popularity of programmes sourced from the United States, such as *The Simpsons,* may be argued to be a result of the cultural similarities that permit local audiences to readily enjoy this imported content, particularly when it is specifically created for adolescent audiences. The second most popular programme, *Home and away,* illustrates the point that cultural specificity also attracts adolescents to content. The trend for the substitution of Thai programmes for imports has reduced the range of content available to audiences but arguably increased the cultural specificity. Moreover, the overwhelming preferences for the drama series *Chingcha Chali,* which is about life in Northeast Thailand (including Si Saket), expressed by the students in Bangkok may be argued to illustrate an interest in content which addresses this cultural specificity.

The results gathered regarding film suggest that the market extends globally across cultural and linguistic boundaries, particularly for material provided by transnational corporations. The preferences also illustrate the fact that the market for these films does not generally extend to Si Saket. In terms of popularity it appears that the adolescents in Thailand also ranked Chinese and Thai productions highly. This high ranking of Australian films is not evident in the Australian sample, with films produced for the United States market dominating preferences.

In summary, globalization of film and television may be argued to be primarily a function of the market development practices of transnational corporations linked to distribution agreements with local exhibitors. The preferences expressed by the adolescents in Australia and Thailand demonstrate that distribution of western and English-language films has limits, with Si Saket largely excluded. Moreover, the cultural and linguistic particularity evident in rural Thailand acts as a break on the distribution of western content, although Bangkok is clearly part of the global market. Further work would be necessary to examine the cultural impact of such distribution and market formation; however, it is worthwhile noting that the distribution and exhibition practices evident in both countries are conducted as commercial operations.

References

Anon. (1996) 'Top ten grossing films in Thailand', *Cinemag,* September.

Anon. (1997b) 'AFI awards spot the difference', *Cinema Papers,* December. Melbourne: MTV Publishing .

Australian Film Commission (1996) *Get the picture: Essential data on Australian film, television and video,* 4th edition. Sydney: AFC.

Bell, P. & Bell, R. (1993) *Implicated: The United States in Australia.* Melbourne: Oxford University Press.

Carr, E. (1998) 'Village keen to give Asia the flicks', *The Australian Financial Review*, 14-15 February.

Crowe, D. (1998) 'Grand ambition: The Packer-Gates connection' *The Australian Financial Review*, 14-15 March.

Cunningham, S. & Jacka, E. (1996) *Australian television and international mediascapes.* Melbourne: Cambridge University Press.

Hamilton, A. (1992a) 'The mediascape of modern Southeast Asia', *Screen*, 33 (1), Spring.

Hamilton, A. (1992b) 'Family dramas: Film and modernity in Thailand', *Screen*, 33(3) Autumn.

Herman, E. & McChesney, R. (1997) *The global media: The new missionaries of corporate capitalism.* London: Cassell.

Kline, S. (1993) *Out of the garden: Toys, TV, and children's culture in the age of marketing.* London: Verso.

Kline, S. (1995) 'The play of the market: On the internationalisation of children's culture,' *Theory, Culture & Society*, (12), London: Sage.

Lent, J. A. (1993) 'Four conundrums of Third World communication' in Nordenstreng, K. & Schiller, H. I. *Beyond national sovereignty: International communications in the 1990s*. New Jersey: Ablex Publishers.

Lent, J. A. (1980) 'The animation industry and its offshore factories', in Sussman, G, & Lent, J. A. *Global productions: Labor in the making of the 'information society'.* Cresskill, New Jersey: Hampton Press.

Lewis, G. & Slade, C. (1994) 'The samurai who came to the world's biggest barbecue: Australia, Japan and globalization', *Media Information Australia*, 71, February.

Lewis, G. (1996) 'Communications regionalism in Southeast Asia: The Thai experience'. A paper presented to the political economy section of the IAMCR conference, Sydney, Australia, August.

Lonner, W. J. & Berry, J. W. (1986) *Field methods in cross-cultural research*. Beverly Hills: Sage Publications.

Masojada, J. & Meichelboeck, P. (1997) *Filmed entertainment industry: Trends, themes, and major Australian participants: Update on listed Australian operators.* Australia: Deutsche Morgan and Grenfell.

MPDAA (Motion Picture Distributors Association of Australia) (1996) 'National box office figures', personal correspondence, 21 October.

O'Regan, T. (1993) *Australian television culture.* Sydney: Allen & Unwin.

Pendakur, M. (1993) 'Political economy and ethnography: Transformations in an Indian village', in Wasko, J., Mosco, V. & Pendakur M. (eds) *Illuminating the blindspots: Essays in honour of Dallas Smythe.* New Jersey: Norwood.

Punya Ubon (1994) Personal interview with proprietor of Punyaporu Pappayon (travelling movie show), Ban Phek village, Kunthalak District, Si Saket province, Thailand. Cited in McElhinney, S.K. 'Globalization of film and television: A comparison of the preferences of Australian and Thai adolescents'. Unpublished doctoral thesis. Australia: Macquarie University.

Suchontan, C. (1996) 'Sahariviya City eyes Disney-style park' *The Bangkok Post,* 4 September.

Sussman, G. (1997) *Communication, technology, and politics in the information age.* Thousand Oaks: Sage.

Sussman, G. & Lent, J. A. (1998) *Global productions: Labor in the making of the 'information society'.* Cresskill, New Jersey: Hampton Press.

Tulich, K. (1994) 'Kids with cash', *The Bulletin with Newsweek,* 12 July, Sydney, Australia.

UNESCO (1995) *Our creative diversity,* Report of the World Commission on Culture and Development. Paris: UNESCO.

Alternative uses of Chinese television and alternative passages to power: An ethnographic study of alternative uses of television in 15 urban Chinese families

Yong Zhong

Introduction

On the basis of an ethnographic study of 15 Chinese urban families, this chapter attempts to examine two research questions regarding the relationship between Chinese viewers and television. The two questions are:

1. What are the subjects' reactions like to their positioning by the television set and official Chinese television?
2. For those who have problems accepting the position imposed on them, how do they escape it and how do they relate to television in a way that empowers them?

Both questions are based on two perspectives developed by recent international television studies theories. One perspective is that television audiences are not masses of cultural dupes who are easily susceptible to the control and manipulation of television. Halloran has discussed the outdatedness of:

> The emphasis on the viewer as tabularasa . . . just waiting to soak up all that is beamed at him. Now we think in terms of interaction or exchange between the medium and audience, and it is recognized that the viewer approaches every viewing situation with a complicated piece of filtering equipment. (Halloran, 1970, p.20)

Cultural studies scholars, especially Stuart Hall (1981) and John Fiske (1987), have more recently delivered a semiotic liberation of the viewers by diversifying the production of meanings and pleasures. They have identified the audiences, whom they regard as *readers,* as ultimate producers of meanings and pleasure because it is they who *read* meanings into a text. According to Fiske, the range of meanings produced by the readers are potentially infinite but can be heuristically coded into preferred readings at one end and oppositional meanings at the other, with negotiated meanings in between. Fiske's theorization has led to his celebration of viewers' semiotic democracy in spite of the homogenizing logic of the financial economy of television. He writes:

> It is decentered, diverse, located in the multiplicity of its modes and moments of reception. Television is the plurality of its reading practices, the democracy of its pleasures, and it can only be understood in its fragments. It promotes and provokes a network of resistances to its own power whose attempt to homogenize and hegemonize breaks down on the instability and multiplicity of its meanings and pleasures. (Fiske, 1987, p.324)

The second perspective is the importance of the contexts of use and relation to television. Morley points out that the starting point of contextualized television studies is 'the household or the family, for it is here that the primary involvement with television is created, and where the primary articulation of meanings is undertaken' (1992, p.183). He also recommends ethnography as an empirical method most appropriate for contextualized television studies. Following is what Morley has to say about audience ethnography:

> Television as 'text' and television as technology are united by their construction, their recontextualization, within the practices of our daily lives and in the display of goods and cultural competence, both in private and in public. If we are to make some sense of the significance of these activities which after all, are the primary ones for any understanding of the dynamics of the pervasiveness and power of contemporary culture, then we have to take seriously the varied and detailed ways in which they are undertaken. (Morley, 1992, pp.182-183)

I have some reservations about the two perspectives, especially Fiske's theorization of semiotic democracy. I fear that the liberation of the audiences and celebration of their ultimate power can be interpreted as an assertion that interpretive resistance is necessarily more common than subordination and overwhelms the reproduction of dominant meanings – a fear shared by Corner (1991) and Morley (1992). Especially in the Chinese context, where propaganda pervades television, a theoretical liberation of the audiences from the textual fetters may be a convenient excuse for justifying, in practical terms, the continued use of television for propaganda purposes. So, the assumption that people habitually use the content of dominant media against itself in order to empower themselves is theoretically sound but politically and strategically problematic and inappropriate for studies of Chinese 'teleVISION', as opposed to Chinese television.[1]

In short, my problem with the semiotic democracy is that, in Chinese teleVISION, it tends to condemn the viewers to a continuous drudgery of reading against the grain. In the name of the contestation of meanings between indoctrination and counter-indoctrination, it condones the transformation of the after-hours television viewing from entertainment into an extension of the political life. If Chinese television, including its offerings, self-positioning and preferred viewing contexts, is so reactionary and suppressive, does it mean that there is no escape from it? Does it also mean that the viewers have no choices but accept its tyranny? Yes, as I have found through the present audience ethnography, there is an escape, an ingenious one, which is using television for a variety of unorthodox purposes. In this article, I will examine in depth such alternative uses of television through ethnographic studies of 15 Chinese urban families.

To wind up the introduction, I would like to emphasize that this is an ethnographic audience study that attempts to analyze the subjects' reactions to the position offered to them by Chinese television and to construct an alternative passage to viewers' power. The construction of the alternative passage is meant to account for the subjects' triumphant escape from a reified position and their occupancy of an autonomous subject position. By autonomous subject position, I refer to those psychological and physical attributes that enable an individual to make informed judgements and decisions and to take responsibilities for his/her own activities. I concede that the new subject position is not one of total and final freedom from all ideologies. In the Chinese context, an end to political propaganda may very well be the beginning of subjection to other ideologies, such as those related to commercial propaganda. But it at least offers an alternative and increases the choices available to the individuals. I believe that the ability and freedom to make one's own choice is exactly what is lacking in modern China.

Next, I will discuss the findings of the project in three sections. Firstly, I will present a brief review of the research procedures and methods used in this project. Secondly, I will discuss the position offered to the viewers by Chinese television and how the subjects reacted to the position. The discussion will lead to a proposition about a majority of the subjects abandoning Chinese television. Thirdly, I will construct a scenario of many subjects making alternative uses of television by presenting a number of case study descriptions. I will conclude with a critique of the popularity of the alternative uses of television, focusing on how they empower the subjects.

---

1. In this article, I distinguish Chinese teleVISION from Chinese television. The former is a vision of the medium and its viewers in China whereas the latter refers to the medium and its characteristic use as a tool for propaganda.

Research procedure and method

The project described in this article has adopted a combination of ethnographic methods, including participant observations and interviews. What I would like to emphasize now is that the ethnographic approach is an holistic one, one that is concerned not only with the act of television viewing but also with the dynamic physical, political, cultural and historical contexts/processes of which television viewing is but a part. Geertz has defined this approach as 'thick descriptions' of activities and events because it takes into account 'a multiplicity of complex conceptual structures . . . superimposed upon or knotted into one another. (1973, p.14)

Adopting the ethnographic approach, I hope to be able to describe and interpret the cultural practices of television viewing undertaken by my subjects in their habitual and familiar contexts. The present project has actually brought me into the homes of 15 families in three of China's cities and has enabled me to furnish 'thick descriptions' of the contexts of, uses of and relations to television in those contexts. The process of the research consists of a number of interwoven aspects, including sampling, fieldwork (i.e. participant observation and interview) and data analysis. Following is a brief discussion of the aspects.

Sampling

This project, which uses predominantly the qualitative analysis methodology to furnish thick descriptions of television viewing, is more concerned with use of television by particular and typical types of audiences. It has no aspiration or ambition to produce any comprehensive generalizations about masses of Chinese television audiences as totalized taxonomic collectives. Therefore, it has not applied the kind of random sampling that is typical of quantitative researches. Instead, great efforts have been taken to select informants of particular interest to the research. I have been enlightened by Ang's (1991) and Morley's (1992) argument that the traditional dominance of the generalizing research should be balanced or, at least, complemented by the opposite concern with particularization. Concerned with particularization, I have intended to examine how five families in each of the three Chinese cities have related to and used television.

I had the following criteria in mind when I selected the families for the ethnographic description. Basically, I wanted five families in each city which were different from one another in social, economic and cultural terms. Secondly, I looked for families of different demographic structures and sizes, including DINK (double income no kid) families, kernel families and extended families. Thirdly, I tried to include both native and migrant families in each city. The main purpose of insisting on the variations was to avoid accidentally targeting one particular narrow segment of the Chinese urban populace.

Nevertheless, I did not harbour a naive wish that the variations could make the samples demographically a truer reflection of the Chinese urban populace. Thus, in every city, I looked for families that could broadly fit into any five of the following heuristic categories:

1. *Guojia ganbu*, i.e. officers employed by the state and entitled to stable benefits provided by the state, including cadres of government departments and managers of government business. Presumably and theoretically, they work for and represent the interest of the state and, in turn, their welfare is looked after by the state.
2. *Zhishi fenzi*, i.e. intellectuals and professionals, such as teachers, scientists, accountants. Presumably they are the segment of the populace that generally has more independent thinking than other segments.
3. *Getihu*, i.e. self-employed trades-persons who make a living on their skills and labour.
4. *Dakuan*, i.e. upstart rich people who are widely believed to have benefited from the recent economic reforms and from their official connections.
5. *Dagongzai*, i.e. people who are paid wages by other people to undertake menial or clerical work.
6. The new urban poor, including *mangliu*, i.e. recent impoverished migrants to the cities, and *Xiagang gongren*, i.e. unemployed or stood-down people who are often perceived to be the losers in the current rounds of economic reforms.

To find the right families for the research, I sought help from a number of people, including Zhong Ni-ya, a neighbourhood administrator in Guangzhou, Mrs Zhang Xinying, a Beijing-based journalist, and Mrs Zhu, a visiting scholar to the University of New South Wales from Wuhan. I discussed my sampling criteria with them and invited them to provide a list of candidates for me to choose from. They also contacted those whom I was interested in visiting, inquiring about their willingness to and availability for participating in the research. After a series of consultations and discussions, I was able to identify the 15 families to be researched in the three cities.

Participant observation and interviews

Following Morley's insight, I have adopted a research methodology combining participant observation and in-depth discussions with the subjects to gain a better-informed understanding of the Chinese television audiences. But what is participant observation? According to Hymes (1962) and Burns (1997), participant observation involves the researcher being there, participating in the activity or event being observed, immersing him/herself amongst the subjects whose behaviours are being studied, and experiencing their life in order to get first-hand knowledge about them. Earlier, in the Malinowskian tradition of ethnography, participant observation was about *being there* to observe the *unconscious, habitual* activities of people in a *natural environment* without disturbing them. It was thought that such an *immersionist* style of investigation would provide a *comprehensive, authentic* and *objective* knowledge about the people in question.

But there has always been scepticism about any claims to *comprehensiveness, objectivity, sincerity and authenticity.* Clifford (1986) argues that there can be no place of overview from which to map human ways of life, thus removing the basis of any claim to a comprehensive overview. Geertz (1973) claims that, as the analyst's account is always an interpretation of what his/her informants are up to, it is necessarily a fiction about, rather than a truthful reflection of, the informants' world. Their arguments suggest that ethnographers should transcend the Malinowskian ideal of 'immersionist ethnography' and seek to neither become nor mimic the native/other and that 'only romantics or spies would seem to find any point in that' (Geertz, 1973, p.13).

In the present project, I have been conscious of the interpretive nature of the participant observation and the dynamic nature of my subjects. I have made the best possible arrangements to be there, to spend extended lengths of time with my subjects, to observe their varied uses of and relations to television, to participate in their television-related activities and to engage them in my discussions. But I have made no attempts to be secretive about my mission, or to disguise my research activities, or to recreate a seemingly natural environment. Instead, I have invited my informants to be active, conscious co-participants in the project.

The ethnographic visits were made from January to February 1997 to the five Beijing homes, from December 1997 to January 1998 to the five Wuhan families and from December 1998 to January 1999 to the five Guangzhou families. I managed to spend maximum time available with each family I visited, five to seven hours a day for three days, including one or two weekend days, i.e. at least a total of 20 hours. In Guangzhou, I was invited to live with three of the families each for the four-day period. In Wuhan, I was invited to live with two of the families during my visit to the city. Naturally, I had even more opportunities to see what was happening in these five families.

The visits to the families usually began at 5 pm or 6 pm, before dinner. Sometimes, I talked with one or two individual informants whilst their other family members were doing family chores, like preparing dinner and washing up. At other times, I helped with some minor chores while chatting with them. After dinner, I participated in their leisure activities, including viewing television, singing karaoke, viewing movies on video compact disc players (VCD), listening to music and playing mahjong. Most visits finished at 10 pm or 11 pm. On the whole, the families were extremely tolerant of my intrusion and tried their best to be helpful to my research needs.

I also engaged the informants in discussions that were based on, but not restricted to, a list of core questions previously written in my notebook, which

I referred to now and again as a checklist. I raised the questions selectively, sometimes while participating in the television-related activities, and sometimes while doing other things. At other times, my informants and I just stopped doing other things and had a concentrated discussion over an issue. I felt that, as I got to know my informants better and vice versa, the discussions became more and more spontaneous, revelatory and candid.

I sought permission to tape the discussions with a cassette-recorder and take notes of the observation and was given permission to do so in most of the families. I gave assurance that each family would receive a copy of the tapes or notes made about the family if they wished, and that I would camouflage their identities in any article that I would seek to publish as a result of the project. As it turned out, many of the informants, especially those in Wuhan and Guangzhou, happily said that they would not mind having their identities revealed in foreign publications – apparently an encouraging sign of sociopolitical liberalization and reduced fear of persecution.

Analyzing observation notes and interview tapes

I agree with Geertz (1973) that it is absolutely important for ethnographers to be introspective about the *fictional* nature of his/her work. However, I must insist that, behind the language used to construct my representation, I witnessed, through my viewpoint, empirical, live and daily activities lived by my informants. I heard their personal accounts of how they used and related to television and what they thought about television related activities. What I saw and heard may eventually prove just diffuse and fleeting moments in the infinite temporal passage. But they were some of the subversive moments in a very recent Chinese history, which I continue to characterize as a period under strict political and thought control.

My processing of these moments went through the following phases. In the initial phase of analysis, I listened to the taped interviews and transcribed them. I also read the notes taken during observation and tidied them up. Next I sorted out the written data, put together all data regarding each family as a case study. Then I wrote up a description regarding each family and indexed the descriptions to facilitate coding. The description of each family focused on both the general television viewing habits of its members and particularities found in their uses of television.

In the second phase, I read through the case study descriptions of all the families, with special attention paid to the similarities between the 15 families in their uses of television. To identify similarities from qualitatively collected raw data I used Strauss and Corbin's (1990) method of open coding. According to them, open coding is the 'process of breaking down, examining, comparing, conceptualizing, and categorizing data' (1990, p.61). In my analyses, I sorted the data in order to identify various forms of commonality among the subjects in their experience with television. For example, what common uses, or otherwise *abuses*, do they make of television? Are there any other similarities, such as the frequency of a certain kind of use or *abuse*?

While examining the commonality between the subjects, I also paid attention to any particularities of any family and/or individual in their/his/her uses of television. I intended to discover if a seemingly particular use shares a kind of common or comparable condition with another particular use. For example, what is in common between the various alternative uses of television? As a result of such open coding, I have been able to group the data into different categories.

In the third phase, I refocused my analysis with a view to the power relation involved in various uses of television. For this analysis, I adopted Strauss and Corbin's (1990) method of axial coding, which is a set of procedures whereby data are put back together in new ways after open coding, by making connections between categories. Through axial coding, I tried to cross-examine a use or alternative uses of television in terms of the relationship of the users to television. For example, when I looked into use of television as a support appliance for karaoke, I considered what conditions gave rise to it, what songs were sung, how the singers behaved, what pleasures were generated, what were the consequences of karaoke on the singers and on television. In other words, axial coding enabled me to explore whether an individual family/informant was related to television in a way that subjugated or empowered them/him/her. Were they/he/she positioned as an active, autonomous subject with whom the power of selection and self-determination rests? Or were they/he/she positioned as a mindless recipient of television and an ignorant pupil aspiring to soak up television's ideology?

Chinese television's positioning of the viewers and viewers' reactions to it

I would like to start with an examination of the position offered to viewers by Chinese television. Generally speaking, Chinese television has traditionally positioned the viewers as passive, homogeneous and accepting masses who are supposed to learn attentively the correct way of thinking and behaving. Should a viewer accept this positioning offered to him/her, he/she would lose his/her autonomous subject position and be subdued into an indistinguishable element of the learning masses, i.e. a psychologically immature being. Thus, I have argued that Chinese television constructs itself as the omnipotent schoolmaster while constructing the viewers as the homogeneous learning pupils (Zhong, 1998; Zhong & Zhong, 1998).

How do my subjects react to such demeaning positioning by Chinese television? This ethnographic audience has identified three typical reactions. One of them is that of acceptance, which is characteristic of a minority of the informants in their relation to Chinese television. A second type of reaction recognizes Chinese television's formative role but rather than accepting it, uses it as an instrument for other practical purposes, such as child minding and teaching. This reaction is typical of many of the parents involved in this research. They deliberately encourage their children to watch certain genres, especially those of Chinese television, for formative purposes. A third type of reaction is that of total rejection of the positioning offered by Chinese television, which is shared by the majority of the subjects, who reject their positioning by official Chinese television by simply turning it off.[2]

I have discussed the three types of subjects' reactions to their positioning by Chinese television in such a manner as if each reaction was consistently distinct of another and each subject always reacted in a totally stable and predictable way. In fact, the reactions are not always consistent or predictable and can vary across different genres and different contexts. For example, some subjects seem to be comfortable with their positioning by CCTV serials but resist their positioning by CCTV news.[3] Some other subjects who allegedly reject their positioning by CCTV do watch some of its programmes, such as *Jiaodian Fangtan* (a daily current affair talk show) and English news. Still some other subjects may watch Chinese television whilst rejecting the position offered by it or even producing oppositional readings. For example, I witnessed some of them watch Chinese television while continuously protesting aloud its distortion of reality. Furthermore, there are also those whose access to Chinese television is their only free entertainment and those who seemingly watch television without really paying attention to it.

After considering all the above grey areas, I am still confident with the proposition that the subjects reject their positioning by Chinese television. Their reaction has caused their massive abandonment of Chinese television, especially CCTV. Maybe I can present a more balanced assessment of attitude to Chinese television by dividing the subjects into three gross rather than precise generations, i.e. the young, the middle and the senior. I can safely state that Chinese television is almost totally irrelevant to the young generation, is losing relevance to many of the middle generation and is only relevant to the majority of the senior generation. Following is a case description of their abandonment of Chinese television.

---

2. I believe that the attitude of my subjects reflects the loss of viewers from CCTV to local television or from Chinese television to alternative television or to alternative forms of leisure activities. In some areas, such as Guangzhou, only a minority of the local population watches Chinese television and even fewer watch CCTV. According to a recent news story on *Guangzhou Daily*, some of the staple shows of CCTV have less than 1 percent audience ratings (http://home.guangzhou.gd.cn/news/gzdl/rb0801/gzdl0605.htm).

3. Like many other subjects, they think that CCTV's news is late and uninformed, and shows lack of concern for ordinary people and real social problems. They watch Hong Kong news on a daily basis to balance their reception of news.

Case study 1: Chinese television switched off

This project has involved 22 members of the young generation, i.e. ranging from preschool age to unmarried people in their 20s. I have been startled to find that rarely any of them watch Chinese television regularly or voluntarily. Instead, almost all school age children, and many high school students and even some university students, are addicted to Japanese and Disney serial cartoons. If they cannot find enough of them on television, they would have their parents buy VCD versions of them. The more mature young people may watch sports programmes and movie channels on Chinese television. But they seem to prefer and can afford other more active, social forms of leisure activities, including karaoke and VCD viewing.

The apathy to Chinese television is shared by many of the middle age subjects involved in this research, totalling 36 in all. These people may have more variant and flexible viewing preferences and tend to fluctuate between Chinese television and alternative television and alternative forms of leisure activities. Their cultural habits and familiarity with traditional Chinese narrative and content may motivate them to pick Chinese television. Their family commitments and responsibilities as wage earners and home makers may compel them to pick Chinese television, which is the main free leisure for many families. But their real-life social experiences are likely to make them more sensitive to and critical of the propaganda on Chinese television than many others. Their busy work schedule and overexposure to political social life in the daytime may make them resistive to further propaganda on Chinese television. It seems to me that most of the middle age subjects would not hesitate to abandon Chinese television if alternative forms of leisure activities were affordable, or if alternative television signals were available to them.

Many of the senior people involved in the present research, 17 of them altogether, seem to care about Chinese television. They are the real audiences of some of its classical genres, including traditional operas, old movies and variety art shows. I would speculate that their viewing preferences have been conditioned and constrained by their discursive and aesthetic habits developed over the years. They are also less able than their children to adapt to the new forms of popular culture. However, these senior people seem to be least interested in those genres, including news and documentaries, which are often associated with propaganda. In addition, at least five of the senior people do not watch television on a daily basis. They are more interested in outdoor and social activities that are more conducive to a healthy life.

Across all age groups, the subjects obviously know what they want and what they do not want from television. When questioned why they do not watch or do not like Chinese television, many would say: *tai sha, buhaokan, meijin, men, tai yansu, tai zhengzhi xiang, tai lei,* or *tai duo shuojia,* which respectively mean too silly, no fun for watching, not exciting, boring, dead serious, too political, too tiring, and too much preaching. When asked what they can do about Chinese television to make it more attractive, they say: Why bother about doing anything about it? One can live on, have a good time without watching it. There are better and more important things to do, such as viewing VCD movies, singing karaoke and playing games.

Case Study No 1 sums up well the current status of Chinese teleVISION. Official Chinese television continues to position the viewers as passive, homogeneous and learning pupils, while more and more empirical viewers reject that positioning. As a result, official Chinese television is quickly losing its relevance to the Chinese viewers. *While it tries to retain yesterday's viewers,*[4] *it is losing today's viewers and has already lost tomorrow's viewers.* The viewers who have abandoned or are abandoning Chinese television have escaped to other forms of leisure activities, including karaoke, viewing VCDs, playing games, and receiving alternative television signals.[5] There is nothing shameful about this escape from the tyranny of propaganda television. In fact, I believe this is a more ingenious and triumphant escape than Fiske's semiotic democracy, because it does not compel the subjects to read against the grain. It is a live re-enactment of active but unconfrontational resistance described by Barmé and Jaivin (1992) as *zhi qu Weihu Shan* (taking Tiger Mountain by wit rather than by force).

Increased appropriation of television for alternative purposes

Singing karaoke, viewing foreign movies on VCD, playing games, and using computers are just some of the many other forms of cultural activities that many of my subjects have escaped to. Next, I will continue to construct a scenario of people engaging in these alternative activities on the basis of my ethnographic study of the 15 families in three Chinese cities. This scenario will lead to a proposition that the television set is transformed from a central carrier of top-down distributed television signals into a monitor that plays a

---

4. During my 1998 visit to CCTV, one of its directors told me that CCTV was serious about appealing to the taste of today's audiences. But it seems to me that Chinese people are changing much faster than CCTV can imagine and that CCTV's perceived audience tends to match yesterday's viewers more than today's viewers. Hence my argument that CCTV, and the rest of Chinese television, is fighting a losing war for viewers.

5. In addition, this research project has identified another development through the audience ethnography, which is the ever-increasing reception of alternative signals, especially from Hong Kong, to the exclusion of official Chinese signals. This development is also reconfiguring Chinese teleVISION by positioning the subjects as selective, autonomous users of television and reducing Chinese television to an irrelevant role. But in this article, I will concentrate the diversified uses of television for alternative purposes.

supportive role in people's pursuit of other causes. As a result of the transformation, television loses its traditional central position and becomes an accessory to other electric or electronic devices, such as VCDs, computers and games machines and plays a supportive and subordinate role in a range of user-centred activities. But for the time being, I will discuss the popular appropriation of the television set for alternative purposes among the 15 families involved in the present research project.

Use of the television set as a visual aid for karaoke

Among the many alternative uses of the television set, singing karaoke is the classic instance and has been popular for a long time. Of the 15 families involved in this ethnographic study, the majority of their members have had more than accidental experiences of singing karaoke. Members of two Beijing families, two Guangzhou families and four Wuhan families reportedly sing karaoke regularly at home, at least once a week on the weekend. In the cities of Wuhan and Beijing, karaoke is regarded as one of the main forms of family and social entertainment. Following is a brief case study description of engagement in karaoke in the four Wuhan families.

Case study 2: Use of the television set as a karaoke line prompter and musical instrument

Of the five Wuhan families involved in this project, four engage in karaoke on a regular basis, ranging from at least once a week to almost every other day. The only other family that does not sing karaoke at all belongs to my categorization of the new urban poor. In this family, the father has a very low income, about ¥400 a month, and the mother has been stood down by her factory. They do not have luxury appliances, except a 12-inch black and white television.

Of the other four families, singing karaoke is found to be the second most frequent pastime for their members, ranging from toddlers to grandparents. Some members of the families also sing karaoke in workplaces, schools, restaurants, commercial karaoke salons and other people's homes. Some of them also use karaoke to entertain business partners, customers and colleagues. In addition, all the four families regard karaoke as a favourite form of entertaining family friends and visitors.

But what is most noteworthy about karaoke is not its popularity, but rather that it is much more democratic than traditional forms of family pastime. Who has the microphone is not to be decided by an authority but rather tends to be sorted out by democratic negotiation and friendly turn-taking. Furthermore, there is little generation- or gender-based conflict and little resentment or dissent about who sings what and how. Grandparents' choice of traditional opera or folk songs, or parents' selection of nostalgic revolutionary marches or patriotic songs and the young generation's preference of Hong Kong songs all tend to be respected rather than suppressed or criticized.

Democracy of choices and pleasures is not the only attractive aspect of karaoke. In a Beijing family, I found its members combining family pastime and business in karaoke. Following is a reconstruction of the alternative use of television for karaoke as a combined form of family pastime and family business.

Case study 3: Karaoke as a combined form of family pastime and family business

The Hans are a migrant family from Jilin, a province in Northeast China. Madam Han, in her 50s, used to work in a medium-sized machinery factory but was stood down in 1993 and was paid only ¥80 a month as living allowance. Her late husband, whilst working as a technician in a factory, had a monthly income of about ¥350. Their income combined was estimated to be less than the local average family income at the time. But, together, they had to struggle to raise three teenage daughters and had to pay for part of the living expenses of her parents. Then her husband died in 1995, leaving them stranded in impoverishment.

She moved to Beijing in 1996, bringing her three daughters with her, aged nine, 13 and 15. She borrowed money from her relatives and friends and bought a 50-seat restaurant where her family both worked and resided. In order to attract customers, she set up a set of facilities that could screen television and play karaoke discs and VCD movies in a corner of the restaurant. Her second daughter is the one who operates the appliances and hosts the entertainment.

Most of the diners are students from a neighbouring aviation university and *dagongzai* (lowly paid migrant manual workers) working and living nearby. She has over 300 movie discs and about 150 karaoke discs for her diners to choose from. She also encourages regular diners to bring their own favourite discs. According to her and her children's account and my field observation, singing karaoke is the most preferred and frequent activity, especially in the evening, and watching Hong Kong movies on VCD is the next. Rarely is the television set used to watch television programmes. According to Madam Han, her television set can only receive CCTV and BTV channels, which very few of the diners are interested in. Many of them are able to receive more interesting programmes at home from cable television. She plans to subscribe to a cable network in order to access programmes from other provinces and especially from Hong Kong. Her eldest daughter believes that Chinese television can never create the same festive atmosphere which Hong Kong movies or karaoke can.

The Hans and their friends also use the appliances for other private purposes. One purpose is to relax and seek pleasure after long hours of work. Madam Han said that she sometimes blamed herself for the need for her daughters to help with the family business, resulting in their discontinuation of schooling. She is glad that her daughters could at least have some fun from singing karaoke after work. Another purpose is to engage the youngest daughter in a safe indoor activity outside the business hours while the mother and the two elder daughters prepare their meals. The little girl told me that she had learned to speak the Beijing style of Mandarin, some Cantonese and Korean and learned to recognize many Chinese characters by singing karaoke and reading karaoke captions – an achievement which her mother takes great solace in. Still another purpose is to entertain friends and acquaintances during the weekends. Madam Han said that meeting and entertaining these people generated a sense of kinship and protection which was important to the well being and security of her family of four females in their adopted city.

To sum up case studies 2 and 3, whether for family pastimes or for business, the television set is but a screen that is used to display song captions and audio and visual effects. It plays a supportive role as a line prompter, i.e. an accessory to karaoke, and as a screen for whatever programmes that are selected by the singers, rather than the centrally disseminated signals. Rather than influencing passive audiences, it is used as an instrument to seek pleasure in a much more precarious, performative, active and selective manner.

These case studies point to some of the reasons that underlie the popularity of karaoke. Generally speaking, karaoke provides a forum of self-expression in Asian cultures that arguably tend to value collectivity at the expense of individuality. I believe that it has an added political subversiveness in China. By appropriating the television set for instant performances, karaoke sabotages television's function as a monolithic *organ* (throat and tongue) of the Party State and as a royal carrier of centrally disseminated signals. It subjugates the television set to a subordinate role as a line prompter and musical instrument. The corollary of the subjugation of the television set is the empowerment of the users who are no longer under any pressure to gaze and decipher the official signals. The users now can actually choose what song to sing, just as they can choose actively and spontaneously between watching performances on the television screen or performing in front of the set. No wonder this subversive alternative use of the set would have aroused the suspicion and disapproval of the government.

I must point out that, beneath the apparent diversity, I see a scenario of individuals using imported popular culture to confront and challenge the dominant official culture. Generally speaking, the most frequently sung titles come from Hong Kong, especially in Guangzhou and Wuhan. Whilst in Wuhan, I spent an evening visiting the Four-Beauty Pond Square at one end of a huge Wuhan Number 2 Bridge over the Yangtzi River. There on the square were four open-air karaoke stalls where patrons could pay ¥3 to sing a song in front of the crowds. Most of the songs sung during my three-hour visit were titles from Hong Kong and Taiwan. In one of the stalls, I counted the volumes printed on its menu and found 82 volumes of Hong Kong songs, 38 volumes of Taiwan songs, eight volumes of Mainland Chinese songs plus several volumes of Japanese, American, Russian and European songs which had been translated into Chinese. According to the stall-keeper, the most popular songs are those originally sung by Faye Wong, Jacky Chang and Alan Tam of Hong Kong and Teresa Tang of Taiwan.

I must also add that karaoke seemed to be going out of fashion towards the end of the 1990s, especially in Beijing. As a sign of its decline in public venues, I noticed during my last visit to the capital in 1999 that many luxurious karaoke clubs had closed down. Some of the other subjects involved in this project report that they used to be very keen on singing karaoke, though they do not do it as often now. There are various reasons for the decline. Some of the subjects, especially those from families that are suffering hardship after the Asian economic melt-down, find themselves too busy with second jobs or too psychologically depressed for any form of pastime, including singing karaoke and watching television. For some other subjects, especially those in Guangzhou and Beijing, Hollywood movies on VCD, bowling, playing tennis, going to the gym, and driving cars have superseded karaoke as a preferred form of pastime. There are also a few subjects, especially older and better-educated people, who reject karaoke as a trashy, noisy and uncultivated activity.

Use of the television set as a screen for VCDs

An increasingly common alternative use of the television set is connecting it to the video compact disc (VCD) player. Though the VCD first appeared in Chinese shops in about 1995, it has already become a commonplace appliance in the Chinese mediascape. In the propaganda discourse, the VCD is another symbol of national progress, prosperity and strength because China is the largest producer and consumer of VCD players in the world. Some of my research subjects seem to view the ever-increasing use of the VCD from a somewhat different perspective. They claim the VCD is a symbol of their enhanced living standard and internationalization. Anyhow, the VCD seems to have penetrated and saturated at an even greater pace than television used to in urban China.

VCD players are a common appliance in the 15 families involved in the present ethnographic study too. Between the families, there are a total of 11 VCD players and four computers with built-in VCD players. One of the families has two VCD players and three others have a VCD player and a computer with built-in VCD each. Of the four families that do not have a VCD player or computer with VCD, two claim that they have plans to buy one. In Wuhan and Beijing, my subjects told me that a VCD player had become a prerequisite for a marriage, like television in the 1980s.

A VCD player, supported by a television set, offers a much wider range of choices than television. An average 1995 model can be used for many applications, including playing movies and karaoke songs. Some of the new models that incorporate VCD, DVD, CD and computer hard disc facilities can be used for even more applications.[6] Whatever uses are made of the VCD, the television set becomes an accessory, a monitor. It is no longer the supreme source or carrier of education, information and entertainment disseminated and regulated by a central authority. The VCD player assumes a more central role in facilitating the users' active and selective pursuit of information and pleasure.

Viewing movies on VCD is an increasingly common activity in many Chinese cities. Within the scope of the present project, it is more common in Guangzhou and Beijing than in Wuhan. For example, three of the five Guangzhou families view VCD movies regularly. One of them has bought about 200 movies and reportedly spends more time watching VCD movies than television programmes. The other two have close to 100 discs. One of the latter, a poor three-member family with one retiree and one unemployed adult, reportedly used to watch one VCD film on a weekday evening and up to three movies on a weekend evening. Then they were able to rent VCDs for ¥2 per film from a local shop until it was shut down by the authorities for violation of intellectual property rights.[7] Now they watch fewer VCD movies and more Hong Kong serials through a local cable network because, they told me frankly, they could not afford to buy VCD movies for ¥7 or ¥8 per disc.

Cheap pirated discs are easily available in all three cities I visited. In Guangzhou, they are sold openly in a shopping centre in North People's Road. In Wuhan, shops that deal in legal or pirated VCDs, or both, flank Baozheng Street. In Beijing, I witnessed numerous street hawkers along the Zhongguancun Street, who approached pedestrians and offered to sell them cheap VCD discs, including forbidden pornography programmes. In all three cities, there are small shops that rent VCD discs for between ¥2 and ¥3 per film. In addition to the purchased and rented discs, some subjects, including two families in Guangzhou and three families in Beijing, reportedly swap discs with friends or neighbours. In short, the VCD has diverted the attention of many of the families from television. Next, I will present a case study of the alternative uses of the television set as an accessory to the VCD in two Beijing families.

Case study 4: Use of the television set as a screen for VCD movies

The first family is that of Mr Huang, a bank clerk, and Ms Lin, a sportswoman turned teacher, who are typical of the new generation addicted to VCDs. Complaining about their busy lifestyle and about the necessity for them to work overtime to make extra money, they say that they do not have time for television. Huang watches only CCTV's daily news and Lin usually watches

---

6. For example, Kingwon Super VCD KW-SC2000, produced in Shenzhen, can be used to playback VCDs, to play games and, as a computer, to operate Windows 98 and to access the Internet.

7. During my visit to China (especially in Guangzhou and Wuhan), I visited many corner shops that still leased pirated VCDs disks for ¥2 or ¥3 per movie a night. Even some of the most recent Hollywood productions were available, including *Titanic, Mulan, The mask of Zorro* and *Lethal weapon 4.*

nothing but a one-hour variety show staged by Hunan Satellite Television[8] on Saturday evening. They claim that their two-year-old son and his nanny were the only patrons of television. I read into their claim a disparaging attitude towards television because it implies that television is intellectually suitable for naïve children and uneducated people.

In spite of their busy work commitments, Huang and Lin do spend a lot of time viewing VCD movies. Sometimes they watch one or two movies in an evening and occasionally they may watch up to six or seven movies on Saturday and Sunday. They have about 300 discs, most of which are Hollywood movies, and boast a collection of every Oscar-winning film and what they call *dapian*, i.e. Hollywood blockbusters, including: *The sound of music, Gone with the wind, On golden pond, Evita, The English patient* and *Saving Private Ryan*. They also regularly swapped VCDs with friends or colleagues. Their exposure to Hollywood movies has made them knowledgeable about different Hollywood genres and well informed about Hollywood actors.

Viewing VCDs has proved to be a luxurious pastime for the family. They bought their Korean-made Goldstar for over ¥3,000 in 1995, about twice the monthly family income at the time, and used to pay up to ¥180 for a commercial disc. Now, commercial discs are cheaper, costing about ¥30 to ¥50 per title. They do not buy pirated discs because they want to have the best quality discs for their collection.

According to Huang and Lin, the money spent on VCDs is a worthwhile investment in lifestyle. The VCD has given them the power to select a more preferable form of pastime, and to collect programmes that are to their liking and taste.

A second family in this case study is that of Mr Jin, Ms Zai and their daughter Xiao Jin in Beijing. Both Jin and Zai are manual workers employed by a hospital and have a combined income of about ¥1,500 a month, not much for a family of three, including a school age daughter, living in the capital city. They have few luxury appliances, only a 21-inch colour television set, placed in a conspicuous position in the family lounge. They have no plans to buy a VCD player even though, according to them, many of their neighbours and acquaintances have one. The family has recently been linked up to the Beijing Cable Television Network and, for an annual fee of ¥140, can potentially access up to 34 different channels. But their television set, an old model, is designed to receive a maximum of eight channels.

---

8. Hunan is a province to the north of Guangdong. Hunan satellite television signals are received in most Chinese cities by local cable television networks and are relayed via cable to individual households. Generally speaking, I have found that Hong Kong television has more audience than Chinese television, and local television has more audience than CCTV in China. The daily news and current affairs seem to be amongst the very few genres of CCTV that have more audience than other television stations. There will be further discussions about the marginalization of CCTV in a later section.

Television is the main source of cheap entertainment for the family. Nevertheless, Jin and Zai refrain from watching television in order not to distract their daughter from her studies. This might not have bothered her as she claims to have no interest in Chinese television, which she described as a combination of excessive political news and boring serials. She would only watch television when it screened cartoons, especially Japanese cartoons. According to her account, BTV has recently screened about 50 episodes of a Japanese cartoon series, which, in Chinese, is entitled *Feng zhi Gu (Valley of the wind)*. She and her classmates are keen to watch episodes repeatedly, as well as the rest of the series, and therefore have been saving their pocket money to buy the series on discs. So far, she herself has bought 22 discs containing the series plus another 10 discs of other cartoons. On a free afternoon or a weekend, they would gather at the home of one of the classmates that has a VCD player to enjoy watching programmes on the discs.

I have discussed VCD-related activities in two Beijing families in Case Study No 2. To sum up, the VCD has provided major viewer-friendly alternatives to state-run television and has reduced the television set to a screen, an accessory subject to the control and selection of the viewers. It transfers the power of programme selection from official television operators to individual viewers. It also reduces the time available for television viewing. Furthermore, as most of the VCD programmes available for sale or in circulation are (pirated) from Hollywood, Hong Kong and Taiwan, the instrumentality of Chinese television for propaganda is weakened.

I would like to further speculate that the pleasure derived from viewing VCDs has to do with viewers' enhanced ability to make choices. Such pleasure is at least twofold. On the one hand, they have an expanded selection of pleasurable programmes outside the conventional official propaganda. On the other, they have cheap access to the best international cultural artifacts in pirated versions without having to pay an arm or a leg for the products, thus sabotaging the interest of those multinational companies that wish to make huge profits from the vast Chinese populace.[9]

Use of the television set as a platform for games

Playing games is still another alternative use of the television set. Electric/ electronic game machines were unheard of in Maoist China. Then in the early 1980s, as the first batch of game machines were installed in a number of hotels open to foreigners in the larger cities, hand-held game machines (e.g. Nintendo Gameboy) began to appear in the hands of the younger generation.

---

9. *Titanic,* a Hollywood blockbuster, costs between ¥70 and ¥100 in cinemas in Beijing and Guangzhou, which is about three to four days' local average daily wage. An original VCD version of the same film costs about ¥150, and costs between ¥10 and ¥15 in a pirated edition, a much more affordable alternative.

Since the late 1980s, new products, such as Sega, Nintendo and Sony Playstation, that use the television set to provide a bigger and more exciting screen have quickly become available to the new generations of pleasure and stimulation seekers. A number of southern Chinese businesses have joined in the chase for consumers and profits by producing their own versions of television-supported game machines such as Xiaobawang. Today, hand-held machine games have largely been superseded by games played via television screens or computer monitors, which are regarded as the new must-haves of family consumer goods.

Many of the subjects involved in this study have had more than occasional experiences of playing games. They include not only school age children and adolescents, but also adults, not only blue-collar workers but also intellectuals. In fact, some of those who have access to VCD players (or computers) say they use the machines to play games more often than viewing movies/serials (or for work purposes). In addition to VCD players and computers that have game facilities, two families in each of Guangzhou and Beijing and one family in Wuhan have separate television-supported game machines, including two Segas, two Nintendos, one Sony Playstation and three Xiaobawangs (a Beijing family has three machines and another Guangzhou family has two). According to my research, playing games is another common alternative use of the television set, though the playing time in itself is not comparable to television viewing time. Nevertheless, in combination with time spent on VCD movies, karaoke and computers, game playing has contributed greatly to the minimization of time spent on watching broadcast television. Following is a case study presentation of two typical families whose members use television sets to play games.

Case study 5: Use of the television set as a platform for games

This case study looks at the alternative use of the television set as a platform for games in two families. The Lus are a low-income family of four members in Guangzhou. Mr Lu works as a handyman and has an average wage of about ¥1,000 a month. Lu's wife Ms Chen is a kindergarten nurse and is paid a regular monthly salary of just over ¥400. Mr Lu's father lives with them and, with a monthly retirement pension of ¥750, is part of the family's economic structure. Together they have to raise a son of 15, a Year 3 high school student, who, as the hope of the family, is under great pressure to achieve. Their monthly expenditure often exceeds the total family income, making it necessary for Lu to work seven days a week and for Ms Chen to baby-sit for a neighbouring single parent family.

Generally speaking, the Lus lead a simple and economical life. According to Lu, in order to save money, he has always had his hair cut by his father or wife. Watching television used to be the only entertainment for the family and Lu's father still spends most of his daytime in front of the set. But the family paid ¥1,450 for a new model VCD player in late 1997 and has since spent another ¥800 or so on accessories, game discs and movie discs. To the family, it is a wise investment as it provides an economical alternative to relax and entertain the family, especially Lu and the son, who are physically or mentally exhausted by their daily routines. More importantly for the parents, their son can play games at home instead of mixing with problem kids in commercial game salons.

As a result, the television viewing time in the family has been greatly reduced. Lu and the son claim that they spend less time watching television than using the television set for alternative purposes (including playing games, singing karaoke or viewing movies on VCD). They usually play competitive games such as car racing or war games. (When I was there in the family observing their behaviour, I noticed that they could not stop fidgeting while watching whatever television programmes. They referred to them invariably as boring propaganda talks. They were more attentive and involved when they were playing games.) Ms Chen always seems to be too busy for any forms of leisure. But occasionally she has a mahjong game with three virtual players, which she often has to abandon halfway in order to cope with housework commitments. Lu's father is the only one in the family who watches a lot of television – Hong Kong channels – during the day and in late evenings. He claims that he has been accustomed to passive entertainment and is too old and too slow to learn the games.

Another Guangzhou family in this case study is one that is usually regarded as an intellectual one, consisting of Mr Mai, an academic, Ms Wei, a high school teacher, and their 11-year-old son, who won an intercity children's piano competition in 1997. They are relatively better off and, according to their own account, can save up to 40 percent of the family income for investment. All the three members of the family claim to be very busy and have no time for television or karaoke, both of which they describe as vulgar and a waste of time. Talking about television, the parents only watch evening news programmes on CCTV and Hong Kong's Asia TV. They always motivate their son to watch nothing but concerts to improve his music competence, and English educational programmes to improve his English proficiency. Occasionally, the family watches a Hollywood blockbuster like *Saving Private Ryan* or *Schindler's list* on VCD.

In spite of their cultivated tastes, both Mai and his son seem to be enthusiastic about playing games. They used to share one Nintendo game machine which they bought in 1995. Then they bought a computer in 1996 and a VCD player in early 1998. Now Mai usually plays games on the computer and lets his son have the television-supported Nintendo. Ms Wei sometimes pleads with her husband not to play too long so that he will not be a bad role model for the son who, she believes, has a good chance to become a master musician. She looked apparently troubled one day when, during our discussion, the son said that he would like to be a game programmer. Mai was not as worried. As a matter of fact, he told me privately and proudly that he and his son had successfully tried to use the software *PC Tools* to alter some of the game programmes.

In summary, I have presented a case study of members of two families playing games on the screen of the television set. I must repeat that game machines are still a luxury to some Chinese families, even in the cities, and that playing games is still a negative concept often associated with waste of time and decadence in the minds of many individuals. On the whole, I believe that the total time spent in playing games by my subjects is less than their total time spent in watching television. However, it has proportionally reduced the television viewing time.

What is more important, playing games reduces the television screen from a carrier of centrally disseminated signals to a stage for personally selected games. Compared to television, which constructs a passive receiving audience, playing games positions an empirical player as an active decision-maker and a competitor who usually begins as an underdog but who may actively accumulate enough skills and experiences to beat the virtual players. Thus, playing games is more (inter)active, and sensually more stimulatory, participatory and selective than viewing television or even viewing movies on VCD on the part of the players. Furthermore, there is the possibility of some empirical players rewriting a game scenario, thus elevating themselves from the position of a competitor to that of a game designer and rule writer, game organizer and privileged winner.

Use of the television set as a computer monitor

In my ethnographic study, I have also come across a family in which the television set is used as a computer monitor. Though it looks like an isolated case in itself, it shares a commonality with the previous instances of alternative uses of the television set in the sense that it reduces the set to an accessory, another appliance.[10] What particular alternative uses the people put the set to is not the real question here. What matters is that this particular use of the television set as a computer monitor contributes to the forming of the scenario of alternative uses of the set prevailing over its conventional use for propaganda. The following is a reconstruction of the alternative use of the television set as a computer monitor in the family.

Case study 6: Use of the television set as a computer monitor

Huo Yinxiang is a 10-year-old single son of a Guangzhou family. As his parents both have to work long hours, sometimes on the weekend too, he is often left

---

10. However, I must point out that, in the general Chinese teleVISION, use of television as a computer is by no means an isolated exception. Panda Television, a prestigious Chinese brand, is designed to play a supportive role to computers by providing a computer connection port in the set.

home alone outside school hours. His parents used to encourage him to watch television, using it as a child-minder. He used to be fond of Disney and Japanese cartoons but has mostly lost interest in them. One day, without seeking prior permission from his mother, he turned on her desktop PC and learned to use its painting facility. His adventure with the computer is endorsed by the parents because it is the best means to keep him safe and sound at home. Now, he spends hours painting pictures whenever his parents are out. According to his own account, television is very dull and noisy with endless talks, and producing graphics (i.e. Christmas cards, greeting cards) is more creative than *ting gushi* (listening to stories). He has also started to surf on the Internet. Whenever she was home, his mother would stop him from working on the computer because it was already impairing his eyesight. Nowadays, before leaving him alone at home, his father will reconnect the computer hard disk tower to the family's 29-inch television set so that the son can have a larger, more eye-friendly monitor. When I was studying his family, I volunteered to be a child-minder, spending a long Saturday afternoon with him. It turned out that he was totally absorbed in creating a New Year's greeting card for his grandmother and did not need much supervision.

What does the last case study tell us? I find a convincing argument in the alternative use of television as an enlarged monitor for the computer in Huo's family. The argument is that, between Huo's family and television, the former are active, ingenious and creative users of the latter and the latter is an inanimate object subjected to the manipulation of the former. The traditional thesis that television can brainwash and manipulate its audiences is simply rendered irrelevant in Huo's family.

As an isolated instance, the alternative use of television as a monitor for the computer in Huo's family may not be significant. But it is significant as part of a massive cultural practice, which I have identified as alternative uses of official Chinese television. I believe that my research into this and other alternative uses in this article so far is only a small representation of the resistive wave against official Chinese television.

Next, I will continue to examine the consequences of the popular alternative uses of television. But first I would like to make a brief summary of my discussions so far. On the basis of an ethnographic study of 15 families in three Chinese cities, I have constructed a scenario of alternative uses of the television set subduing and displacing television's conventional use. This scenario leads to my proposition that alternative uses have reduced or even usurped television's centrality and that they have tended to marginalize its role in the cultural life of the subjects. When it is used for alternative purposes, including screening VCD movies, karaoke and games, the television set is transformed from a central role in propaganda into a supportive role in popular culture. It supports and facilitates its users in their active and selective consumption of popular culture and their rejection of centrally disseminated messages and centrally dispensed entertainment.

The creation of the empowered user-subjects and marginalization of television

Now, I would like to discuss the consequences of the various alternative uses of television. There are two mutually related issues of concern to me. One is the consequence of the alternative uses of television for the users and the other is the consequence for official Chinese television.

Let me first consider the consequences for the users. Fiske, among many other scholars, has enlightened my perspective on seeing the people as the ultimate source of power. I do have a problem fitting his theory to studies of Chinese teleVISION for two related reasons. Firstly, the theory condemns the virtual Chinese viewers to the incessant mental drudgery of making oppositional readings of a medium characterized predominantly as propaganda by many scholars. Secondly, a semiotic liberation of the viewers from the dominant meaning may provide a convenient excuse for justifying, in practical terms, the continued use of television for propaganda purposes, which seems to be politically and strategically problematic to me. I perceive the Chinese viewers to be too clever and pragmatic to be coerced into struggles with the dominant text and its dominant meaning.

There is a more workable passage to power than semiotic democracy in the Chinese situation, especially in relation to the subjects involved in this ethnographic study. This passage is the alternative uses of television. My argument is that alternative uses of television, including some ingenious ones, provide real opportunities for the alternative users to acquire power. It is precisely these opportunities that have motivated the television viewers to appropriate the television set for alternative purposes and to reconstruct themselves as users of television.

But how do users gain power with the alternative uses of television? I believe that the power mainly comes from their self-positioning through alternative uses. Compared to television, alternative uses diversify the positionings available to the people. On the one hand, they may continue to subject the people to a range of passive positions, such as consumers/viewers of commercial discs and recipients of the consumerist ideology. On the other hand, they may unprecedentedly offer a range of other positions to the people, which empower them by transforming them into active, selective and subjective users of the once formidable television set. More importantly, because our new constructs are users, not passive recipients of anything, it makes more sense to say that they construct a positioning for themselves through their alternative uses.

The position to be occupied by the alternative users has three impacts on their relation to television and other appliances in various cultural practices. First of all, it centralizes the users by redefining them not as passive consumers or recipients but rather as decision-makers and selection-makers of their cultural and leisure activities. It is they who decide what song to sing, what VCD to watch, or what game to play. And, as importantly, they can independently adopt their own pace, frequency and mode of activity. Furthermore, in order to be resourceful alternative users, they must reach out to the black market, private rental shops and their social connections rather than relying on the central supplier of programming, i.e. the official television. In other words, the alternative uses enable the users to acquire an autonomous subject position.

Next, the positioning animates the alternative users by transforming them from passive listeners and beholders into active performers. According to Butler (1990), identities are performatively constituted. I believe that the inaction, which is typical of television viewing, subdues the viewers into an inanimate object position. In Marxist terminology, television reifies the viewers into statistics or commodities for television and advertisers. The alternative users assume the subject position of active performers and makers of meaning, when they act out in various performative acts and parodies, including performing karaoke, interacting with virtual competitors in games, cheering up fellow singers or hurrahing after winning a virtual game. Instead of watching to digest passively and quietly what is offered on the screen, they demote television to a supportive role. As a result, they transcend the conventional positioning offered to them by television. In short, the performative activities, which are typical of the various alternative uses of television, facilitate their identity building and inflate their autonomous subject position.

Still next, the assumption of an autonomous, performative subject position enables the users to transcend the official agenda of television and pursue individualized agendas. In the official discourse, television is a medium that links up individual families to the central state by disseminating centrally distributed programmes that aim to educate the audiences through entertaining them. Now that the alternative uses of television have deconstructed the mass into autonomous, performative individuals, the users can pursue a diverse range of alternative and individualized agendas. Among them are, notably, the search for information, the pursuit of pleasure and self-expression, which are initiated by personal needs and aspirations rather than centrally organized or supplied by official television.

After a consideration of the consequences of the alternative uses of television on the users, let me briefly discuss the issue of Chinese television. I must say that a logical corollary of the ascent of the users' power and their subject position is the descent of the power and the status of the television set. Prior to the appearance of the alternative uses of television in the Chinese mediascape, the television set was relevant to the Chinese populace mainly as the only free window to the world or the only free source of entertainment. As the alternative uses become more and more available and pervasive, official Chinese television is quickly losing its monopoly on information and entertainment and becoming irrelevant to the lives of many of my subjects, and presumably also to the majority of the Chinese populace.

With the loss of the official Chinese television has come the loss of the power and central status of its seemingly ubiquitous terminal, i.e. the television set. There are many manifestations of this loss of power and status, including reduction of television's conventional use, reduction of time spent on viewing it, reduction of its influence on the people, and the removal of its centrality in the cultural, symbolic and semiotic life of the people. What is most humiliating is that it is subjugated to a minor supportive role in its uses for alternative purposes, including screening VCD movies, karaoke and games. Whereas it used to occupy the viewers' sensual and mental attention, now it merely supports and facilitates its users in their active and selective consumption of popular culture and their rejection of centrally disseminated messages and centrally dispensed entertainment. In other words, the alternative uses of the television set have resulted in its huge degradation and marginalization, which is proportional to the elevation of the users to the empowered subject position.

I must also add that alternative uses of television have indeed created some real moments of subversion that threaten to sabotage some of the grand narratives often used to legitimatize the rule of the Chinese Communist Party. Suffice it to name but a few examples. Hong Kong and Taiwan karaoke corroded the official discourses of, I quote Liu Xiao-bo, 'revolution, selfless dedication in the name of "fear neither hardship nor death", merciless class struggles and the right of violence' (1993). China has protested the international release of *Seven years in Tibet, Red corner, Kundun* and BBC's famous documentary of Mao Zedong but has had difficulty stamping out their VCD versions on the domestic black market. These are some of the instances of subversion that have contributed to loosening up the monolithic dictatorship of the Communist Party.

But on a number of occasions, alternative uses of television have joined forces with some of the worst evils of the current sociopolitical evils in creating what I regard as new social injustices, corruption and immoralities. Well-known examples include rampant prostitution and exploitation of women in commercial karaoke salons, and uses of VCD to spread pornography. In 1998, a businessman became a county-level Party and government official by treating high-ranking officials to extravagant karaoke parties that cost him more than ¥400,000 (AU$80,000).[11] In 1996, games that re-enacted Japan's World War II bombardment of Pearl Harbor and invasion of China were made widely available for sale in many shops, causing a noisy uproar of public opinion.[12]

---

11. According to Yan (1998), this scandal was widely covered by local media in Guangdong province. Yan, L. S. (1998) *'KalaOK Zhengzhi* (Karaoke politics)' in Wang, H. (ed.) *Zhenshi de Yanshuo (True Words)*. Beijing: China City Publishing House.

12. Chinese media have published many articles condemning the games. Among them was *'Lishi Qineng Youxi* (History not for games)' by Lu, G., Tian, J. & Zhao, X. in *Nanfang Zhoumo (South China Weedend)*, 12 July 1996, p.4.

However, these and many other evils not only sabotaged the rule of the Party State but also harmed public interest and, therefore, must not be associated with the subversion of Chinese television's role in propaganda.

Conclusion

As a conclusion to my discussion of the three developments in Chinese teleVISION, I would like to say that many of the subjects involved in this ethnographic audience study have liberated themselves from the yoke of the seemingly powerful medium of official propaganda television. Their liberation is not a result of what Fiske calls 'semiotic democracy', i.e. the hard mental labour of struggling to read oppositional meanings into the dominant texts. Rather it is a clever accomplishment achieved through alternative uses of television.

The invention places the subjects on a vantage point in a new power relation to television, especially official Chinese television. The power of the subjects enables them to make alternative uses of television, which in turn further empower them in their relation to television. Alternative uses of television position them as selective, performative, autonomous, manipulative subjects. By subjugating television to the capricious, scandalizing selections and manipulations of the subjects, the invention rewards the daring subjects with unprecedented pleasure and condemns television to a supportive role. In other words, it is reconfiguring the current Chinese teleVISION by elevating the alternative users to the status of an autonomous subject while marginalizing and decentralizing official Chinese television to a supportive and sometimes irrelevant status.

But I have a number of postscripts to make regarding the arguments made in this chapter. Firstly, they are based on a qualitative, ethnographic research that involves a non-randomly selected sample of only 15 families in three cities of China. Because the research is meant to be concerned with particularity, its findings do not have claims to generalization regarding use of television in the whole country. Nevertheless, I believe that the findings of this project must be taken seriously when we attempt to consider the generality of Chinese television. In addition, the data collected for this project include not only what the 15 families did with television and what they said about their use of television, but also what they perceived as the common practice outside their immediate families.

Secondly, when I talk about the marginalization, decentralization and appropriation of television, I am referring to two separate concepts. One is that of a terminal appliance, i.e. the television set, and the other is television as a mass medium, especially official Chinese television, which continues to aim to educate the masses through entertaining them. Surely, the television set is turned on less and less frequently, for shorter and shorter length of time to receive television signals in a society evolving further away from mono-culturalism. What is more significant is the active boycotting of the use of television for propaganda purposes. For many ordinary Chinese people, reception of television, especially of alternative television signals,[13] is still an important free option in their everyday cultural life.

Thirdly, alternative uses of television in themselves can hardly be regarded as the ultimate liberation of the users, especially in a culture that places great emphasis on formative moral education. One might argue that the alternative uses are an escape from social reality, which pampers the users rather than motivates them to combat the current social injustice and oppression. I must point out that the alternative uses of television are not about bringing the people into direct confrontation with the social or textual suppression and domination. Their beauty lies in fermenting a condition that is more tolerant of choices made by individuals. They may not eradicate propaganda and reform official Chinese television, but they effectively render the latter irrelevant.

---

13. By alternative television signals, I refer to foreign and Hong Kong television programs, which have become easily available, in spite of the official ban, in most Chinese urban areas, especially on coastal areas.

English-language references

Ang, I. (1991) *Desperately seeking the audience*. London: Routledge.

Barmé G. & Jaivin, L. (eds) (1992) *New ghosts, old dreams: Chinese rebel voices*. New York: Times Books.

Burns, R. (1997) *Introduction to research methods*, 3rd. edition. Melbourne: Longman.

Butler, J. (1990) *Gender trouble*. London: Routledge.

Clifford, J. (1986) 'Partial truths', in Clifford, J. & Marcus, G. (eds) *Writing culture*. Berkeley: University of California Press.

Corner, J. (1991) 'Meaning, genre and context: The problematics of "Public knowledge" in the new audience studies', in Curran, J. & Gurevitch, M. (eds) *Mass media and society*. London: Edward Arnold.

Fiske, J. (1987) *Television culture: Popular pleasures and politics*. London: Routledge.

Geertz, C. (1973) 'Thick description', in Geertz, C. (ed.) *The interpretation of cultures*. New York: Basic Books.

Hall, S. (1981) 'Encoding and decoding in television discourse' in Hall, S., Hobson, D., Lowe, A. & Willis, P. (eds) *Culture, media, language.* London: Hutchinson.

Halloran, J. (1970) *The effects of television.* London: Panther.

Hymes (1962) 'The ethnography of speaking' in Gladwin, T. & Sturtevants, W. C. (eds) *Anthropology and human behaviour.* Washington DC: Anthropological Society.

Lu, S. H. (1996) 'Postmodernity, popular culture, and the intellectual: A report on post-Tiananmen China', *Boundary 2*, XXIII, Summer, pp.139-169.

Morley, D. (1992) *Television, audiences and cultural studies.* London/New York: Routledge.

Strauss, A. & Corbin, J. (1990) *Basics of qualitative research: Grounded Theory procedures and techniques.* Newbury Park: Sage Publications.

White, M. (1992) 'Ideological analysis and television' in Allen, R. C. (ed.) *Channels of discourse, reassembled.* London: Routledge.

Zhong, Y. (1998) 'Mass or master medium: A case study of Chinese television talk show', *Asia Pacific Media Educator,* 5, pp.92-102.

Chinese-language references

Liu, X. B. (1993) *'Wang Su li Zou he Wu Linghun* (Going pop without spirit)', *Zhongguo zhi Chun (China Spring)*, May, p.120.

Yang, D. P. (1994) *Chengshi Jifeng: Beijing he Shanghai de Wenhua Jingshen* (Monsoons of the cities: The cultural spirit of Beijing and Shanghai). Beijing: Dongfang Publishing House.

Zhong, Y. & Zhong D. Y. (1998) 'Dashi Meijie haishi Dazhong Meijie? Zhongguo Dianshi Tuokouxiu Chuanbo Moshi Kaocha ji Ge'an Fenxi (A mass medium or a master's medium? An observation and a case study of the communication model adopted by Chinese television talk shows)', *Hong Kong Journal of Social Sciences,* 12, Autumn, pp.67-81.

Transnational communication: Establishing effective linkages between North and South

Anura Goonasekera

Introduction

It is common knowledge that the effects of modern communication technologies are not uniform across all countries of the world. It means different things to different people in different countries. While many of us speak of a phenomenon called globalization created as a result of the impact of new communication technologies, we also realize that many of the poorer countries in the world, and poorer communities among the richer countries, are yet to be touched by this phenomenon. Transnational communication and the potential that it provides for the establishment of effective linkages between South and North or between the poorer world and the richer world needs to be understood within these global trends.[1]

It is now well recognised that transnational communication cannot be reduced only to its technological dimensions. Nor is its primary impact confined to economics and trade. Transnational communication has important legal, moral and cultural implications. These need to be recognized in a discourse about the establishment of efficient linkages between North and South using transnational communication. International agreements such as that of the World Trade Organization (WTO), agreements on trade-related intellectual property rights (TRIPS) and technological convergence, most conspicuously seen today in the Internet, all raise fundamental issues relating to the establishment and maintenance of communication linkages between the richer North and the poorer South.

The communication scene in Asia

Asia has taken a big leap in transnational communication in recent years. A large number of local, regional and multinational satellite television companies have established a strong presence. Hong-Kong-based STAR TV, owned by the Murdoch empire, carries programmes from NBC, the BBC and CNN, and can potentially beam programmes to 220 million households in Asia and the Pacific.[2] The Hong Kong Chinese Television Network carries a 24-hour Mandarin language news channel. Regional news is broadcast from Singapore by Asian Business News (ABN), owned by Dow Jones.

Realizing the need to provide programmes in Asian languages, the multinational satellite companies, such as STAR TV and the BBC, have launched a series of television productions in association with Asian companies. For instance, the BBC has commissioned a series of television productions in India; CNN has established bureaus in Asia; and Asian companies in Hong Kong, Taiwan, Singapore and India have also commenced television programme productions aimed at regional audiences in Asia. Local television stations have launched new programmes to win back the audiences lost to STAR TV. Suddenly, the Asia-Pacific region has become a testbed for multicultural television programming (Chan & Ma 1996). We see emerging in Asia a Chinese-language audience, an Indian-language audience and a Malay-language audience. Very soon Japanese- and Korean-language

---

1. At present the dominant force behind these trends is the advanced, industrial nations ably led by the United States. In March 1994, the International Telecommunications Union (ITU) held a World Development Conference in Buenos Aires, at which it was recognized that restructuring the information industry was shifting to the private sector and to forces of competition. US Vice President Al Gore called upon all the representatives of the member countries of the ITU to start reorganizing their information infrastructures to build a Global Infobahn. He said that the creation of this network of networks was an essential prerequisite for the sustainable development of all members of the human family. This would lead to economic development, political stability and a larger volume of international trade. In February 1995, the G7 countries (seven advanced industrial nations) and the European Union convened a first-ever ministerial conference in Brussels on the Information Society. The objective was to design a shared vision for building a Global Information Infrastructure (GII). Again, the emphasis was on the IT sector, not on the broadcasting/social communication sector. At that meeting, Al Gore called on the G7 members to open their markets to foreign suppliers of equipment and services and in turn offered to lift the 25 percent ceiling on investment by foreign companies in the US telecommunications sector. At the same conference, Japan spoke of reforms towards an intellectually creative society, that is, a society in which intellectually creative activities play a dominant role and become economic assets. The conference also featured an exhibition of interactive and multimedia application by leading information and communication manufacturers of G7 countries. The emphasis was patently on the creation of international markets for communication equipment and advanced technologies.

2. The Murdoch empire includes television (Fox Network and eight US station affiliates; BSkyB Satellite delivery system for Britain; STAR TV for Asia, Middle East and India); film (Twentieth Century Fox); book publishing (Harper Collins); magazines (*TV Guide*) and multimedia (Delphi Internet Services and MCI Joint Ventures).

programmes will join the competition. Unlike in the past, when television audiences were seen as entities within nation states, we now see emerging in Asia regional audiences transcending national boundaries and forming geolinguistic communities.

While transnational television is a prominent example of the changes taking place in the communication scene in Asia, other forms of communication, both new and old, continue to have an impact on the Asian media scene. The Internet is spreading quickly, with even the poorest of countries aspiring to join the network. Cellular phones, faxes, email, databases, electronic networks and cable are spreading rapidly and cutting down isolation in a historically unprecedented manner. On top of this, a large number of communication satellites are being placed in orbit by Asian countries.

Policies

The establishment of effective and efficient linkages utilizing modern communication technologies depends on the policies followed by National governments. At the first ministerial meeting of the WTO, held in Singapore in 1996, trade ministers from 28 countries, including many Asian countries, agreed in principle to sign the Information Technology Agreement (ITA) – an ambitious trade liberalization measure which seeks to eliminate tariffs on information technology equipment such as computers, modems, automatic data processing machines and teller machines, by 1 January 2000.[3] However, in the absence of such formal agreements in many other areas, Asian countries follow markedly different traditions and policies. One such example is in policies relating to the reception of satellite TV transmissions. Due to a confluence of historical, political and economic factors, India has adopted an open skies policy in relation to satellite broadcasts. India today is completely open to transborder television programmes via satellite. The Indian government has made policy pronouncements that it would not ban or interfere with foreign TV transmissions entering India via satellite. In this respect, Indian policy is similar to that of Japan, where there is no bar to the access of foreign satellite television by its citizens. However, the effects of this policy in creating an audience for satellite programmes are quite different in India and Japan. An industry providing foreign TV satellite fare, through a network of terrestrial cables, has sprung up in India. These cable companies provide a direct link between Indian TV viewers and foreign satellite transmissions. Consequently, there is a large segment of Indian urban

---

3. The following countries and territories have acceded to ITA. These countries account for almost 93 per cent of the $750 billion in ITA trade. Australia, Canada, Costa Rica, Czech Republic, El Salvador, Estonia, EC, Hong Kong, Iceland, India, Indonesia, Israel, Japan, Korea, Macau, Malaysia, New Zealand, Norway, Panama, Philippines, Poland, Romania, Singapore, Slovak Republic, Switzerland and Liechtenstein, Chinese Taipei, Thailand, Turkey, United States.

households linked via cable to foreign satellite TV programmes. This is not the case in Japan.

Japan, like India, has an open skies policy in relation to satellite broadcasts, to the extent that people are free to use satellite dishes to receive foreign programmes. However this has not resulted in the creation of a large audience for foreign programmes. Hagiwara (1998) observes that US television programmes have not fared well except in the early years of Japanese television history. From the late 1950s to mid-1960s quite a few American social dramas were broadcast and enjoyed high ratings. After the mid-1960s imported programmes gradually lost popularity. The main reason was the improvement in the production capability of Japanese television in the wake of the strengthening of the economy. The ownership of television sets by the rural population was also an important factor for the drop in ratings of imported programmes. Rural people had a strong preference for domestic programmes, often complaining that western programmes were too complicated or confusing (Ito, 1994). Furthermore, English, which is the language in which most satellite TV programmes are broadcast, is not a language used very much in Japan, even by the elite.

While India and Japan are open to foreign satellite TV programmes, some other Asian countries, such as China, Malaysia and Singapore, remain virtually closed to such transmissions because dish antennas cannot be freely owned by citizens of these countries. In Singapore, households with cable TV get access to satellite TV programmes such as CNN. In Malaysia, the audience for foreign programmes is limited to programmes broadcast through national television. Malaysia amended its Broadcasting Act in 1996 to allow its citizens the use of satellite receiving dishes. But the permitted size of the dish is 60 cm, so that only programmes beamed by Malaysia's own satellite, MEASAT, can be received. Furthermore all satellite programmes beamed to Malaysia from outside are downlinked to government stations, checked and uplinked to MEASAT and relayed to Malaysian households an hour later (Karthigesu, 1998). TV Malaysia has a policy of increasing locally produced TV programmes. In spite of this policy, however, foreign programmes (not necessarily western programmes) occupy around 40 percent of broadcast time. This is partly due to the multiethnic and multilingual character of the Malaysian population. Foreign programmes are needed to cater to different ethnic groups. Chinese-language programmes are imported from Hong Kong and Taiwan; Indian-language programmes imported from India. Another reason for the presence of foreign programmes is the high cost of producing local programmes and an apparent preference for some foreign programmes.

An economic model

It is possible to find a correlation between a country's economic growth (GDP) and increases in a country's domestic television programme productions. This is particularly so for local drama programmes. However, empirical studies in

Asia have shown that significant non-economic variables impinge on domestic TV productions. These include the presence of a large English-speaking population as a result of British colonial rule. India, Sri Lanka, Pakistan, Malaysia, Myanmar and Singapore are some of the countries in Asia that have a substantial audience for English-language programmes. Furthermore, while a purely economic model would predict that foreign television programmes would come from wealthier countries such as the US and the UK, there are again exceptions to this in Asia. For instance, although Japan is Asia's wealthiest country, there are very few Japanese programmes on the TV menus of other Asian countries. Japan, thus, appears to be culturally isolated. US programmes seem to satisfy Asia's cultural common denominator. Apart from economics, factors such as culture, politics and proximity influence the television menus of Asia (Waterman & Rogers, 1994).

While economic development increases the potential market for production industries all over the world, this increase is relatively greater for home producers from the countries experiencing economic growth. However, such growth in local media programmes must be carefully stimulated by the governments of these countries through appropriate media policies. The imposition of quotas for foreign programmes and the offer of effectively captive local audiences for local productions may not, in the long term, be in the interests of local programme producers. Such policies will create an uncompetitive, overly protected cultural sphere that will require huge financial subsidies to stay afloat.

Despite such economic logic, leaders in many parts of the world continue to look for ways to restrict foreign media influences in their countries. This is because of the perceived harmful effects of such programmes, and the belief that these outweigh the beneficial economic effects. Two areas in foreign television fare have caused considerable concern among leaders of the Third World. These are violence on television, and the effect of such programmes on vulnerable groups in society such as children. These concerns have shaped the response of many countries to television programmes from the West – particularly from the US. Some of these programmes are seen as featuring too much sex, violence, drug use and the glorification of other types of hedonistic behaviour, particularly among youth, to be suitable for people living in societies with different traditions and values.

The information rich and the information poor

While developments in communication technologies have brought immense wealth to some countries, particularly those in the industrialized parts of the world, many of the poorer countries of the world are left behind by these technologies. This has created a great divide between the information rich and the information poor. This is the stark reality of the ecology of international communication in the world today.

The governments of developed countries, led by the United States, are pressing ahead with the creation of an international trade regime that would enshrine legal principles immensely beneficial to the transnational companies in the business of communication. A regime of public international law is being created to legitimize the self-interested action of the richer countries. International mechanisms such as GATT and the WTO are being used as instruments in this quest for profit. Forces behind the Global Information Infrastructure (GII) are known to use international trade and financial institutions, such as the WTO and the World Bank to impose an ideological, political and economic order beneficial to the industrialized wealthier countries. This in turn has created greater inequality. To quote a recent writer on the subject: 'Of all the issues that have been brought on the agenda of GATT in the Uruguay Round, the subject of trade-related intellectual property rights (TRIPS), including trade in counterfeit goods, is one area where the most determined and combined effort of the industrialized countries is deployed against the Third World. What the industrialized countries, led by the US, have sought to establish are new international rules to protect the monopoly profits of their TNCs, deny Third World countries access to knowledge, block their capacity for innovations and technological change and prevent any rise of competitive capacity in the Third World' (Raghavan, 1990, p.115).[4] Economic interests in the fruits of new technologies have led to a shift in regulations from culturally based legal regimes to economically based ones; from legitimization based on cultural interests to legitimization based on economic interests; from trusteeship to an open market.

While a great deal of effort is made to create and sustain an international legal regime conducive to the interests of the richer countries, very little effort is made to assist the less fortunate countries to gain even a modicum of benefits. Universal access to basic communication and information services still remains

---

4. 'The US with the help of the media have injected some value loaded words like "piracy" and "counterfeiting" to describe those who were not prepared to accept their demands. In such media discourse the US became the champion of artists and creative peoples' rights and others were painted as criminals indulging in immoral activities . . . While the US insisted that a corporation's trade secrets be given protection it was unwilling to advance similar protection to knowledge held by Third World peasantry. For example seeds that have been nurtured by the peasants for hundreds of years and perfected to suit the soil and environmental conditions of a particular region have not been patented by anyone . . . Under the US proposal a TNC such as Cargill, could obtain a patent to that seed and resell it to the peasants . . . for a fee' (Pendakur, 1995, pp.36, 37.). Moral rights are also excluded from the Berne Convention and TRIPS does not include coverage for moral rights because the US, together with some other countries, did not want to recognize such rights and lobbied for their exclusion. See Michael Pryles, Jeff Waincymer and Martin Davis in *International Trade Law*, p.1083, 1996, Sydney: The Law Book Co., Information Services.

a distant dream for many of the poorer countries in Asia. Many would accept the right to communicate as a basic human right. However, without universal access to basic communication facilities, such a right remains an empty principle. As Pekkar Tarjanne, Secretary General of the International Telecommunication Union (ITU), remarked 'without action on the part of the world community there is a very real danger . . . that the global information society will remain global in name only; the world will be divided into information rich and information poor' (Tarjanne, 1997, p.10).[5]

An obvious reason for the inability of poorer countries to provide universal access to information and communication services is the lack of economic resources. It is common knowledge that different countries in the world are at different stages of development. For instance, on the basis of wealth, Asia will fall into two distinct parts: the rich Asia and the poor Asia. Japan, Singapore, Hong Kong, Australia, New Zealand, Taiwan and South Korea are countries that comprise rich Asia. Japan is leading rich Asia with a per capita income of nearly US$39,000. Even among the countries in rich Asia there is a wide disparity of incomes. The per capita income of Japan is over four times that of South Korea. Among the countries in poor Asia are Afghanistan with per capita income of only US$150; India's per capita income is US$310 and Cambodia's US$215.

These discrepancies in levels of income are reflected in the access to communication that people have in the different countries. Bangladesh has two phones, five television sets and 10 newspapers per 1,000 people, whereas Singapore has 378 phones, 199 television sets and 289 newspapers per 1,000 people (Goonasekera & Holaday, 1998). While unevenness in development is a fact in most parts of the world, there is another equally important fact that we need to recognize. Despite the uneven levels of development, leaders of most countries have recognized the need to keep in step with technological developments in communications if their countries are to ever develop. The leaders of even the poorest countries aspire to benefit by linking up with the economic grid of the developed world. In fact most of these countries are rushing to link up with the electronic superhighway. Opening up hitherto tightly controlled sectors of their economies, inviting multinational companies to invest in their countries and making substantial investments themselves in the telecommunications sectors of their economies, are some of the strategies followed to bring about rapid social and economic development. These are indicative of the seriousness with which countries in Asia consider the development of the communications sector as a path for rapid economic and social progress.

---

5. The ITU Administrative Committee on Coordination endorsed the declaration on Universal Access to Basic Communication and Information Services. The endorsement follows a year-long project by the Organizations of the United Nations Common System to promote the right to communicate as a basic human right (*AMCB*, 1997, pp.10–11).

Out of 53 countries in Asia, 20 already have or are planning to have their own national satellites. It is estimated that Asia will account for 40 percent of the world's GNP within the next 25 years. By 2040 half of global output will be from Asia.

By the end of 1993 China had already installed 18 million new telecommunication lines, achieving a growth rate of 54.1 percent from 1992 to 1993. A number of international donor agencies have pledged large amounts of money to developing countries in Asia to develop their telecommunication infrastructure. World Bank loans alone toAsian countries amounted to US$2,865 million from1987 to1990. The Asian market potential for telecommunication equipment is therefore substantial by any standards. We shall see major inroads made by large and small equipment manufacturers to participate in this market. The major players will be from the us, Europe and Japan, and their strategies will clearly have an impact on investment patterns. However, over the past decade, new cable and satellite delivery options have provided access to a variety of new entrants to the communication equipment industry.

We see in the world today the twin but opposite forces unleashed by advanced communication technologies. On the one hand we see the division of the world into two groups: the information rich and information poor. On the other hand we also see massive efforts by some of the poorer countries to catch up with technological advances by investing heavily in communication hardware. Still, it is quite possible that some countries may get left behind unless the international community steps in to assist them. There are areas, such as education and training, basic research, advice on planning and policies, in which the international community could render assistance, particularly to the poorer countries of Asia that are trying to harness new communication technologies for the development of their economies.

Openness

Recent research on the attitudes of people in Asia to foreign television broadcasts beamed to their countries has shown a remarkable openness to such exposure amongst the ordinary people. The findings of a recent study on broadcasting and cross cultural relations in five Asian countries, viz. India, Hong Kong, Japan, Malaysia and the Philippines, show that the overall opinion towards foreign programmes, mostly western programmes, was positive. The discourse on cultural imperialism, which postulated foreign media programmes as a threat to indigenous cultures, is thus being critically re-examined. Recent research writings question the validity of the assumptions underlying this thesis (Goonasekera and Lee, 1998).

According to the survey in India, more viewers liked foreign programmes such as news, current affairs and sports better than their Indian counterparts. However, when the programmes were culture specific, like films and serials, Indian programmes were preferred. Elements disliked in foreign programmes were sex, vulgarity, violence and crime. Though foreign programmes were considered better, some viewers also considered them harmful as they were likely to create an undesirable impact on lifestyles, particularly of youth. The study found that there was a distinct difference between Indian and foreign programmes, but this difference was determined more by the channel's philosophy rather than by the country of origin. Door Darshan, irrespective of where the programmes were from, preferred the more purposeful programmes, which meet certain social objectives and conform to Indian values and lifestyles. The Indian study surveyed 263 viewers in two metropolitan cities – Bombay and Ahmedabad. Most of the respondents believed that Indian culture, values and lifestyles were strong enough to withstand any foreign influence. They agreed that foreign programmes would bring both good and bad influences. The way to check the bad influences was to produce better Indian programmes. The overall view of the sample was firmly against banning of foreign programmes (Joshi, 1998).

In Japan, except for feature films shown by commercial networks during primetime (mostly Hollywood movies), western programmes rarely get high ratings. The reason for the low rating of foreign programmes is not antipathy amongst the Japanese toward foreign programmes. In fact, the survey results clearly indicated that the Japanese are, on the whole, quite favourably disposed towards foreign programmes. There was an overall tendency for respondents to agree with positive statements concerning imported programmes, and to disagree with negative statements. The majority of the respondents expressed the view that the number of foreign programmes imported should be increased. Very few said it should be decreased. The researchers concluded that the major reason for the failure of foreign television programmes in Japan is the strong competition posed by local programmes, not any xenophobic attitude held by the Japanese audience (Hagiwara, 1998).

In Malaysia, too, the overall attitude towards western programmes was positive. Very few (16.7 percent) said there were too many foreign programmes. The respondents said that western programmes were of good technical and production quality, were educational, enjoyable and creative. They believed that western programmes do have an influence on their children and neighbours. The good influences are that these programmes provide education, teach open-mindedness, help Malaysians to learn English, teach modern lifestyles, and influence people to care for others. The negative influences are that these programmes expose young people to sex, teach loose morals, disrespect for elders and disrespect for authority, promote a lack of discipline, inculcate materialistic values, and cause an increase in crime.

The respondents were presented with a list of statements about western programmes. These included positive, negative and neutral statements. Of the 10 negative statements, the respondents rejected eight. The majority of respondents did not consider western programmes to be harmful to their way of life, nor did they think that imported western programmes were more harmful than Asian programmes. The overwhelming majority of respondents (92.1 percent) disagreed with the suggestion that the government should ban western programmes. They did not see western programmes as corrupting their culture; nor did they feel that foreign programmes increased their dissatisfaction with their own cultures (Karthigesu, 1998).

The findings in Hong Kong were quite similar to those in the three other countries discussed so far. There was little or no support for banning foreign programmes in Hong Kong. The respondents did not find foreign programmes repulsive, nor did they find the values in foreign programmes more deleterious than those in local programmes. On the contrary, they considered foreign programmes to be of better quality, both helping them to better understand foreign cultures and enriching their knowledge.

The results of this empirical study on the attitude of audiences toward western programmes is clearly contrary to the thesis of media imperialism, which postulates a deleterious effect of foreign media culture on indigenous traditions and values. At least this is not how ordinary people, exposed to foreign media programmes, feel about them.[6]

Perhaps one reason for the favourable attitude of audiences toward western media products is the relatively dominant position that local productions hold in these countries. For instance, India is the largest producer of movies in the world and is an exporter of movies. The state-run TV network, Door Darshan, produces and broadcasts quality programmes. India undoubtedly has one of the finest traditions of music in the world. Malaysia is economically rich and invests substantial resources in local productions. Hong Kong has a vibrant media production industry and is an exporter of Chinese TV programmes and movies. Japan is perhaps the strongest producer of movies and television programmes in Asia. When local productions are abundant and dominant, foreign productions of low quality are less likely to be selected and shown on local television. Hence, the high quality of foreign programmes and favourable audience perception of them. If there is a situation where foreign productions dominate and people have no alternative choices, they will have a greater chance of watching inferior foreign programmes and their attitude toward foreign programmes may not be favourable any more. Moreover, when local productions dwindle to a negligible amount, people's views about foreign programmes may also be different, and they may value local productions more than foreign ones as the former becomes something uncommon or novel (Lee, 1998).

International agreements

Many of the areas opened up by transnational communication require agreements amongst states in order to gain mutual benefits from their utilization. These can take the form of international conventions or bilateral agreements. Such agreements are particularly important in relation to international dissemination of cultural products.

---

6. It is possible for critics of these findings to argue that ordinary people cannot see the dangers of cultural imperialism. This again can be dismissed as a patronizing position of elitist researchers.

Recently some issues in this area have been the subject of international debate and negotiations. In the European Community (EC), for instance, transborder TV has been the subject of EC directives. A 1984 EC Green Paper refers to the establishment of a common market for borderless satellite and cable TV operations. Transborder television is also the subject of a 1989 EC Directive. In the European context, transborder could mean a common TV culture for Europe. The objective of the 1989 EC Directive was to develop TV cultures in Europe and to establish the identity of a European culture. In February 1996, a reform bill was passed to strengthen the EC Directive, and in this endeavour European broadcasters were obliged to observe the European content clause which states that European-made programmes must account for 51 percent or more of total broadcasts (HBF, 1996). This is obviously a way of restricting the market for cultural products from non-European countries.

In the Asia-Pacific region it is difficult to envisage transnational television or any other type of communication as a means of establishing a common culture. Unlike Europe, the countries in the Asia-Pacific region have very different traditions and different historical experiences. These countries are far more diverse, sometimes are suspicious of each other, and jealously guard their indigenous cultural heritage.

In 1994, the General Assembly of the Asian Broadcasting Union (ABU) met in Kyoto, Japan, and adopted a resolution specifying the Guidelines for Transnational Satellite Broadcasters in the Asia-Pacific Region. The objective of the guidelines was similar to that of the EC Directive, but the content was very different. Unlike the EC Directive, the ABU guidelines placed an emphasis on respecting the cultural diversity of the Asia-Pacific region, rather than creating a common transnational culture. In the introduction, the guidelines state that the development of satellite television services will undoubtedly foster free flow of information in the Asia-Pacific region. At the same time, the document asserts that there is a serious concern that this situation could have deleterious effects on the values and cultures of the different countries of the region. A series of similar guidelines called Guidelines on the Programme Contents of International Satellite Television Broadcasting in the Asia-Pacific Region were also adopted at a Tokyo meeting of government policy makers from 21 Asian and Pacific countries.

These guidelines reiterated the need to respect the principles of free flow of information, and to protect the sovereignty and domestic systems of those countries that the satellite signals reach, (HBF, 1996).

It is quite possible that such guidelines will eventually provide a common ground for the development of a pan-Asian TV culture. However, in order to achieve this it would be necessary for the members of ABU and the relevant government agencies to work out a consensus or a common vision amongst the countries involved. This will require, at some stage, international covenants to bind the countries to a common course of action.

GATT/WTO

There are many other areas in which transborder communication has necessitated such international understanding or agreements. Liberalization of trade in cultural products consequent to GATT/WTO[7] decisions is one such area. There was a time when cultural products such as movies, performing arts and music were exempted from trade liberalization. In 1947, when GATT was drafted, Article IV of the agreement authorized the imposition of national screen quotas for the 'exhibition of cinematographic films of national origin during a specified minimum proportion of the total screen time actually utilized'. This was based on a dichotomy between trade and culture – trade liberalization and cultural protection. International trade officials were scarcely involved in issues relating to broadcasting and telecommunications. The recognition of the special character of cultural products is not limited to GATT/WTO. The 1989 Free Trade Agreement between the US and Canada specifically exempted cultural products covering films, videos, TV, radio broadcasting, sound recording and print media. In many countries foreign ownership of the media of communication is either prohibited or severely restricted. The usual reasons are national security and social and cultural considerations. However, under the Uruguay Round of Talks in 1986, the sector of trade in services was brought under the GATT commitments to open markets and discipline. The rules of GATT/WTO[8] will now apply to cultural products and services, as they apply to all other services. Thus, traditionally regulatory areas have become market access issues under GATT Uruguay Round Negotiations (Kakabadse, 1995).

The question therefore is whether the rules of trade liberalization could be sensibly applied to cultural products. If trade in cultural products is liberalized, and cultural protection withdrawn, will this result in the flooding of Asian markets with products from the more powerful economies, particularly the US?

While it is true that GATT/WTO rules make no special distinction between cultural products and other goods, this by itself does not open up hitherto restricted markets in cultural products. This is because of the principle, under GATT/WTO, of allowing individual countries to make commitments in the market access areas. This mechanism gives all countries considerable flexibility in handling cultural products and services. Each country can decide whether it wishes to offer market-opening guarantees for any particular cultural product

---

7. General Agreement of Trade and Tariff (GATT). World Trade Organization (WTO). GATT was replaced by WTO in 1995.

8. There are 27 separate legal agreements and 25,000 pages of liberalizing commitments on market access for goods and services, which entered into force in January 1995 with the creation of WTO.

or service. 'In addition GATT provides particular flexibility for developing countries wishing to open fewer sectors or liberalize fewer types of transactions in future negotiations, thus making explicit their rights to extend market access in line with their development situations' (Kakabadse, 1995, p.76).

From the point of view of international trade in cultural products, perhaps what is more significant is the agreement on intellectual property protection (TRIPS agreement), which obliges all member countries to apply the Berne Convention standards, enforceable through dispute-settlement mechanisms. For instance, producers of sound recordings must be granted an exclusive rental right – the right to authorize or prevent the commercial renting of their work. Protection provided for performers and producers is effective for at least 50 years, and applies to all signatories of the agreement. The agreement also contains detailed obligations for governments to provide effective enforcement, including criminal sanctions against copyright violations. GATT signatories are obliged to provide remedies under their municipal law to guarantee that intellectual property rights can be effectively enforced by foreign nationals who hold such rights. These very detailed and strict provisions are expected to build investor confidence, thus leading to more trade in cultural products in the international market.

However, intellectual property rights still remain a major concern. This is a particularly sensitive issue in Asia. One reason for this is relatively weak and ineffective legal and policing mechanisms. It has been claimed that violations of software licenses in the Asia-Pacific region alone have amounted to losses exceeding US$2 billion in 1994 (Low, 1995). Without protecting intellectual property rights and building inventors' confidence in their patent rights, Asian countries will not be able to attract foreign investment. Laws and regulations necessary for the enforcement of WTO decisions are still not in place in some of these countries.

The Internet

Another concern among Asian leaders is the proliferation of international electronic networks. The Internet, for instance, is fast becoming a household word in Southeast Asia, particularly in the more affluent countries of the region. This has opened a vast area of issues ranging from cyber-trade, cyber-dollars and cyberporn, to censorship. Many governments in Asia have assumed it as their moral duty to preserve core cultural values and protect society as a whole from what they perceive as corrupting foreign influences. This fear of foreign cultural domination is fuelled by the historical antagonism between the colonized, subordinated countries of Asia, and the colonizing, hegemonic imperial powers. This attitude has been reinforced by the popular discourse of media imperialism, which became a powerful intellectual theme in the 1960s. Western media products were perceived as culturally and morally harmful for the well-being of Asian countries.

There is little or no contention regarding pornography on the Internet. Very few, if any, would argue in favour of it. But in other areas there is much room for contention. For instance, it often happens that what is legal in one country is illegal in another. And with cyberspace being seamlessly global, it has been argued that cyberspace censorship requires stricter laws (*The Straits Times,* 12 April 1995). The application of such laws becomes very difficult, particularly in the case of electronic mail. Furthermore, it is clear that existing laws are not in step with developments in cyberspace. It is difficult to frame laws to control and censor information considered offensive and, at the same time, allow a free flow of information.

Cyber-trade is another area of concern. According to one report there were an estimated 100,000 websites in early 1996 and their number is doubling every three months. Business activity has begun to grow on the Web. It has been estimated that commercial websites numbered 50,000 in 1996 (Ang, 1996). Business deals through the Internet were said to account for around 4.1 percent of purchases in the US in 1994 and are expected to grow to 16 percent by the year 2000 (*The Straits Times*, 14 August 1994). Such activities could lead to a rise in currency and credit exchanges beyond the control of national governments, and could create problems in the implementation of monetary policies. Imposing import duties and sales taxes could become increasingly difficult, leading to losses in government revenue (Low, 1995).

As the trend towards transborder satellite multi-channels in the Asia-Pacific region increases, the competition for market shares is likely to intensify. Most of the current satellite programmes are in English, or Chinese or Indian languages. Japan and Korea are also likely to enter this market. In addition to the current commercial transnational broadcasting services by private companies, several governments in the region have also launched international services or are planning such services. Notable among these services are CCTV International of China, Korea Channel and the Japanese international TV broadcasts. These telecasts are intended for nationals of these countries living abroad.

The main characteristics of Asian satellite services at present can be summarized as follows: Singapore and Hong Kong have become the centres of Asian satellite TV services; satellite subregions have been formed based on cultural similarities. For instance, the Chinese-language region and the Indian-language region; an ASEAN subregion has been formed as a result of the seven member countries of ASEAN and neighbouring countries launching broadcast satellites for domestic services

It is not an exaggeration to say that there is a scramble for domination of the skies. Large numbers of satellites are being placed into orbit by governments and multinational corporations. For as little as US$25,000, China can uplink a communication satellite using its long march rocket. The skies have become open territory. This is looked upon with apprehension by many countries in Asia. Organizations and individuals are now examining ways by which the international community can bring some order to this situation before it spins out of control. The Kuala Lumpur-based ABU has already formulated a series of guidelines to be followed by transnational broadcasters. This however is not binding on any of the members of ABU. They remain only guidelines for voluntary compliance. International agreements will be required to bind countries to such rules.

National laws

Decisions of national courts based on national laws have become quite important in relation to transnational communication in recent times. The following case material is important as it elucidates current thinking of influential persons in Asia on this subject. The legal principles that emerged through these court decisions and the efforts to create space for coexistence between multinational media and Asian governments is an interesting study of an emerging culture of transnational communication. It is a sociological study of how communities create meanings in new situations brought about by the introduction of advanced communication technologies. It has much relevance to the question of freedom of expression in a world with porous borders – a world with differing geopolitical, commercial and cultural interests competing for ascendancy.

During the years 1986/87, the Singapore government restricted the circulation of *Time, Asian Wall Street Journal (AWSJ), Asiaweek* and *Far Eastern Economic Review (FEER)* – all having wide circulation in Singapore. The restrictions were imposed by a *Government Gazette* notification, under the Newspaper and Printing Act, and hence this procedure is referred to as gazetting. The disputes with *Time, AWSJ* and *Asiaweek* have been over the right to reply considered by Asian leaders as an integral part of freedom of expression. All three publications had carried stories about events in Singapore which the Singapore government said were factually incorrect. The government replied. *Time* and *AWSJ* refused to publish it. *Asiaweek* edited the reply without the knowledge of the Singapore government and attributed the edited version to the Singapore government.

---

9. The article in question was about a Marxist conspiracy revealed by the government in which some members of the Catholic Church were implicated. The report was about a meeting held between Mr Lee and Catholic leaders led by Archbishop Yong. In his suit Mr Lee alleged that the article depicted Mr Lee as being intolerant of the Roman Catholic Church and that he set out to victimize Catholic priests and workers (*The Straits Times,* January 1988). The Singapore courts found all four defendants guilty of ill will, spite or wrong or improper motive. It awarded Mr Lee $230,000 in damages. Eight years after this incident *FEER* remain gazetted under the Newspaper and Printing Act. However, after many years, the permitted circulation has been increased to 4,000 copies.

FEER's report, it was alleged, was not only false but was also defamatory of Mr Lee Kuan Yew, the Prime Minister of Singapore at that time. The government wrote to *FEER* to either substantiate or withdraw the allegations. *FEER* refused on grounds of editorial prerogative. Its circulation was restricted from 9,000 copies to 500 copies and a libel case was filed in Singapore courts.[9]

A more recent case involved charges of contempt of court and libel against the *International Herald Tribune* (*IHT*). The article in question was written by an American academic who at that time was a Senior Fellow at the National University of Singapore. It alleged that some intolerant regimes in Asia, which he did not name, rely upon a compliant judiciary to bankrupt opposition politicians. The Singapore courts found the writer, the Asia Editor of *IHT*, *IHT's* publisher and CEO, and *IHT's* printer, Singapore Press Holdings, guilty of contempt and libel. Fines were imposed on those convicted.[10] When *IHT* was criticized for agreeing to pay damages, *IHT* president, Mr Richard Simmons, said that the courts have found *IHT* to have committed libel and that it would not contest the High Court decision. It would continue to operate from Singapore. Critics who were demanding that *IHT* try to impose American liberal standards abroad were uninformed (*AWSJ*, 18 January 1995).

Apart from recourse to legal proceedings, there are also other ways in which Asian leaders make known their displeasure to journalists who publish disparaging articles. Malaysia's Pergau Dam case is instructive in this regard. The *London Sunday Times* of 24 February 1994, in a story headlined 'Wimpey offered contract bribes to Malaysian Prime Minister' alleged that the giant construction company, Wimpey, had offered initial payment of $50,000 through a middle man to the Malaysian Prime Minister, Dr Mahathir Mohammed. The Malaysian Prime Minister was furious at what he alleged were totally false allegations. In retaliation, the Malaysian government decided to shut out British contractors from all infrastructure projects in Malaysia. Announcing the new policy, the Deputy Prime Minister of Malaysia at that time, Mr Anwar Ibrahim, said 'the British media may have their own political agendas but we detest their patronizing attitude and innuendoes that the governments of developing countries, particularly a Muslim led nation such as Malaysia, are incompetent and their leaders corrupt' (*Sunday Times*, 13 March, 1994). Because of these press reports, it was argued that to deal with British companies was to have shady undertones. Therefore the Malaysian government had decided not to award any new contracts to British companies. This decision affected some big contracts that may have been won by big industries in Britain, including General Electric, Balfour Beatty and British Aerospace. Britain lost thousands of jobs. The end result was that the editor of the *Sunday Times* was removed by Rupert Murdoch. Dr Mahathir said that the editor was sacked.

---

10. *IHT* was ordered to pay Mr Lee Kuan Yew $300,000 in damages, $350,000 to Prime Minister Mr Goh Chok Tong and $300,000 to Deputy Prime Minister, Mr Lee Hsien Loong.

The Gandhi gaffe involved a STAR TV programme called *Nikki tonight*, which is beamed to audiences in India. The programme features Bombay film industry gossip, and in one of its programmes the host, Nikki Bedi, egged her guest, Ashok Row Kavi, a gay activist, into repeating scandalous remarks that Mr Kavi had made a long time ago in the press against Mahatma Gandhi, father of modern India. Kavi called Gandhi a bastard *Bania*. He implied by this that Gandhi was a miser and a sharp dealer. This was a totally false allegation because money meant very little to Gandhi, who lived a very simple life. The allegation went unchallenged in the programme. While such a remark may have been tolerated in western countries it created a roar of angry protests in India. The Indian parliament accused Murdoch of cultural terrorism. The fiasco led to the issuing of an open warrant in India for the arrest of Murdoch and some others working for STAR TV, under Indian law of criminal libel (*Independent*, 6 July 1995). This incident illustrates the tension that could exist between cultural policies of Asian countries and commercial interests of transnational broadcasters operating beyond the borders of recipient countries. Freedom of expression gets caught between such conflicting interests.

The fourth case I want to take is from Sri Lanka. STAR TV took a commercial television company in Sri Lanka to court for allegedly infringing its copyright. The TV station in Sri Lanka, called Extra Terrestrial Vision (ETV), had been downloading STAR TV satellite programmes and re-telecasting them on terrestrial transmitters. In addition, it was alleged that the company was blocking STAR TV commercials and inserting local commercials for a fee. It was not paying STAR TV any royalties for the use of its programmes nor had it sought STAR TV authority to re-telecast its programmes in any form. The Sri Lankan court decided in favour of the defendant. In the light of this decision, the current position appears to be that international TV broadcasters cannot complain against unauthorized use of their material once they telecast these programmes freely to other countries. Such decisions sit uneasily with WTO agreements on intellectual property rights and copyright. Undoubtedly local laws have to be brought in line with provisions in international agreements once these agreements have been ratified by these countries.

The (Indian) Cable Act 1994 (ICA) is another instance of Indian efforts to regulate the TV broadcasting scene in India. This law clearly applies to transnational TV broadcasts to India when such broadcasts are re-telecast though Indian cable companies. A majority of households in India receive foreign satellite programmes through cable services. Dish antennae are too costly for most Indian families to own. ICA stipulates that no programme or advertisement can be transmitted in India unless it is in conformity with prescribed programme and advertising code. The programme code bans material which 'offends good taste and decency, criticizes friendly countries, encourage violence or anti-national attitudes, affects the integrity of the nation, encourage superstition or blind belief, denigrates women or children and which contain visuals or words which reflect a slandering, ironical and snobbish attitude in portrayal of certain ethnic, linguistic and regional groups'. The Act also limits foreign ownership of local channels to 49 percent (Banerjee, 1996). I believe that many a foreign programme would fall foul of such a programme code.

The manner in which Hong Kong and Macau settled their differences in transborder broadcasting highlights the different ways in which economic interests could impinge on such decisions (Lee, 1998). At the centre of the differences between Macau and Hong Kong was the need for Hong Kong to secure its internal market for Cantonese TV broadcasts. The moment Hong Kong's local Cantonese TV market is adversely affected local programme operators such as TVB, ATV and Wharf Cable will apply pressure on the Hong Kong government to secure this market.

In 1991, Macau TV (TdM), which is government owned, decided to boost up its signals to cover vast areas of Hong Kong. This would make TdM virtually another free-to-air TV station in Hong Kong without getting a Hong Kong licence. Furthermore, one of the TdM channels broadcast in Cantonese. This would affect adversely the incomes of local programme operators. The advertising standards in Macau were freer, with few restrictions on cigarette and alcohol commercials. This would result in loss of advertising revenue for local TV stations. Consequently pressure was brought on the Hong Kong government to stop Macau from broadcasting to Hong Kong. In the absence of any covenants, laws or understandings governing transborder broadcasting, the Hong Kong government had no formal way of addressing this problem. It used economic pressure on the Macau government to get them to stop the intended TV expansion. They did this by threatening to legalize casinos in Hong Kong. Legalization of casinos in Hong Kong would affect adversely Macau's most important source of revenue – gambling. People in Hong Kong are the major customers of Macau casinos. If Hong Kong was not a major source of revenue to Macau, probably the Hong Kong government would not have been able to persuade Macau to drop its intention to boost up its TV. There was no legal basis on which the two countries could have settled their differences.

Ideology

The permission given to international media to operate in any country is a privilege granted by the government of that country on its own terms. The basic understanding is that these foreign journalists report events in these countries as outsiders for outsiders. It is alleged that many of the foreign media reports are meant for the countries about which the news item is written. English is spoken and read by influential people in these countries and therefore has an impact on an important section of the population. Local-language newspapers pick up these stories and thereby give them wide publicity even amongst people who cannot read English. In short, the international press has become an offshore press to be read and consumed by the people in these countries. Some of the journalists assume a role that the American journalists play in America. They become invigilators, adversaries and inquisitors of the government. In other words, many Asian leaders see journalists in the offshore press as interfering in the domestic affairs of their countries.[11]

Most of the foreign journalists have little or no understanding of the language, history, culture or forms of governance in the countries that they try to report on. Some of these journalists approach their subject with a cultural arrogance and superiority, which is resented in Asia. No Asian country can withstand such an insidious and irresponsible onslaught from the foreign press.

The libertarian ideology of the press is not a universal model that is applicable all over the world and at all times in the same country. The libertarian view is that the press should be free to publish or not to publish what it chooses, however irresponsible or biased its actions may seem to be. In this model, the audience is seen as freely choosing in the market place of ideas. The 'logic' is that where the media are free, the market place of ideas sorts out the irresponsible from the responsible and rewards the latter. But this model cannot be applied to all countries. The free market place of ideas in multicultural, multiparty democracies in Asia can result in heightening of racial and religious tensions, mobilizing sectional constituencies and arousing emotions (Goonasekera & Ito, 1999). A partisan media can flood the market place with racially divisive information, confuse the people and set the country in a course of racial strife and civil war. In such a media environment, basic issues such as economic growth and equitable distribution are rarely tackled by the press. Instead easy solutions are peddled for complex problems that require hard political decisions. In this situation the free market brings about confusion and violent dissension rather than enlightenment and consensus.

The important point is that a body of legal decisions, customs, conventions and treaties are continually evolving. Transnational communication is being regulated in one form or another. It is important to elucidate the principles based on which such regulations are being made or attempted. Cultural considerations and commercial considerations seem to be competing with each other in the evolution of these principles. Flow of information, at present, depends more on national policies than on international agreements. Systematic research is needed to elucidate the processes involved.

---

11. It is even argued that the purpose of such interference is to achieve an outcome favourable to the international media organizations for which they work or to the interests of western countries in general. This they do in many ways: by setting the agenda for influential groups in these countries; by publishing stories that question the honesty and integrity of government leaders, thereby making such leaders fearful of the foreign media. This is a strategy to soften their stand against such media. Freedom of the press is seen as a battle cry to impose western hegemony in emerging Asian nations. Refusal to publish rebuttal of their stories by international media, which is controlled by companies based in western countries, is seen as cultural arrogance.

We are also seeing changes in the very concept of foreign media programmes. Earlier we identified such programmes on the basis of the countries of origin. The US was identified as providing the bulk of such media programmes. In the future, the world will see 'generic' multimedia entertainment software, created by the confluence of technology and capital from the US, Japan, Europe and other nations, servicing the newly deregulated and privatized media systems in Asia and elsewhere. In the future, it may not make much difference whether an increasingly 'generic' cultural product is owned and produced by companies in America, Japan, Europe or Asia. The challenge is this: how can one identify a path toward autonomous national cultural production in a system that is increasingly catering to the marketing imperatives of transnational monopolies? Will the overarching developments in global media leave room for such autonomous, national cultural productions? There is no guarantee that market forces by themselves will allow for such an outcome. Moves such as those by Microsoft to use its monopolistic position (Windows hegemony in this instance) to squeeze out competitors are worrisome developments for international competition.[12]

Law of the Sky

In a world that is divided on the basis of wealth and power, we need international agreements and common understandings if fairness is to prevail in the way we share the opportunities created by advanced technologies. The formulation of international agreements relating to the common use of the skies will be a first step in this direction. Many would agree that it is no longer desirable to allow only those with the technological capability to harness the skies either for transborder communication or for any other use. This will

---

12. We are currently witnessing an effort by the US government to prevent Microsoft from using its Windows hegemony to force Microsoft's hardware partners, such as Compaq and Micron Technology, to install its Web browser, Internet Explorer, into every PC they make. Failure to do so by hardware manufacturers will result in losing the right to sell Windows-based computers. By doing this Microsoft will effectively squeeze out competitors, such as its primary rival Netscape Navigator. Netscape Navigator, Compaq, Micron and Microsoft are all American companies. US anti-trust laws will apply to these companies and provide relief under US laws. An important question from the point of view of other international players in this field is: What if the competition is from outside the US, say India, Australia or Japan? What relief is there for such businesses from monopolists like Microsoft who want to squeeze them out of business by using strong-arm tactics based on their monopolistic position? International copyright laws provide full protection for companies such as Microsoft from so-called piracy. It is necessary to examine the international obligations that accompany such protection so that, under the cover of international protection, monopolists do not use their position to squeeze out international competition.

obviously require an examination of both international and municipal laws, conventions and customs that apply to the use of the skies at present. This requires both legal and social scientific research, preferably by an international community of scholars. The findings of this research will form the basis for initiating discussions amongst nations on how the resources in the sky are to be used. We already have a Convention on the Law of the Sea. Perhaps this could provide a model, though not an exact one; a starting point for an examination of the emerging Law of the Sky. Principles enshrined in the Law of the Sea, such as the recognition of certain areas of the sea as the 'common heritage of mankind', would probably find parallels in the skies.[13]

In any such inquiry, the international community should consider the rights and responsibilities of governments and countries that receive unsolicited material, such as TV broadcasts, from foreign commercial companies. Already, international conventions exist in areas such as civil aviation, activities on celestial bodies, exploration and the use of outer space and the allocation of the radio spectrum (Evans, 1991). It can be argued that cultural products in the form of TV programmes beamed to one's territorial skies are as important as any other object in the sky. Therefore, in fairness to both senders and receivers, the international community should agree on rules and regulations governing such conduct.

Modern communication technologies have created social situations where the traditional and older systems of conducting business will not do. It has created new situations which require new modes of response. As it stands, some countries that have to decide how to respond to new situations have no option but to use the prevailing municipal law. India's response to the Gandhi gaffe, Sri Lanka's response to STAR TV's allegation of copyright infringement, and India's Supreme Court decision regarding the use of the air waves are all instances of interpretation of legal principles applicable in the countries that decided these cases.

However, transnational communication generated by modern information technologies requires a consensually agreed set of rules and expectations. The WTO provides a broad framework in relation to both goods and services. The principle of free trade has been enshrined in WTO decisions.[14] In the absence of covenants or understandings among countries as to the use of the skies for transborder communication, international cultural exchanges operate on different principles and expectation in different countries. Fear of cultural annihilation of the powerless countries, on the one hand, and the division of the world into cultural markets by the powerful countries on the other, need

---

13. Convention on the Law of the Sea: articles 1(1), 136 and 140.

14. The Uruguay Round has been described as the biggest and most difficult trade negotiations in history. It produced results that no one thought would be possible when the Round commenced in 1986. It is said that there has been no comparable achievement since the creation of Bretton Woods institutions in 1944.

to be reconciled on an agreed basis. International conventions on transborder communication are therefore a pressing need, particularly in Asia.

It is clear that a new form of civic organization is emerging, as a result of the impact of new communication technologies. Such communities are variously referred to as intelligent communities, smart communities, para-social communities, virtual communities and cyber communities. The social relationships among the members of these communities are not necessarily based on physical proximity. Strategic locations such as transportation crossroads and easy access to raw materials and labour, which were very important for the emergence and sustenance of communities in earlier periods of history, are no longer the deciding criteria for the emergence of intelligent communities. New telecommunication technologies have made it possible for business to produce consumers to purchase and workers to interact without the need for common physical location.[15]

However, the policies governing these social processes are still influenced by an old mode of thinking. Even the scientific community has not been very helpful in this regard. Social scientists, researchers and popular writers use metaphors borrowed from earlier periods of history to describe futuristic developments in the field of communications. We speak of global villages, electronic superhighways, multi-media supercorridors etc. These metaphors are much too simple and one-dimensional to capture the momentous changes that are taking place in the intelligent communities. However, policies continue to be influenced by this thinking. We bring in regulations, deregulation and re-regulation, which may be entirely irrelevant to the processes that are going on in the newly emerging communities. There appears to be a vast chasm between the needs of transnational communication generated by modern communication technologies and the policies that are used for its social applications. This has serious implications for important issues in communication, such as freedom of expression, censorship, privacy, and cultural representation in transnational media.

What is significant in the changes that are brought about by new communication technologies is that the traditional centres of control are withering away. Mass communication under the previous modes of production, both capitalist and socialist, were controlled by a group of functionaries. It was easy for the owners of the media to design policies to control the media, including its content, at various stages of production. The owners could be media moguls or governments. However, in the emergent communities, linked to the information superhighway, such direct controls through ownership are becoming increasingly difficult. Furthermore the traditional distinction between different kinds of media such as print, broadcasting, film are getting blurred. Multimedia is becoming the vehicle of the future. Old-fashioned censorship will now be very difficult to impose. With the advent of new communication

---

15. 'Building Smart Communities: How California's communities can thrive in a digital age.' Sandiago State University, 1997.

technologies the medium, the message and the audience will not be discrete entities. They are interacting and merging to become parts of civil society – an intelligent community. A different morality will emerge. The question is what kind of a morality will this be. Will it support values such as openness, freedom and tolerance which are sorely needed for civil life in any human community? Or will it bring about a hegemony that will be a threat to smaller communities and their cultures?

The loud and clear message of transnational communication is that we live in the same world. But different groups see different meanings in this world. Communication across cultures facilitated through advanced technologies makes for more informed and more aware persons with, possibly, a less parochial outlook. It can promote unity among diverse people and contribute to the emergence of a more tolerant, consensual culture crossing national borders. The very same forces have also raised fears of cultural domination and obliteration of ethnic identities. History has shown us that traditional indigenous cultures are strong and adaptable and at times are strengthened in the face of challenges. History has also shown that there is danger of a destructive backlash against all foreign influences – good and bad – when countries are faced with foreign cultural intrusions. However, trying to shut oneself off from the 'intrusion' of foreign cultural influences may be like blinding oneself in the hope that one may walk with more safety in a jungle of pit and precipice. The global spread of communication media is here to stay; it cannot be wished away and we must learn to live with it. In order to harness its potential for good, one should look at it as an opportunity to open one's eyes through education and experience, and not to blind them in fear and ignorance. Perhaps what is required most at the present stage of development of transnational communication is to provide systematic education, both formal and informal, as to the nature of this phenomenon.

This requires continuing research. We need an informed public discourse through the media, through the schools and through public debate. If the enormous possibilities for commerce across cultures, opened up by modern technology, are to be harnessed for human freedom, betterment, tolerance and understanding, it is necessary for the international community to act on the basis of a common vision.

References

Ang, Peng Hwa (1996) 'Free expression and the Internet: Limits and possibilities' in *The Report of the 8th MacBride Round Table*. Seoul: Korean Broadcasting Academic Society, pp.513–519.

Banerjee, I. (1995) *Media ownership and control in the age of convergence,* International Institute of Communications Global Report Series. London: IIC.

Chan, Joseph M. & Eric K. Y. Ma (1996) 'Asian television: Global trends and local processes' in *The Report of the 8th MacBride Round Table.* Seoul: Korean Broadcasting Academic Society, pp.21–42.

Clarke, Arthur C. (1996) 'New communication technologies and the Developing World', in Goonasekera *et al.* (ed.) *Opening windows: Issues in communication.* Singapore: AMIC.

Evans, Malcolm D. (1991) *Blackstone's International Law Documents.* London: Blackstone.

Goonasekera, Anura & Ito, Youichi (1999) *Mass media and cultural identity: Ethnic reporting in Asia.* London: Pluto Press.

Goonasekera, Anura & Lee, Paul S. N. (1998) *TV without borders: Asia speaks out.* Singapore: AMIC.

Goonasekera, Anura & Holaday, Duncan (1998) *Asian communication handbook 1998.* Singapore: AMIC.

Hagiwara, Shigeru (1998) 'Changing role of foreign programming in Japanese television' in Goonasekera, Anura & Lee, Paul S. N. (1998) *TV without borders: Asia speaks out.* Singapore: AMIC, pp.171-206.

HBF (1996) *Asia speaks out: Towards greater programme diversity in Asia.* Tokyo: Hoso-Bunka Foundation Inc.

Ito, Youichi (1994) 'Why information now' in Wang, Georgette (ed.) *Treading different paths: Informatization in Asian nations.* New Jersey: Ablex.

Joshi, S. R. (1998) 'Transborder television in India' in Goonasekera, Anura & Lee, Paul S.N. (1998) *TV without borders: Asia speaks out.* Singapore: AMIC, pp.3-37.

Kakabadse, M. A. (1995) 'The WTO and the commodification of cultural products: Implications for Asia', *Media Asia.*

Karthigesu, R. (1998) 'Transborder television in Malaysia' in Goonasekera, Anura & Lee, Paul S. N. (1998) *TV without borders: Asia speaks out.* Singapore: AMIC, pp.38–77.

Lee, Paul S. N. (1998) 'Foreign television in Hong Kong: Little watched but favourably received' in Goonasekera, Anura & Lee, Paul S. N. (1998) *TV without borders: Asia speaks out.* Singapore: AMIC, pp.141-170.

Low, Linda (1995) 'Social and economic issues in Information Society: A South East Asian perspective', paper submitted at the Workshop on chances and risks of the Information Society: Its social and economic effects in Europe and South East Asia, organized by the School of Communication Studies, NTU, and FES, 18–20 September 1995, Singapore.

Pendakur, Manjunath (1995) 'International institutions and power in a period of recolonization' in Tankha, Brij (ed.) *Communications and democracy: Ensuring plurality.* pp.30-38. Penang: Southbound.

Raghavan C. (1990) *Recolonization: GATT, The Uruguay Round and the Third World.* London: Zen Books (quoted in Pendakur op. cit.).

Tarjanne (1997) *Asian Mass Communication Bulletin* Vol. 28, No. 1, p.10.

Waterman, D. & Rogers, E. (1994) 'The economics of television programme production and trade in Far East Asia', *Journal of Communication,* 44(3), pp.89–111.

Ethnic distance in the different contexts: A Japanese case

Momoyo Shibuya

As a globalized world illuminates the boundaries of ethnic groups, groups active in counterbalancing the trend of convergence, these groups are invested increasingly with meaning even at the level of interpersonal-level communication. Attitudes toward other ethnic groups, which are one of the most crucial causes of inter-ethnic miscommunication, are determined by ethnic labelling. Accompanied by socially created images, ethnic labels direct individuals within particular ethnic groups toward judging, treating or distancing others.

Each ethnic group has its own scale of other group preference, which reflects how the group views the world. Although examinations of ethnic preference/distance scale, generally called 'social distance scale', conclude that the scale would be formulated in social context, it is proven only from the chronological trend of certain groups; few inquiries report from the point of view of the spatial shift of a group. There is consequently a significant gap in knowledge about ethnic distance.

Seeking to explore remedies, this study examines the ethnic distance of groups who have relocated to different societies. It focuses on the Japanese, the dominant group of Japan. Since the Japanese ethnic group is almost coterminous with the Japanese nation in terms of culture and size of population, its intra- and extra-social ethnic distances render comparison straightforward.

After a review of ethnic distance and cross-cultural adaptation strategy, employing Chitty's matrix framework, this study's methodology, results and discussion of results are provided. The study reveals that the way we map other groups is relatively fixed, even in a globalized world with migrant populations.

Ethnic distance

The matrix model

Chitty's matrix model (Chitty, 1997, 1998; for details see Chapter 1) depicts the world as a number of matrices, one within the other. The matrices of the social system include individual (I-matrix) through ethnic (E-matrix), national (A-matrix), regional (R-matrix) and global political economic system (P-matrix); each matrix is interrelated to others.

The P-matrix is composed of interacting R- or A-matrices, each of which consists of particular collectivities of I-matrices known as E-matrices. This means that I-, E-, A- and R-matrices influence the shape of the P-matrix. Meanwhile, the opposite flow of influence also occurs. As environment (an N-matrix) and the P-matrix shape/regulate R-, A-, E- and I-matrices. Each matrix, in short, is a co-production with other matrices.

Due to the process of European-led modernization, the present P-matrix is mostly influenced by Western European and American A-matrices. Although Asian (especially Chinese) E-matrices have grown in power, they have not overtaken the West in terms of influencing the P-matrix. A- or E-matrices other than Western European and American matrices also have to play under the P-matrix rules mainly governed by Western European and American matrices in order to maximize their own interests or to make their own identities secure in the P-matrix. Consequently, the position where each A- or E-matrix stands gives it a different vision of the P-matrix, which connotes certain images of other A- or E-matrices.

Ethnic distance

Socio-psychological ethnic distance, which is normally called 'social distance', is the tacit rank of 'out groups' in order of preference in an ethnic group (Bogardus, 1925; Park, 1926; Sherif, 1948). For instance, North Americans prefer American, Canadian and English people, and least prefer Turks, Chinese and Hindus; Japanese prefer English, French, German and American people most and Philippine, Korean and black people least (Sherif, 1948; Agatsuma & Yoneyama, 1967).

What makes the degree of socio-psychological intimacy/distance towards out groups diverge is difficult to identify due to the complexity of the phenomenon. Many variables are involved directly or indirectly. Yet, some factors are discussed by social distance researchers.

Cultural similarity seems to contribute to the scale of the distance to out groups. Bogardus, for instance, measured the distance to other ethno-cultural groups by his 'Racial Distance Scale', and found that people normally feel closer to the people from similar cultural backgrounds than to the people from dissimilar cultures (Bogardus, 1947). The following studies, for instance, by Brewer (1968) or by Triandis and Triandis (1960) also confirm the correlation between social distance and familiarity, liking, and perceived similarity.

Others view that the attitudes towards out groups are formed by social context (Kato, 1995). Economic and social status in the social context on the distance seems to be an especially influential determinant of the ranking (Park, 1926). Bogardus claims that Americans down-ranked Japanese, Germans and Italians just after World War II (Bogardus, 1947). This is because the dominant group in social and economic terms leads socially prevalent values on which ethnic distance is based (Lewis & Slade, 1994). As Sherif writes:

> The ordering of prestige among the various groupings, the social intimacy or distance permitted and deemed desirable between them, and the prevailing images flow from the powerful and mighty downward to the subordinated. (Sherif, 1966, p.33)

Often the dominant group intentionally sets ethnic distance by propagating stereotypes of groups in order to create a favourable social system or to maintain a status quo in which they can get advantages. Even though it is unintentional, the view of the most powerful group reflects that of the whole society.

However, social context is not necessarily limited to a society in one's immediate environment. In the matrix world the P-matrix always affects A- and E-matrices and therefore social context should in this case include the global context as well. Currently, Western European and American E- and A-matrices drive the P-matrix. In terms of determining perceptions, the ethnic distance of each group in the P-matrix is affected by the view of Western European matrices. In the case of subordinate groups in an A-matrix, the view of the dominant E-matrix is added to that influence.

Cross-cultural adaptation strategy from an ethnic distance perspective

This ethnic distance, which is determined by images of groups, sets a new criterion of judgement of them, affecting communication behaviour. When social distance becomes greater, communication becomes less effective (Gudykunst, 1986). As the dominant group in a society treats other ethnic minority groups by its ethnic distance scale, attitudes of subordinate groups towards the mainstream society, or the dominant group specifically, are also determined by ethnic distance of the groups.

There are four varieties of attitude of groups toward the mainstream society, organized under two criteria: retention of cultural identity and the acceptance of the society based on the social distance. The four varieties are assimilation, integration, rejection and deculturation (Berry, 1980). Assimilation is the form in which 'relinquishing cultural identity and moving into the larger society' occurs. Integration refers to the form in which both the maintenance of cultural identity and the movement to join the mainstream society are seen. In the form of rejection, cultural identity is retained whilst moving into the mainstream society is denied. When loss of cultural identity and striking out against the larger society are engaged at the same time, it is called deculturation (Berry, 1980, p.13).

The retention of cultural identity and the acceptance of the mainstream society are deeply related to the degree of tolerance for cultural diversity in the society and to social identity of the group. In other words the four forms are determined by the two factors. When a group has a positive social identity, assimilation will not easily occur; integration will take place if the degree of tolerance for cultural diversity is high, or rejection if the group despises the mainstream society. In contrast, when a minority group has weak or negative social identity, assimilation and deculturation tend to be preferred options.

Migrants' cross-cultural adaptation makes these four forms of attitude more complicated due to the change of influence of the A-matrix on their ethnic distance. Their strategy for adaptation is derived from the ethnic distance that the migrants have brought with them. However, their shift to a new society might modify their distance scale, because the change of A-matrix means the change of depiction of conceptual social hierarchy, the way of recognizing the world based on power relations in the global political economy and that it might reflect ethnic distance. When the influence of the A-matrix is significant for migrants' distance scale, then the scale would be changed. Nonetheless, if a global system (P-matrix) has strong influence on the distance scale of the group, the shift of A-matrix would not influence a modification of the distance scale.

Research design

The purpose of this study is to examine ethnic distance of a group that has shifted to a new A-matrix. In order to make a clear-cut contrast of before and after A-matrix shifting, the study looks at the Japanese case. The Japanese are the cultural and demographic dominant group of Japan, constituting about 98 percent of the national population. This means the Japanese E-matrix and A-matrix are almost co-terminous and Japanese people do not have to negotiate their ethnic distance with other E-matrices as long as they stay in Japan. However, Japanese E-matrix influence is limited to the Japanese A-matrix. Once Japanese go abroad, then they find themselves in totally different situations, where they need to negotiate their carried views with views within the new A-matrix.

Japanese ethnic distance
It has been claimed that Japanese have a tendency to elevate Westerners and denigrate Asians (Kosakai, 1996). Not a few studies concerning overseas students in Japan reveal this problem, saying Japanese have the discriminatory attitude towards non-Westerners, mainly Asians, in addition to the psychological 'barrier' toward other groups generally (e.g. Iwao & Hagiwara, 1987; Ogita, 1986; Suhara, 1996). As already mentioned, Wagatsuma and Yoneyama (1967) have found Japanese prefer western (white) people to Asians despite cultural and racial similarity to Asians. Similar results to this have been repeated by others (e.g. Nozawa, 1996).

As this difference in Japanese ethnic attitudes towards Westerners and Asians is problematic, the study focuses on the distance towards those two E-matrices rather than creates the list of distance. Therefore, the aim of the study is, in other words, to examine if trends in the formulation of ethnic distance of Japanese in western and Asian countries are similar to those of Japanese in Japan.

Selection of countries

Singapore and Australia were selected because, despite the fact that their A-matrices are culturally and demographically dominated by Chinese (Hokkien) and Anglo-Celtic E-matrices respectively, the two matrices have similar social backgrounds. They are both so-called multicultural societies, both having adopted multiculturalism as a policy. This enables each ethnic group to choose whether or not they maintain their own culture, that is, to select the adaptation strategy.

Regarding the relationship with Japanese in both societies, it is stable in spite of the detrimental experience of World War II. They are good business partners of Japan and popular destinations for Japanese tourists. Moreover, the Japanese communities in both societies are similar in size (about 28,000 in Australia and 26,000 in Singapore) and in character, the first generation being in the majority.

Method

No matter how individuals think about other groups, actual behaviour as a group is the meaningful, true distance for others. Thus, even though ethnic distance can be studied by several research methods, such as questionnaire survey, interview, experiment and observation, actual collective behaviour observation is the method to be used. A social product of the community, especially the one that is observable from outside, is suitable to observe actual behaviour objectively. In this sense, the ethnic press is one of the great indicators of the group's attitude toward the host society.

Mass media would propagate or reinforce immigrants' attitudes toward the host society. This is because mass media contribute to 'expanding the immigrant's experiences in the host society beyond the immediate environment' and that information 'about the broader ranges of the various elements of the host socio-cultural system', which is a basis of attitude formation, are delivered by mass media (Kim, 1991, p.386). Ethnic media are a particularly successful information conveyer (Bednall, 1992).

Ethnic media has stronger influential power on immigrants because the environment is more ambiguous in societies different to their own. According to Ball-Rokeach, the degree of dependency on media is determined by the situation wherein receivers of the message find themselves; the more ambiguous, threatening and/or rapidly changing is the social environment, the more intense media dependency becomes (Ball-Rokeach, 1989). This is because:

... the media system is not only accessible to most people, but is also the information system that is best situated to father/create, process, and disseminate relevant information, we naturally develop dependency relations with it to help us, individually and collectively, to resolve the chronic ambiguities or daily life. (Ball-Rokeach, 1989, p.316)

Even the influential power of mass media fades as time passes (Kim, 1991); still it is true that the content of ethnic media keeps affecting groups' attitudes towards the host society. Therefore, the content of ethnic press is examined to clarify how it connects to two A-matrices, home and host, by categorizing the content, and advertised products, and examining the viewpoint of articles.

A study of Japanese press in Australia and Singapore

Publications in Sydney and Singapore

Japanese ethnic publications amount currently to ten titles in Sydney and eight in Singapore. They may be categorized into three styles: newspapers, magazines and phone directories. In the newspaper category, Sydney has *Japanese Weekend Post* (*JWP:* general), *Nichigo Press* (general) and *Cheers* (entertainment), while Singapore has *Shinnichiho* (general) and *Shinnich Business News* (business). Even though they take on the newspaper format, frequency of circulation varies from twice a week to once a month.

The magazine is more popular format than the newspaper. Sydney's list goes from *In-Form* (general) to *Golf Journal* (golf), *JP Australia* (travel and life in Australia), *Move* (city guide map), *Orokamono Tengoku* (travel for working holidaymakers) and *Sydney-Eats* (restaurants). In Singapore, *Mangostine Club* (general), *Parti* (general), *Gurutto Gourmet* (restaurants) and *J-Plus* (entertainment) are of this category. Most of them are monthly, though there are some titles issued fortnightly or quarterly.

The phone directory is little different to other two categories in terms of accessibility. It consists of *Moshimoshi-page* in Sydney and *Hello Singapore*, *Singapore Benri Denwacho* in Singapore. All of these are issued annually. They are sold at Japanese bookshops, whilst other newspapers and magazines are available also at Japanese grocery shops free of charge.

The content of the press

Press content may be illustrated by the study of an established paper in each city: *Nichigo Press* in Sydney and *Shinnichiho* in Singapore. Both papers have been published for more than 20 years with stable quality and circulation.

What these papers tell about is sorted under five categories and counted. The categories are (1) the host society's affairs (including political economy, social matter, sports, entertainment, culture and history), (2) Japanese affairs (political economy, social matter, sports, entertainment, culture and history), (3) other countries' affairs (political economy, social matter, sports, entertainment, culture and history), (4) Japanese community information (activities, living information, site introduction, education and shops) and (5) others.

Nichigo Press covers the host society's (Australia's) affairs most, in 43.3 percent of all content. It takes a broad view of Australia, including news, review, readings and features. Information about the Japanese community, found in reviews and reading, accounts for 22 percent of content. Japanese and other countries' affairs follow with 16.4 percent and 13.3 percent respectively. Most of the information about Japan and other countries is found in news and reading. In contrast, 34 percent of the content of *Shinnichiho* is taken up by news of Japan, following the host society's (Singapore's) affairs for 35.3 percent, found in news, features and information notes. The third category, taking up 20.3 percent, is other countries' affairs, mainly news. Japanese community information is dealt with only in 9.2 percent of the content. The information regarding the Japanese community is provided under reading, information notes and reviews, rather than news stories.

Countries mentioned in text indicate the editorial policy. In the case of *Nichigo press*, 25 percent of articles mention 'Australia', 19.7 percent mention 'Japan and Australia', 12.2 percent mention 'Japan, Australia and other country(ies)', but only 9.9 percent mention 'Japan'. In *Sinnichiho*, 17.2 percent of articles mention 'Japan', while 13.3 percent mention 'Singapore'.

Viewpoint of article also shows the editorial direction of the press. Of the articles in *Nichigo Press*, 44 percent are written from Japanese community's point of view. The articles from Japan's viewpoint occupy 27.5 percent, and those from Australia's 21.3 percent. On the other hand, 39.8 percent of articles in *Shinnichiho* are written from Japan's viewpoint. The articles from Singapore's point of view follow with 29.3 percent, and then those from the Japanese community's viewpoint with 16 percent.

Advertising is another significant measure by which to examine the connection to the A-matrix. Advertisements in the Japanese press cover a very wide range; goods (new and second hand), cars, computers, communications, travel, education, relocation, accommodation, sitters, food, beauty care, medical care, finance, legal matters, information centres, clubs, and employment (Japanese restaurants, tour guide and other).

Main categories of advertisements in *Nichigo Press* are employment (24.3 percent), education (13.4 percent), food (10.5 percent) and accommodation (8.6 percent). In *Shinnichiho*, on the other hand, food (32 percent), education (11.7 percent) and goods (9.7 percent) are main categories. Regarding the country of origin of advertised products, 40 percent of advertised products in *Nichigo Press* are from Australia, and 33.5 percent are Japanese. Even the Australia government places advertisements in *Nichigo Press*. The main advertisements in *Shinnichiho* are for Japanese products and these constitute

36.9 percent of the total. However, advertisements placed by the Singapore government cannot be found; Singapore products take up only 9.7 percent of the total.

Discussion and conclusion

The Japanese press in Australia and Singapore display how the Japanese communities situate themselves in those societies. The first notable point is the flourishing state of the Japanese press. The number of the Japanese publications is large relative to the community's size. This suggests that most of the members read more than one kind of publication. Japanese community members are highly exposed to information conveyed by the local Japanese press.

Comparing the content of two major papers, *Nichigo Press* in Sydney may be seen to be more community oriented than *Shinnichiho* in Singapore. Not only quantitatively but also qualitatively, *Nichigo Press* offers more community information and shows more affinity to Australia than to Japan, even though Japaneseness is not denied. As for *Shinnichiho*, it does offer information about Singaporean affairs, but, unlike in the case of *Nichigo Press*, the Japanese community is slighted. The Japanese community is not the central issue in *Nichigo Press*. Clearly, the viewpoint of *Shinnichiho* is focused on Japan.

Advertisements also show that the press in Australia is connected to the host A-matrix more than the press in Singapore is to the Singaporean A-matrix. In a way, a wider range of products indicates that the Japanese community relies on the Japanese press as an information source, which means the community forms a 'ghetto'. However, advertisements in *Nichigo Press* are for Australian products, connecting it to the Australian society. For the community, Australian society matters more than Japanese society. *Shinnichiho's* advertisements are for Japanese products and they are mostly consumer goods, less connected to a specific A-matrix. Therefore, being in Singapore society does not seem to have so much meaning for the Japanese community.

Which is closer in ethnic distance terms, then? From the points above, Australia seems closer to Japanese than Singapore does. The Japanese in Australia identify themselves as a part of Australian society. With loyalty to their own ethnicity, however, their attitude is not simple 'assimilation' but more integrative. The Japanese in Singapore identify themselves as Japanese even though they live in Singapore physically. Yet, since they do not totally ignore Singapore society, they might be placed between rejection and integration strategies.

The result coincides with the Japanese ethnic distance in the domestic context. When the A-matrix one belongs to is exchanged for another, the ethnic distance scale, the view of the world, can be changed. However, the ethnic map remains the same if only physical surroundings are changed but people's mentality remains unaltered. Or, in a global society, where the view of the P-matrix dominates E-matrices quite strongly, the influence of the A-matrix might be quite limited.

This chapter seeks an answer to the question 'does ethnic distance change in the different context?' The study of Japanese E-matrices in Australian and Singaporean A-matrices suggests that the answer is 'no'. A group is likely to retain its view of the world and attitudes toward other groups even in a different A-matrix from its own. Once the ethnic distance map is set in the mind, it is difficult to change, even after getting more information about other groups or having more direct experience of them. Ethnic distance at home and within expatriate E-matrices may be considered to be relatively consistent across A-matrices in a globalized world.

References

Agatusyma, H. & Yoneyama, T. (1967) *Henken no Kozo*. Tokyo: NHK.

Ball-Rokeach, S. (1989) 'Media System Dependency Theory' in DeFleur, M. L. & Rokeach, S. *Theories of mass communication* (5th edition). New York, NY: Longman, pp.297-327.

Bednall, D. (1992) *Media and immigrant settlement*. Canberra: Australian Government.

Berry, J. W. (1980) 'Acculturation as varieties of adaptation' in Padilla, A.M. (ed.) *Acculturation: Theory, models and some new findings*. Boulder, Co: Westview Press (for AAAS), pp.9-25.

Bogardus, E. S. (1925) 'Measuring social distance', *Journal of Applied Sociology*, 9, pp.299-308.

Bogardus, E. S. (1947) 'Changes in racial distances' *International Journal of Opinion and Attitude Research*, 1, pp.55-62.

Brewer, M. B. (1968) 'Determinants of social distance among East African tribal groups', *Journal of Personality and Social Psychology*, 10(3), pp.279-89.

Chitty, N. (1997) 'A Tale of Two Cities: Contiguous moments of reported political and cultural reality in Sydney and Singapore'. Paper presented at the Political Economy session of the IAMCR Conference held in Oaxaca, Mexico, 4-7 July 1997.

Chitty, N. (1998) 'Mapping Know-ware Land'. Paper presented at the session on Communication Education and Training: Staffing the Information Marketplace, AMIC Conference held in May 1998.

Gudykunst, W. B. (ed.) (1986) *Intergroup communication*. London: Edward Arnold.

Iwao & Hagiwara, S. (1987) *Ryugakusei ga Mita Nihon*. Tokyo: Simul.

Kato, Y. (ed.) (1995) *Shakai Shinrigaku*. Tokyo: Yuhikaku.

Kim,Y. Y. (1991) 'Communication and cross-cultural adaptation' in Samover, L. & Porter, R. (eds) *Intercultural communication: A reader* (6th edition). Belmont, California: Wadsworth.

Kosakai, T. (1996) *Ibunka Juyo no Paradokkusu*. Tokyo: Asahi Sensho.

Lewis, G. & Slade, C. (1994) *Critical communication*. Sydney: Prentice-Hall Australia.

Nozawa, K. (1996) 'Communicating with strangers: A comparison of Japanese and Australian attitudes toward ethnic groups and the acceptability', in *Hibarino*, 18, pp.59-98.

Ogita, S. (1986) *Bunka Sakoku Nihon no Ryugakusei*. Tokyo: Gakuyo Shobo.

Park, R. E. (1926) 'The urban community as a spatial pattern and a moral order' in Burges, E. W. (ed.) *The urban community*. Chicago, Illinois: University of Chicago Press, pp.3-18.

Sherif, M. (1948) *An outline of social psychology*. New York, New York: Harper.

Sherif, M. (1966) *Group conflict and co-operation: Their social psychology*. London: Routledge & Kegan Paul.

Suhara, S. (1996) *Ajiajin Ryugakusei no Kabe*. Tokyo: NHK.

Triandis, H. C. & Triandis, L. M. (1960) 'Race, social class, religion, and nationality as determinants of social distance', *Journal of Abnormal and Social Psychology*, 61(1), pp.110-8.

Part Three

Reporting crises

Migrant workers: Myth or reality?

Suda Ishida

Introduction

The 1997 economic crisis in Southeast Asia offers an opportunity for this researcher to study news patterns and narratives in mass-circulated English-language Thai newspapers – *The Nation* and *Bangkok Post*. In an analysis of news stories about migrant workers from Indo-China and Burma, which were published in the two English-language Thai dailies during the period of one year before and six months after the Asian financial slump beginning mid-1997, we see the media's use of news patterns and historical narrative to make meaning of news in ways that reflect bias against these migrant workers. Thai journalists employ news narratives to tell stories about outsiders that fit into a socially and culturally constructed frame of 'them' versus 'us'. The narrative patterns, the author will argue, can be traced to the pro-nationalist history of Thailand written by the 1930s, and may be seen as perpetuating stereotypes about Thailand's foreign neighbours.

In retrospect, uneven development in Southeast Asia and the economic boom of the late 1980s to the mid-1990s contributed to an influx of labour into Thailand from some of its poorer, formerly communist neighbours, including Burma, Cambodia, Vietnam and Laos. Between 1993 and 1997, the Thai government granted work permits to roughly 600,000 foreign workers in an effort to alleviate domestic labour shortages. Mostly unskilled labour, they found work in low-paying industries largely shunned by Thais, such as farm work, fishing, salt farming, building construction and rice mills. In spite of the large number of such permits, a daily English-language Thai newspaper, *The Nation,* reported that nearly one million of these labourers were working illegally ('Thailand to deport 300,000 illegal', 16 January 1998).

The Asian financial crash in mid-1997 and the resulting economic slump created a local job-market squeeze. Millions of Thai citizens lost their jobs and new university graduates were unable to find work. The government, which had previously ignored the existence of unauthorized workers, cracked down on illegal entry and unlawful employment. On 19 January 1998, the Labour Ministry announced a plan to repatriate illegal immigrants, especially those from Burma, Laos and Cambodia. The plan received strong support from local labour unions but drew angry protests from those businesses that relied heavily on the cheap labour of non-Thai workers ('Rights and wrongs of repatriation', *Bangkok Post,* 1 March 1998). In the face of domestic political pressure, the government nonetheless remained adamant, claiming that once the foreign workers were deported, unemployed Thai nationals would be able to fill the job vacancies. The Thai media played a significant role in setting the public agenda concerning this issue. When the public debate on illegal immigrants was most intense, two nationally circulated newspapers – *The Nation* and the *Bangkok Post* – ran extensive coverage of the government's deportation plan.

By integrating a social and a cultural theoretical approach, this chapter attempts to demonstrate that the English-language Thai press produces news based on stereotypes and story lines that resonate with cultural myths about Burmese and Indo-Chinese. These mostly pro-nationalist story lines are based on themes and plots that have appeared throughout much of Thailand's history since the 1930s, when the Thai military elite came to power.

This study primarily employs a qualitative textual analysis of news and feature coverage of migrant workers appearing in *The Nation* and the *Bangkok Post* between January 1997 and July 1998 – one year before and six months after the Thai government's official announcement to deport illegal migrant workers. This period is important because it covers the timeframe that clearly illustrates the press's attitude toward migrant workers soon after the onset of the Asian economic crisis until after the Thai government's official announcement of the deportation. By analyzing how a specific news frame was used by the Thai press, this chapter attempts to outline the evolution of the news media's attitudes that in turn affected the manner in which the news was chronicled and meaning was made.

Conceptual frameworks

For the past half century, media scholars have attempted to answer two questions: 'What is news?' and 'Why does news appear as it does?' Different perspectives focus on various aspects of news and journalistic practices. Berkowitz (1997) suggests that there is no way that only one perspective can explain the entire nature of news and the process of news-making; each perspective reveals a different aspect of the same picture.

The notion that 'the world has to be *made to mean*' (Hall, 1982, p.67) raises questions about the role of the media as a centre for the process of meaning-making. Communication scholars firmly contend that communication media need to share a minimal quantum of mutual cultural and ideological values with their audience. Within a given political, economic, social and cultural milieu, the media work to create and reinforce specific images of the world that surround both themselves and their audience (Hardt, 1992, p.172).

Various approaches have addressed the question of why media coverage of news concerning subcultures, subordinated class groups and foreign nationalities tends to be more negative than positive. Lippmann's *Public opinion* (1922) provides a classic explanation of stereotypical and biased reporting in the media. Lippman believes that the media rely on certain stereotypes, based on their cultural and social values, to create a picture of the world to their audience. Meanwhile, the study of racism maintains that the media engage in 'institutionalized racism' by being prejudiced toward different races and portraying them as social deviants (Dates & Barlow, 1990; Entman, 1990, 1992; Lule, 1995; van Dijk, 1996). The political economy perspective argues that the media are used as propaganda tools 'to mobilize support for the special interests that dominate the state and private activity' (Herman & Chomsky, 1988, p.xi).

However, the social meaning of news frameworks can also be used to explain why the process of news production leads to a media bias against certain minorities, including women and homosexuals. Since news production is constrained by such factors as the journalists' knowledge about topics, timing, sources, budget constraints, and institutional ideology (Gans, 1979; Fishman, 1980; Tuchman, 1978), journalists tend to rely on certain patterns and themes to provide templates for new stories in order to accomplish their work within a limited time budget. Presenting news in the narrative form helps make journalists' work easier, since they often must produce many stories within a limited time frame; their storytelling skills help them meet deadlines (Colby & Peacock, 1973; Tuchman, 1978; Vincent, Crow & Davis, 1989; Berkowitz, 1997).

Social and cultural perspectives, or what Schudson (1991) calls a 'culturological' framework, are concerned with news as a human construct that evolves around the social and cultural worlds from which it emerges. Zelizer (1993) explains this work of journalism as interpretive community. She posits that journalists create community through discourse that grows out of informal talks and professional gatherings. Through the discourse, 'journalists create share interpretations that make their professional lives meaningful; that is, they use stories about the past to address dilemmas that present themselves while covering news' (Zelizer, 1993, p.85).

Berkowitz explains that 'when journalists typify an occurrence to expedite the reporting effort, they must decide on the general narrative structure that best applies' (1997, p.321). The main components of the narrative are based on the traditional who, what, where, why, how and when format (Vincent, Crow & Davis, 1989). Bennett and Edelman further note that popular plots require the identification of those who are 'virtuous, who are threats to the good life, and which courses of action are effective solutions' (1985, p.159).

Bird and Dardenne (1988) state that journalists, as members of a particular culture, are bound by a 'cultural grammar' (Colby, 1975) in framing the rules of the narrative construction. The narrative structures, therefore, are based on cultures and values shared by journalists and their audiences. Galtung and Ruge (1965) note that the mythical elements of news as derived from 'resonance' refer to the notion that readers read – and journalists write – the same stories over and over again. The principle of consonance ensures that events that may actually be different are encoded into frameworks that are already understood and familiar (Galtung & Ruge, 1965). The narrative, then, incorporates the past into the present (White, 1987), with news patterns giving them a 'skeleton on which to hang the flesh of the new story' (Bird & Dardenne, 1988, p.73).

Bird and Dardenne (1988) further find that most news accounts are reported as 'chronicles' of sequences of events or stories, rather than as individual stories. Referred to by Tuchman (1974) as 'the routinization of the unexpected', through the chronicle the overall structure of myth is emphasized while individual stories are not. In fact, the criteria for what should be chronicled changes over time. By tracing the changes in news chronicles, we can learn a great deal about a culture and its dominant values. Schudson (1989) further points out that journalists' views of their world are formed by the cultural frameworks in which they function.

In our relations with different social and cultural groups, group ideology and collective identity need to be clearly defined by answering such questions as: 'Who are we?', 'Where do we come from?', 'Who is included in our group?' and so on (van Dijk, 1998, p.121). Rivenburgh (1997) states that relations amongst different cultural groups can arouse feelings of national identity in the evaluative and competitive senses. According to Tajfel and Turner (1986), discriminatory conduct may occur merely because people are aware of the existence of an 'other'. For example, research that focuses on coverage of international news has shown that the media not only carefully select issues and stories, but also position and evaluate them in relation to the perspective of their governments' policy. 'Once selected for coverage, nations are not simply described, but often positioned vis-à-vis the home nation in cooperative (friend, ally) opposition (enemy, threat) or stratified (developing, admired) postures' (Rivenburgh, 1995, p.10). Other researchers find that the media tend to represent those with amiable/similar policies as 'us', adversarial/different as 'them' (Dahlgren with Chakrapani, 1982; Stevenson & Gaddy, 1994). Smith (1992) finds that historians often use symbolic representation of 'self' and 'others' as an instrument to 'construct' or 'invent' the sense of a nation, especially during periods of nationalism.

Journalism and historical narrative

Although there is a general assumption that news media in different cultures have different aims and emphases, Bird and Dardenne (1988) argue that writing news as a narrative is a skill learned and generally adopted by journalists to organize information more clearly and effectively. The journalists' use of the narrative as a means of shaping the social and cultural constructions of reality is also paralleled by the narrative methods that historians rely upon to construct a national history. Reynolds (1993) states that historians reconstruct the past by making stories out of chronicles, reducing the richness of history to a mere sequence of events. 'Histories that are particularly successful at conveying an explanation of the past do so because they tell a story that fits a sequence of historical events like a hand in a glove' (Reynolds, 1993, p.313).

White (1981) uses the term 'employment' to describe the process of selecting a story line to fit historical evidence, 'essentially a literary, that is to say fiction-making, operation' (White, 1985, p.85). Grossman (1978) also notes that nationalist historians believe that the use of employment as fiction-making is 'liberating'. 'It is a source of freedom, because it restores to human beings their role as makers of meaning' (Grossman, 1978, p. 33).

Bird and Dardenne (1988) assert that news is a particular kind of mythological narrative with its own symbolic codes that are easily recognized by the audience. 'We know when we read or hear a news story, that we are in a particular "narrative situation" (Barthes, 1982), that requires a particular kind of stance to be understood. News stories, like myths, do not "tell it like it is", but rather, "tell it like it means"' (Bird & Dardenne, 1988, p.71).

Myths, according to Hall (1984), must be constantly retold to be effective, with themes being rearticulated and reinterpreted over time. Stories, then, do not have to be recreated every time the need arises; instead, they are constantly derived from themes that already exist (Hall, 1984). Narratives are coauthored by those who tell stories and those who read them. Oschs (1998) states that how we think about ourselves and others is influenced by both the message content of jointly told narratives and the experience of working together to construct a coherent narrative.

Historical myths in the Thai context

In his study of the Thai media and foreign policy, Lewis (1996) finds that the official Thai view of foreign policy usually stresses its historical success by emphasizing that Thailand is the only Southeast Asian nation never to have been colonized by the West. This view holds that even though Thailand was a 'front line state' during the Vietnam War (according to the Domino Theory), it has managed to not only survive but to thrive in the world market economy. Many scholars also note that the Thai government has always closely linked its own national security – the preservation of national sovereignty and the promotion of national well-being – with that of its neighbours (Snitwongse & Paribatra, 1987; Neher, 1990; Buszynski, 1994; Lewis, 1996).

Varunpitikul and Tangwisutijit (1998) note that Thai officials often point out that, even though they have been sharing the region with a myriad of races for centuries, they have little knowledge of their own neighbours. Hence, prejudice in foreign policy results from allowing myths and stereotypes to dominate the view regarding neighbour's traditions and cultures.

Kasetsiri (1998) claims that the relationship between Thailand and its poorer neighbours is not based on mutual respect. In modern economic terms, Thais perceive their neighbours primarily as sources of cheap labour and natural resources, and markets for their products. In historical terms, Thais view Burmese and Vietnamese as threats. While the Burmese are thought of as national enemies because of the Burmese occupation of Thailand's Ayutthaya Kingdom (1569-1584 and 1767), the Vietnamese are seen as rivals in Thailand's effort to expand its territory into Laos and Cambodia. Thais also see Laotians and Cambodians as inferior. Between the mid-1800s and the early 1900s, Thailand's expansionist military took control over some parts of Laos and Cambodia, and today Thais generally believe that Laos and Cambodia are better off under Thai protection (Varunpitikul & Tangwisutiji, 1998).

Samudavanija (1991) states that the national identity of the Thai state was created in the late 1930s in an effort to legitimize the shift of power from a monarchy to military rule. Influenced by the rise of nationalist sentiment in Europe at the time, Thai military intellectuals construed a national history deliberately aimed at building a sense of national identity and unity (Reynolds, 1993). Despite the fact that the country has never been colonized by foreign powers, the historical narrative of the Thai state is built upon themes and plots of Thai leaders defending their homeland, warding off foreign aggression, expanding territories, and subjugating such 'inferior' neighbours as Vietnam, Laos, Cambodia and Burma (Tarling, 1998). The plot and meaning of the 'melodramatic past', says Winichakul, became a dominant paradigm of Thai historical discourse, 'making history an ideological weapon and a source of legitimation for the state' (Winichakul, 1995, p.100).

During the Cold War, the consensus in favour of maintaining unity in nation-states was at its height. After the 1950s, Burma, Vietnam, Laos and Cambodia had turned to communism and were receiving massive military support from the Soviet Union or China. In response to the perceived threat outlined by the Domino Theory, the Thai military government instituted a policy of anti-communist propaganda and repression. When anti-communist sentiment was at its peak, the Thai national media were used by the government to spread rumours about their communist neighbours' conspiracy against Thailand.

One rampant story, for example, told of Vietnamese magic potions that shrank penises and induced impotence in Thai men. The mysterious penis-shrinking additives were said to have been mixed in food sold in Vietnamese-owned restaurants in Thailand. National radio stations broadcast stories of blood-sucking vampires who kidnapped children in order to feed wounded communist guerrillas (Bowie, 1997) who were hiding themselves along the Thai-Laos-Cambodia borders. By describing these vampires as 'wearing indigo-dyed shirts, flip-flops, shoulder bags and significantly, eyeglasses', the government-sponsored popular movement exacerbated xenophobia and anti-communist sentiment that ultimately resulted in the massacre of students (who mostly dressed in the attire of the so-called vampires) at Thammasat University in October 1976 (Bowie, 1997).

The legacy of its deliberately constructed political history may make it difficult for Thailand to maintain an indifferent attitude toward its neighbours, despite the fact that communism in Eastern Europe has collapsed and Thailand's formerly communist neighbours have embraced capitalist economic systems. According to the official Thai view, Thailand remains a 'front-line' state, confronting perceived threats that come from political instability and economic poverty in neighbouring countries such as Burma and Indo-China (Lewis, 1996).

Methodology

Altheide (1996) explains that the study of theme and frame is used in ethnographic textual analysis to capture the emphasis and meaning of news created by the media. Altheide explains that frame, theme and discourse are related to the communication format of selection, organization and presentation of information (1996, p.29). By recognizing the format, researchers are able to recognize frames that give a general definition of what is before us.

Goffman (1974) believes that frame can be used as a schematic of interpretation that enables researchers to locate, perceive, identify, and label 'occurrences of information'. Further, the study of theme provides researchers with ideas that 'connect different semantic elements of a story into a coherent whole' (Pan & Kosicki, 1993). Lule also suggests that 'though press portrayals are complex and subject to multiple interpretations, textual analysis can be valuable in pointing out how stereotypical depictions are invoked through the language and conventions of the press' (Lule, 1995, p.177).

In the examination of how the English-language Thai press frames news coverage of migrant workers, three questions are addressed:

1. What are the predominant themes that appear in the Thai press concerning migrant workers from Burma and Indo-Chinese countries?
2. Do these themes explain news narratives found in the Thai newspapers?
3. Do these themes reflect the common myths about foreign neighbours that are perpetuated in Thai history?

For a number of reasons, two English-language newspapers – the *Bangkok Post* and *The Nation* – were chosen for this research. First, the two newspapers provide daily on-line publications that can be easily accessed through the Internet. Second, the two newspapers are mostly read by the Thai elites and policy-makers even though their circulation of both newspapers is not large – approximately 50,000 for *The Nation* and 60,000 for the *Bangkok Post* (Eng, 1997). A total of 40 news articles and editorial commentaries that appeared during the studied period were examined to see how these two influential newspapers presented the picture of migrant workers during the economic crisis.

Findings

Migrant workers: A perceived threat to national security

Migrant workers are often depicted by the English-language Thai press as criminals, social deviants, job stealers, and diseased predators who pose a distinct threat to Thailand's national security. The Thai authorities are said to have their hands tied because of concerns regarding relations with other countries and human rights violations.

Evidently, the dominant image that Thais see of their neighbours through the media's lens is almost exclusively that of the threat that these neighbours pose to the national security and economic well-being of Thailand. In *The Nation* (14 April 1997) a police chief stated that the presence of illegal immigrants in Thailand posed a threat to national security and had given rise to social problems because they were 'part of criminal gangs and a major source of new diseases'. According to the police chief, the police department was too short of funding to be able to crack down on the illegal entry of foreign labourers due to the increasing cost of detaining them. On 28 May 1997 *The Nation* echoed this negative theme by quoting an academician who warned that the huge number of Burmese immigrants posed a 'big threat to Thailand's national security concerning crime, sociopolitics, economics, health care, and foreign policy'.

The *Bangkok Post* on 13 July 1997 presented a feature on the increasing flow of foreign workers seeking jobs in Thailand as being at the root of problems associated with 'human smuggling' activities, narcotics and other illicit goods. This 'has given the Thai government a headache', and any attempt to solve these problems would 'become a continuing war', said the

Bangkok Post. 'Our major task now is smashing the gangs', reported the *Bangkok Post* in the same issue.

Both of these publications repeatedly presented stories in which all foreign workers from neighbouring countries were depicted as being plagued with various diseases. For example, the *Bangkok Post* issue of 9 December 1996 discussed the practice of testing migrant workers for HIV. Under the same theme, *The Nation* (27 April 1997) had a bold headline claiming: 'Disease still rampant with influx of migrants'. The story began with a lead paragraph that used an accusing tone regarding migrants bringing various diseases into Thailand, despite the Thai government's hard efforts to curb infectious disease such as AIDS, malaria, tuberculosis, syphilis, elephantiasis and leprosy.

According to the *Bangkok Post* (1 March 1998), medical expenses for illegal immigrants were estimated to be as high as 100 million baht (roughly US$3 million) a year. Further, migrant workers from poorer countries were said to have entered Thailand for the primary purpose of taking advantage of medical resources that are provided for Thai nationals. The reporter quoted a high-ranking public health official: 'Say we have 100 beds in a hospital, 60 beds might be taken up by Burmese immigrants. It is a dilemma because if we do not treat these people, they might spread new strains of diseases to Thais. But if we spend our resources on them, the locals will complain.'

Foreign workers were also associated with increasing crime rates in cities with large numbers of migrant workers. On 13 January 1998, *The Nation* interviewed a metropolitan police chief concerning the increased rate of criminal activity resulting from the economic slump. The police chief was quoted as saying 'This [illegal immigrants who commit crimes] is a very big problem for us alone to deal with . . . There are many types of illegal immigrants. Some come to commit crimes directly in this country, and some use Thailand as a gateway to other countries. Nonetheless, they either directly or indirectly cause a rise in illegal activities. These criminals are often violent, as has been shown in cases involving business disagreements, killings, and the mutilation of the corpses . . .' The increase in criminal activities, according to the police chief, was indirectly caused by the fact that 'immigrants take away jobs which would otherwise have gone to Thais, resulting in a rise in unemployment'.

The *Bangkok Post*'s report on 1 March 1998 wrote that Thais had not been getting along well with illegal immigrants and saw them as 'bad people' who instigated social unrest and street fights. Another article appearing in the *Bangkok Post* on 1 March 1998 raised concerns regarding the export of capital earned by foreign workers who repatriated a large portion of their salaries to the family that remained in their home country. 'The outflow is huge', the *Bangkok Post* quoted a source in a commercial bank as saying. On 23 August, 1997, *The Nation* reported on a call by the Employers' Association to lay off alien workers because it would 'help heal the country's ailing economy'. The same article also echoed a 'suggestion that the government speedily launch a program to push out foreign workers'.

Before the deportation plan was announced in early 1998, *The Nation* portrayed problems perceived to have been caused by foreign workers as being a permanent threat. On 5 May 1997, the newspaper reported on a labour policy seminar in Thailand that criticized the government's decision to grant permission to a number of foreign nationals to work in the country as a hasty and risky decision. According to the press, the government had not thoroughly investigated whether the country faced a serious labour shortage. In the same report, the government was said to have legalized foreign labour 'merely to serve the interests of a small group of selfish employers who wanted to exploit illegal cheap workers to boost products from their labour-intensive, export-oriented industries'. The uncontrolled number of foreign labourers, said *The Nation* on 26 March 1997, 'could pose a threat to national security'. That threat, repeated *The Nation* on 4 April 1997, was due to the influx of migrant workers that rose to 'unmanageable levels'. Therefore, the report stated, it might be impossible to solve the problems.

The migrant worker as exploited victim

In contrast to the primary theme of migrant workers who posed a threat to the nation, a secondary theme in the Thai press depicts migrant workers as being victims or as being weak. On 19 February 1998, *The Nation* compared migrant workers to flies that could be 'swatted' at any time by Thai authorities. 'They are easily hidden or ignored when times are good', and 'easily disposed of when thing turns sour'.

On 1 March 1998, the *Bangkok Post* ran an extensive feature questioning the 'Rights and wrongs of repatriation'. The story questioned the morality of the Thai government in deporting migrant workers to their home country. A 'typical' illegal worker was portrayed as being 'obedient', 'hard working', and 'reliable'. According to the same report, most of these people, unprotected by Thai law, were abused by unscrupulous Thai businesses that paid wages lower than the legal minimum wage. 'Those who [are] sick simply leave or die', said the *Bangkok Post*.

The Nation's editorial on 8 April 1998 echoed the same theme found in the *Bangkok Post*. The article told its readers that migrant workers were 'victims to the worst kind of abuses – low pay, horrendous working conditions, unsanitary living quarters, seizure of their travel documents, sexual assault especially for those working as domestic helpers, and those duped into the sex industry. Some never make it home. Again, *The Nation* questioned the government's repatriation policy by arguing that these foreign workers were merely victims of the economic crisis in Southeast Asian countries. These 'workhorses', said *The Nation*, 'are made convenient scapegoats, rounded up and deported'.

On 1 June 1998, the *Bangkok Post* quoted a labour expert who claimed that 'Thai authorities [are] too critical of alien workers. They [are] regarded as criminals or separatists who wanted to destroy the country, rather than victims of the economic downturn.' Also on 31 July 1998, the *Bangkok Post* pointed out that the Thai government's policy of repatriating migrant workers who had contracted HIV/AIDS was inhumane. The report quoted a non-governmental organization as saying 'deporting a person living with HIV to a country where treatment doesn't exist means condemning that person to a death sentence'.

In addition to being portrayed as victims of the Thai system, migrant workers were further depicted as being unwanted by their own country. On 16 January 1998, *The Nation* cited an army general who said 'it is urgent they [migrant workers] be deported because they could pose short and long-term problems for us, particularly where security is concerned. Deport first and discuss later. Deportation is not an easy job, we could be criticized of not being aware of human rights.' In the same article, a high-ranking national security official expressed doubt about whether the country of origin of the migrant workers would take their own citizens back. The story implied that the unfortunate migrant workers were caught in a hopeless situation. Hence, the migrant workers could be better off under Thai protection.

Discussion and implications

In the analysis of the press coverage of migrant workers, two dominant and conflicting themes emerge. While one evolves around stories of migrant workers being threats to national security, the other portrays them as victims of the Thai government's political expediency. The findings support the hypothesis that the Thai press uses certain patterns to report stories about foreign neighbours. Whether consciously or not, the press compresses the more complicated issues concerning illegal immigrant workers in Thailand by compiling them into two superficial and uncomplicated themes – threat versus victim.

These two themes, repeated over and over again throughout the studied period of more than one year, are drawn mainly from the Thai government's views of foreign neighbours and the mytho-historical relationship between Thailand and its neighbours. Since the stories are reported in chronicle form, readers can easily recognize and assimilate the symbolic codes, mythic structures, themes and plots that are used in the reports.

First, by framing the theme of 'threat', the press fills in minor details such as the migrant workers' threat to public health, economic well-being, crime and social disorder. All of these problems are linked to national security concerns and appear to justify the government's repatriation plan. The second picture of migrant workers is framed to show that migrant workers are weak, unfortunate, and helpless victims. In this case, the English-language Thai press appeared to rely heavily on official sources, reflecting historically patronizing Thai attitudes toward their foreign neighbours. By following these two dominant themes, this author will argue that the English-language Thai newspapers generally ignore the more complicated socioeconomic and political causes of labour migration, unequal development pace in Southeast Asia, and Thailand's domestic political conditions that are linked to migrant labour. Other humanistic elements concerning migrant workers are also overlooked. Not all migrant workers are 'weak' and 'obedient' victims, and it is also doubtful that they are the main cause for rising crime rates and social unrest in Thailand.

According to the sociological approach, the use of the news narrative by English-language Thai journalists can be learned by socializing within and among media organizations. Also, as stated previously, journalists tend to rely on certain patterns and themes as templates for new stories in order to accomplish their work within a limited time. By presenting news in the narrative form, the journalist is able to produce more stories in a shorter timeframe; their storytelling skills also help them meet deadlines. Indeed, the English-language Thai press's utilizing of the mythological narratives to make the meaning of news might be a subconscious one, perhaps with the need to 'humanize' and 'sensationalize' events to attract a larger readership. Yet, the press's reproduction of certain images of foreign nationals is problematic.

References

Altheide, D. (1996) *Qualitative media analysis.* Thousand Oaks: Sage.

Barthes, R. (1982) 'Introduction to the structural analysis of narratives' in Sontag, S. (ed.) *Barthes: Selected writings.* London: Fontana-Collins, pp.251-295.

Bennett, W. & Edelman, M. (1985) 'Toward a new political narrative', *Journal of Communication*, 35, pp.156-171.

Berkowitz, D. (1997) (ed.) *Social meanings of news.* Newbury Park, California: Sage.

Bird, E. S. & Dardenne, R. (1988) 'Myth, chronicle, and story: exploring the narrative qualities of news' in Carey, James (ed.), *Media, myths and narratives: television and the press.* California: Sage, pp.67-86.

Bowie, K. (1997) *Rituals of national loyalty: An anthropology of the state and village Scout Movement in Thailand.* New York: Columbia University Press.

Buszynki, L. (1994) 'Thailand foreign policy', *Asian Survey*, 39 (8), pp.721-737.

Colby, B. N. (1975) 'Cultural grammars', *Science*, 187, pp.913-919.

Colby, N. & Peacock, L. (1973) 'Narrative', in Honigman, J.J. (ed.) *Handbook of social and cultural anthropology.* Chicago: Rand McNally, pp.613-636.

Dahlgren, P. with Chakrapani, S. (1982) 'The Third World on TV news: Western ways of seeing the "other", ' in Adams, W. (ed.) *Television coverage of international affairs.* Norwood: Ablex, pp.45-63.

Dates, J. & Barlow, W. (1990) *Split image: African American in the mass media.* Washington, D.C: Howard University Press.

Eng, P. (1997) 'Media rising', *Columbia Journalism Review*, May/June, p.20.

Entman, R. M. (1990) 'Modern racism and the images of blacks in local television news', *Critical Studies in Mass Communication*, 7 (4), pp.332-345.

Entman, R. M. (1992) 'Blacks in the news: Television, modern racism and cultural change', *Journalism Quarterly*, 69 (2), pp. 341-361.

Fisher, W. R. (1985) 'The narrative paradigm: In the beginning', *Journal of Communication,* 35, pp.74-89.

Fishman, M. (1980) *Manufacturing the news.* Austin: University of Texas Press.

Galtung, J. & Ruge, M. (1965) 'The structure of foreign news'. *Journal of Peace Research*, 2, pp.64-91.

Gans, H. (1979) *Deciding what's news: A study of CBS evening news, NBC nightly news, Newsweek and Time.* New York: Pantheon.

Goffman, E. (1974) *Frame analysis.* New York: Harper and Row.

Grossman, L. (1978) 'History and literature' in Canary, R. & Kozicki, H. (eds) *The writing of history, literary form and historical understanding.* Madison: University of Wisconsin Press, pp.3-39.

Hall, S. (1982) 'The rediscovery of "ideology": Return of the repressed in media studies', in Gurevitch, M., Bennett, T., Curran, J. & Woollacott, J. (eds) *Culture, society and the media.* London: Methuen, pp.56-90.

Hall, S. (1984) 'The narrative construction of reality: An interview with Stuart Hall', *Southern Review*, 17 (1), pp.3-17.

Hardt, H. (1992). *Critical communication studies: communication, history and theory in America.* London/New York: Routledge.

Herman, S. & Chomsky, N. (1988) *Manufacturing consent.* New York: Pantheon.

Kasetsiri, C. (1998) an interview in Varunpitikul, Y. & Tangwisutijit, N. 'TRF-sponsored project dispel myth', *The Nation*, 22, August.

Lewis, G. (1996) 'Communications regionalization and internationalization in Thailand', *Journal of International Communication*, 3 (2), pp.7-18.

Lippman, W. (1922) *Public opinion.* New York: Simon & Schuster.

Lule, J. (1995) 'The rape of Mike Tyson', *Critical Studies in Mass Communication*, 12, p.176-195.

Oschs, E. (1998) 'Narrative', in van Dijk T.A.(ed.) *Discourse as structure and process.* London: Sage, pp.185-207.

Neher, C. (1990) 'The foreign policy of Thailand' in Wurfel, D. & Burton, B. (eds) *The political economy of foreign policy in Southeast Asia.* London: Macmillan.

Pan, Z. & Kosicki, G. M. (1993) 'Framing analysis: An approach to news discourse', *Political Communication*, 10, pp.55-75.

Reynolds, C. (1993) 'The plot of Thai history: Theory and practice', in Wijeyewardene, G. & Chapman, E. C. (eds) *Patterns and illusions: Thai history and thought.* Singapore: Institute of Southeast Asian Studies. pp.310-330.

Reynolds, C. (1998) 'Globalization and cultural nationalism in modern Thailand' in Kahn, J. (ed.) *Southeast Asian identities: culture and the politics of representation in Indonesia, Malaysia, Singapore and Thailand.* Singapore: Institute of Southeast Asian Studies, pp.115-145.

Rivenburgh, N. (1995) 'Images of others: The presentation of nations in the 1992 Barcelona Olympics', *Journal of International Communication*, 2 (1), pp.6-25.

Rivenburgh, N. (1997) 'Social identification and media coverage of foreign relations' in Malek, A. (ed.) *News media and foreign relations.* Norwood: Ablex.

Samudavanija, C. (1991) 'State identity creation, state building and civil society' in Reynolds, C. (ed.) *National identity and its defenders: Thailand, 1939-1989.* Monash University, Australia: Center of Southeast Asian Studies.

Schudson, M. (1989) 'What is a reporter?' The private face of public journalism' in Carey, J. W. (ed.) *Media, myths, and narratives: Television and the press.* Newbury Park, CA: Sage, pp.228-245.

Schudson, M. (1991) 'The sociology of news production revisited' in Curran, J. & Gurevitch, M. (eds) *Mass media and society.* London: Edward Arnold.

Smith, A. (1992) 'Nationalism and the historians' in Smith, A. (ed.) *Ethnicity and nationalism.* New York: E.J. Brill, pp.58-80.

Snitwongse K. & Paribatra S. (1987) *Durable stability in Southeast Asia.* Institute of Southeast Asian Studies: Singapore.

Stevenson, R. & Gaddy, G. (1984) 'Bad news and the Third World' in Stevenson, R. & Shaw, D. (eds) *Foreign news and the new world information order.* Ames: Iowa State University Press.

Tajfel, H. & Turner, J. (1986) 'The social identity theory of intergroup behavior' in Worchel, S. & Austin, W. (eds) *Psychology of intergroup relations.* Chicago: Nelson-Hall.

Tarling, N. (1998) *Nations and states in Southeast Asia.* Cambridge: Cambridge University Press.

Tuchman, G. (1974) 'Assembling a network talk-show' in Tuchman, G. (ed.) *The TV establishment programming for power and profit.* Englewood Cliffs, New Jersey: Prentice Hall.

Tuchman, G. (1978) 'Television news and the metaphor of myth', *Studies in the Anthropology of Visual Communication,* 5 (Fall), pp.56-62.

van Dijk, T. A. (1996) 'Discourse, power and access' in Caldas-Coulthard, C. R. & Coulthard, M. (eds) *Texts and practices: Readings in critical discourse analysis.* London: Routledge, pp.84-104.

van Dijk T. A. (1998) *Ideology: A multidisciplinary approach.* Thousand Oaks, California: Sage.

Varunpitikul, Y. & Tangwisutijit, N. (1998) 'TRF-sponsored project dispels myth', *The Nation,* 22 August.

Vincent, R., Crow, B. & Davis, D. (1989) 'When technology fails', *Journalism Monographs,* 117, pp.1-6, 21-26.

White, H. (1981) 'The value of narrativity in the representation of reality' in Mitchell, W. (ed.) *On narrative.* Chicago: Chicago University Press.

White, H. (1985) *Topics of discourse: Essays in cultural criticism.* Baltimore/London: The

Johns Hopkins University Press.

White, H. (1987) *The content of the form: Narrative discourse and historical representation.* Baltimore/London: The Johns Hopkins University Press.

Winichakul, T. (1995) 'The changing landscape of the past: New histories of Thailand since 1973', *Journal of Southeast Asian Studies*, 26 (March), pp.99-120.

Zelizer, B. (1993). 'Has communication explain journalism', *Journal of Communication*, 43 (4), pp.80-88.

Newspaper articles

'Over 1,000 illegals nabbed in immigration crackdown', *The Nation*, 1 January 1997.
'Getting through the back door', *Bangkok Post*, 9 March 1997.
'Illegal immigrants targeted', *The Nation*, 26 March 1997.
'White-collar layoffs loom', *The Nation*, 29 March 1997.
'Official vows to crack down on illegal aliens', *The Nation*, 1 April 1997.
'Diseases still rampant with influx of migrants', *The Nation*, 27 April 1997.
'Research agency sees benefits from foreigners', *The Nation*, 27 April 1997.
'Academics flay govt.' alien policy', *The Nation*, 27 May 1997.
'Warning sounded over illegal foreign workers', *The Nation*, 27 May 1997.
'Repressive Slorc rule blamed for Burmese influx', *The Nation*, 28 May 1997.
'Labour chief attacks policy', *The Nation*, 8 July 1997.
'War against flesh smuggling gangs', *Bangkok Post*, 13 July 1997.
'Employers want foreign workers to lose their jobs', *The Nation*, 23 August 1997.
'New holding centers sought for Burmese', *Bangkok Post*, 31 October 1997.
'Alien workers held in raid on factory', *Bangkok Post*, 1 November 1997.
'Human trafficking on rise in region', *The Nation*, 11 November 1997.
'Fishing maybe lifeline', *The Nation*, 10 December 1997.
'Police chief foresees hard year for force', *The Nation*, 13 January 1998.
'Thailand to deport 300,000 illegals', *The Nation*, 16 January 1998.
'At the bottom of economic barrel', *The Nation*, 19 February 1998.
'Mae Sot in dilemma over deportation', *Bangkok Post*, 1 March 1998.
'Rights and wrongs of repatriation', *Bangkok Post*, 1 March 1998.
'Immigrants can bring powerful influences', *The Nation*, 12 March 1998.
'Ouster of Burmese "impossible", ' *Bangkok Post*, 15 March 1998.
'Illegals seek edge over poverty', *Bangkok Post*, 31 March 1998.
'Alien workers find El Dorado no city of gold', *The Nation*, 20 April 1998.
'Reprieve from illegal labour purge pain', *The Nation*, 30 April 1998.
'Businesses protest huge crackdown on aliens', *Bangkok Post*, 1 June 1998.
'Rice labourers fear repatriation', *The Nation*, 3 July 1998.
'Rice mills close in protest over alien worker crackdown', *The Nation*, 3 July 1998.

'Final decision on illegal labour pending', *The Nation*, 4 July 1998.
'Shift in policy on alien staff hinted at', *The Nation*, 5 July 1998.
'Rice millers press govt on alien workers', *The Nation*, 6 July 1998.
'Trairong's labour plan backfires', *The Nation*, 7 July 1998.
'Rice millers agree to resume operations', *The Nation*, 7 July 1998.
'Rice millers ask for leniency', *The Nation*, 8 July 1998.
'Two agencies to study issue of alien workers', *The Nation*, 11 July 1998.
'Govt committee eases ban on illegal workers', *The Nation*, 16 July 1998.
'Illegal immigrants found with diseases on list face deportation', *Bangkok Post*, 31 July 1998.
'Crackdown on alien workers', *The Nation*, 31 July 1998.

Thailand in the
International Herald Tribune:
A content analysis

Jan Servaes & Patchanee Malikhao

Introduction

This chapter deals with the media coverage on Thailand of the international daily newspaper *International Herald Tribune* (international edition, Paris, France). It is primarily based on a seven-month content analysis undertaken by the authors from April to October 1998. The objective of the study is to determine how much (quantity) and what kinds of news (quality) are reported (and how they are reported) about Thailand during the study period.

A four-stage content analysis methodology was utilized, as follows:

Stage 1: Literature review on related research projects and theoretical perspectives.

Stage 2: Compilation of news reports, inclusive of listing, classification and determination of typology; 59 news items were listed and classified.

Stage 3: In-depth analysis, including a qualitative analysis.

Stage 4: Drafting of final report.

The main objective of the study was to determine how much (quantity) and what kind (quality) of news on Thailand is reported in the *International Herald Tribune* (*IHT*) within the specified time period. Research questions posed in this study were:

1. Who were the personalities highlighted?
2. What were the major events covered by the *IHT* and how were they treated?
3. What stories were published in the front pages?
4. What were the types of news published?
5. What were the sources for news in Europe?
6. From which cities/places did the news originate?
7. Which topics got highlighted or emphasized by illustrations or cartoons to attract special attention?
8. Are the news stories covered from a positive, negative or neutral perspective?

There were 59 news items listed in the *IHT* coverage on Thailand. Most of the items can be classified as 'economic' news issues (including business, financial and labour news stories).

The hypothesis that the interest which the *IHT* attached to Thailand would be dependent on the proximity or involvement regarding the country was found correct. However, 'proximity' is not only a geographical criterion; proximity or involvement has to be assessed in a combined fashion with political, economic, cultural and social rationales which define the attitude of a nation and its press concerning the subject under study. This hypothesis can be considered to be correct not only for the *IHT* in general; also the attitude of the *IHT* in particular cases seems to be nourished by specific political, socio-psychological and economic motives.

Major events reported in the *IHT* were:

- Financial and economic measures taken by the Thai government to comply with International Monetaary Fund (IMF) conditions (more than 50 percent of all the stories)
- Mr Clean (Seri Temiyavej), a Thai policeman, leads fight against corrupt politics
- Changes within Thai political and banking system
- Thailand's unemployment figures on the increase
- Financial news on specific Thai companies
- Reshuffling of the Cabinet
- Religious leaders speak out
- Trafficking in children
- The fluctuations of the Thai baht
- The Thai crisis in the Asian economic context
- Thai international relations.

Worth mentioning is also the full-colour full-page advertisement for the 'Amazing Thailand' tourism promotion campaign.

Our findings show that the *IHT* covered Thailand from a US nationalistic, and to some extend, also 'ethnocentric' perspective. More than half of the articles are of an economic or financial nature. Most often the writer attempts to assess the impact of the Thai economic crisis from a US or international perspective. Therefore, a second general conclusion can be that the broad political framework in which the newspaper covered Thailand was the dependency axis. This dependency axis has two major components: on the one hand stories which assess the changes which may occur on a geo-strategic and political-economic level; on the other hand the 'domino effect' of the Thai economic crisis on other neighbouring countries (especially the Association of South East Asian Nations [ASEAN]) or the world at large. Almost exclusively these stories were assessing the consequences of this dependency axis from a western (mainly US) perspective in general. Consequently, it is noteworthy that the *IHT* leaves the Thai perspective largely under-illuminated. Few or no examples of a comprehensive Asian perspective have been found.

The so-called news values, which form the 'structure' of the news product, have also been confirmed in this analysis. Values of composition and continuity, of elite nations and personality treatment, of negative reporting and human interest stories, etc, were identified.

In sum, the *IHT* covers Thai issues from its own political, economic and strategic interest points. The starting or reference point is somebody or something from the newspaper's 'homefront'.

Theoretical framework

It will be useful at the outset to state what this chapter is and is not trying to accomplish, and to specify the premises on which it builds.

The basic idea is that the production of news is influenced generally by the political, economic and cultural systems, as well as by the actual situation, in which the production and transmission of information takes place.

Firstly, we claim that news may never be considered as only a series of facts or a window through which we look at the external world: 'Rather it is a cultural product and the accounts and description of the world which it gives are produced from within a specific interpretative framework' (Glasgow University Media Group, 1980, p.3). Therefore, a fundamental question is whether 'misrepresentations' are the result of the *structure and culture* in which news (or media content in general) is produced (and therefore, of an unintended nature), or more intentionally aimed to distort and sometimes falsify reality.

Secondly, news is an *organizational product*, generated by routine occupational practices in an institutional setting with specific performance demands and limits of time and resources. These organizational and institutional factors also shape the structure in which news is being produced (Brown, 1995).

Thirdly, news is *manufactured by journalists* who – often unconsciously – select and interpret a number of facts, based on an 'unclear vision on society'. Hence Golding and Middleton (1982, p.112) correctly state that 'we should never forget that news production, like all other social activities, involves real people doing real jobs about which they are able to reflect and over whose content they have considerable autonomy'. Our task as sociologists or communication researchers is to discover and to explain the limitations of that autonomy.

Therefore, we perceive *news* as the result of combined action based on institutionally determined and collectively made choices under the current economic, political and cultural interest constellations (further elaborated upon in Servaes & Tonnaer, 1991).

News production has a lot in common with other social practices which are carried out on a routine basis in a formalized institutional context. It is at this point that the concept of *professionalisation* comes into play. On the one hand journalists and media workers in general use a specific paradigm of reality to cover recent events in the world; on the other hand professionalism also provides newsmakers with a set of 'implicit' practices of production routines. In other words, professionalism offers journalists 'a legitimate (and legitimating) way of seeing the world as well as practical frameworks which stipulate how to assemble stories to report on perceived happenings' (Dahlgren, 1984, p.6). In addition, professionalism not only gives a handhold to newsmakers, it also contributes to the general perceptions about news for the public at large.

In our opinion the news production process contributes to the *societal ideation process*. We mean by that the manner in which not only the rational or cognitive, but also the irrational or intuitive elements of knowledge, ideas and information are passed on. In this case ideation is not only to be seen as a distribution of specific facts or events but rather as a generalized angle of vision on social reality with strong affective and subjective components. Thus Davis and Walton (1983), in their analysis of the 'Aldo Moro story', found that the visual and verbal content of the news about the death of the murdered Italian Christian-democrat more distinctly stated how the media contribute to the preservation of an ideological consensus rather than how this can be studied by a research of the 'events' which constitute the news: 'There is a universally assumed consensus (in western media) within which, with some cross-cultural variation, to complex causes and impact of armed opposition and revolutionary violence are reduced by the inferential frameworks of "law and (dis)order", the "violent society", the threat to democracy, and international terror, to a simple picture of a temporary and unprovoked outbreak of irrational violence in an otherwise ordered and peaceful society' (Davis & Walton, p.48). An analysis of the international news coverage about the assassination of Lebanese president-elect Beshir Gemayel arrives at the same kind of observations. It concludes that there are two major factors, closely interrelated, that determine the content, format and style of international news: an 'international consensus of implicit news structure rules' and the role of the international news agencies (van Dijk, 1984).

One classic study on the 'implicit news structure rules' was published in 1965 by Johan Galtung and Mari Holmboe Ruge of the Peace Research Institute in Oslo. Their study on 'The structure of foreign news' (1965) analyzed how the Congo, Cuba and Cyprus crises of the early 1960s had been reported in four newspapers in the Norwegian capital. They found that the vast majority of 'spot news' items originated from a very limited number of international news agencies. They also identified a dozen *factors* that seemed to mark an event as newsworthy:

1. the time-span needed for an event to unfold itself and acquire meaning
2. the scale and intensity of an event (both in absolute and in relative terms)
3. the clarity of an event
4. the meaningfulness (meaning both 'cultural proximity' and relevance)
5. the consonance
6. unexpectedness
7. continuity, and
8. composition (balance) of the available news.

These eight news values were considered to be of a general or 'universal' nature. Four additional news values were culture-specific:

9.   elite nations and
10. elite persons
11. personification and
12. negativity in the news.

Galtung and Ruge formulated a number of hypotheses concerning the interrelationships of these news values. The hypotheses of *selection* ('the more events satisfy the criteria mentioned, the more likely that they will be registered as news'), of *distortion* ('Once a news item has been selected what makes it newsworthy according to the factors will be accentuated'), and of *replication* ('both the process of selection and the process of distortion will take place at all steps in the chain from event to reader') have been tested by several researchers since (for an elaboration and overview, see Boone & Servaes, 1982; McQuail, 1994; Mowlana, 1997).

With such a vision on news production, we try to exceed the traditional research approaches on news production. This kind of research mainly deals with 'transmission problems', i.e. questions concerning the 'selection' (how does the news selection happen on the basis of a mass of events?), the 'translation' (how do events become news?), the 'control' (how are journalists checked?), the 'choice' (how objective, comprehensive or newsworthy is the news?) and the 'effect' (how much or what does the public understand of the news?)

This kind of research certainly is useful if one wishes to study the 'rationalistic' issues of news. Nevertheless, the impact of news may well lie behind this rationalistic dimension and may well be of a more fundamental subjective dimension from a rather *ideological or mythical* nature. According to Roland Barthes, 'A myth has a double function: it points out and it notifies, it makes us understand something and it imposes it on us'. Joseph Campbell (1988, p.10) adds: 'A dream is a personal myth; a myth is the public dream of a society'. Myths are generally expressed through the narrative form of storytelling. Myths are human phenomena (creations of the human mind and spirit); at the same time they are cultural phenomena (they effectively organize the way we, as a group, view portions of our world).

One fundamental premise in this approach is that 'national cultures are structured around myths which explain the origins of the particular national grouping, their specific national identities and their concepts of national destiny. Such national mythologies seek a grounding in broader cosmic myths, and thus gain a sacred, timeless character. Myths function more at the unintentional, symbol level, defining that which a national society is trying to become. Mythological functions are likely to be especially strong at times of national crisis, rapid change or external threat' (White, 1985, pp.19-20). In our opinion the invasion of Grenada in February 1982 was such a period wherein myths are strongly emphasized (see Servaes &

Drijvers, 1986; Servaes, 1991). The handover of Hong Kong by Britain to China was another opportunity for such a study (see Servaes & Malikhao, 1997; Ramanathan & Servaes, 1997).

From what precedes it should be clear that we wish to state the thesis that *'news is a myth-maker'*. Dahlgren (1984) suggests that the mythic domain of (TV) news performs four basic operations on a regular basis:

1. It establishes and concretizes the social order as part of our cognition.
2. It legitimates and celebrates the basic and dominant structures, functions and leadership of the social order.
3. It serves to explain and interpret that which transpires which is of relevance for the social order.
4. For the viewer or media consumers in general, it integrates and implicates, and evokes identification and loyalty to the social order.

These observations should not lead to the conclusion that the mythic denies or camouflages social tensions. On the contrary, tensions are brought out and are part of the social order's dynamics. 'The point is, however, that they are rendered safe for the social order as a whole: the boundaries and limits of the issues, their significance, the stakes involved, the array of perceived and reasonable options, etc. are presented, interpreted and (usually) resolved such that the contours of the social order remains intact' (Dahlgren, 1984, p.77).

In other words, *news is one of the ideological clockworks by which mythical themes are transmitted.* The 'message' of the myth – and what this myth means and does in a certain culture or national context – is not only framed in its patent content, but also in its structure.

Research design and methodology

How then can this mythic domain of ideation be studied in the news coverage of Thailand in the *IHT*. Referring to our above definition of news, and starting from the assumption that there is a basic coherence and logic to the domain of the mythic, which runs 'parallel' to the informative dimensions of news, we would argue that the subliminal mode of ideation is operating under circumstances which are of a *discursive* ('content'), *technical* ('medium') and *contextual or societal* nature.

The fundamental issue hereby is: *how can this be studied methodically?*

The outlining of a new study methodology is an activity which more often than not comes about with trial and error. Furthermore, this kind of research cannot be carried out but in an interdisciplinary fashion. One of the fundamental problems, however, is 'how to combine a variety of methodologies in the same research design so that these mutually reinforce and complement each other' (White, 1985, p.23). Nevertheless, that is precisely what we have been trying to accomplish by combining normally separately used research methodologies, i.e. the quantitative and qualitative content analysis.

For our research we selected a so-called 'quality newspaper', namely the *IHT*. Some general data on the *IHT* (international edition) are as follows.

General data on the International Herald Tribune
(International Edition)

Language:	English
Primary range of distribution:	Europe
Kind of publication:	Newspaper
Periodicity:	Daily (except on Sundays)
Circulation:	192,195 per day (67% is distributed in Europe) (1995)
Ideology/ target groups: global	Perspective; focus on main international developments; 80% of the readers is male and age between 40 and 50 years; 92% of its readers have a university degree; 40% speak at least four languages
History:	The paper was established in 1887 in Paris as the European edition of *The New York Herald*. It was the world's first real international newspaper.

Though headquartered in Paris, France, the 'home-base' of the *IHT* can be considered 'international with US roots'. The *IHT* has an editorial agreement to publish articles and commentaries with *The New York Times* and *The Washington Post*, two US-based elite papers. Usually elite papers give much more attention to foreign and feature news than other dailies do. They also have a network of correspondents. Hence one may suppose that the *IHT* is less dependent on the structurally determined news supply, which is in the hands of the world news agencies. To this may be added that the *IHT's* coverage of foreign events is at least quantitatively big enough to speak of a policy in this matter. On the other hand the so-called myths are, unlike in the popular mass newspapers, less explicitly perceivable in the coverage of quality newspapers and hence more difficult to detect.

A four-stage content analysis methodology was utilized, as follows:

Stage 1: Literature review on related research projects and theoretical perspectives.

Stage 2: Compilation of news reports, inclusive of listing, classification and determination of typology; 59 news items were listed and classified.

Stage 3: In-depth analysis, including a qualitative analysis.

Stage 4: Drafting of final report.

We did not take the usually used constructed week/weeks-period as the *time-unit* for our research design. We decided to study the coverage on Thailand from 1 April to 31 October 1998. This seven-month period can be considered representative. No major Thai events occurred, with the exception of the first anniversary of the devaluation of the Thai baht on 2 July 1997.

As a study method we opted for a *subject or theme-analysis* instead of a classic content analysis. Beardsworth (1980) elaborates on both analysis methods. He notes that each study method carries distinct purposes and limitations in it. The research-design of a theme-analysis is more of an explorative than a hypotheses-testing nature. A certain number of significant indices, frequencies and data are searched for, explained and interpreted. On the other hand, in a content analysis one tries to test the available facts by comparing them to preliminary formulated hypotheses. The choice and definition of the variables (e.g. date, item, dateline, source, type of item, subject, headline direction etc) are very important. They have to be as precise as possible, and certain categories have to be enlarged during the study, others to be narrowed. It is very important that the different coders are attuned to each other (there were two coders for this project, i.e. the authors of the paper). Since coding is a human and hence subjective activity it goes without saying that so-called intercoder-reliability and coder-reliability problems are involved. The reliability of this project can be said to be very high. In addition one coder reviewed the codes of the other and adjusted when necessary.

The main objective of the study was to determine how much (*quantity*) and what kind (*quality*) of Thai news is reported in the *IHT* within the specified time period. *Starting questions* posed in this study were:

1. Who were the personalities highlighted?
2. What were the major events covered by the *IHT* and how were they treated?
3. What stories were published in the front pages?
4. What were the types of news published?
5. What were the sources for news in Europe?
6. From which cities/places did the news originate?
7. Which topics got highlighted or emphasized by illustrations or cartoons to attract special attention?
8. Are the news stories covered from a positive, negative or neutral perspective?

It probably needs no argument that the interest for a country in foreign news coverage *almost never* correlates with the geographic size of that country. Also arguments like 'strategic position' or 'political interest' seem to us rationalizations for politicians, who hereby try to justify their deeds and decisions, rather than a direct indication of interest of the newsmakers.

Therefore, the interest which the media have in a subject is difficult to measure. First of all the *notion of importance* implicitly assumes a comparison to something else. From that premise one could try to weigh the attention the *IHT* devoted to Thailand against other 'important' international events that happened in the same period. We are not able to make such a comparative study here. Such an exercise would ask for a content analysis of the complete foreign news coverage.

To estimate the degree of importance the *IHT* devoted to Thailand, we had to look for indices in the news coverage itself. Basing ourselves exclusively on the news product, which is the final outcome of any journalistic activity, we risk overlooking a number of the above-mentioned underlying factors which influence the news production process and thus also have an impact on the external interest for the subject. Hence the constraints of the editorial staff, the lack of resources, the dependence on the readers, the degree of autonomy of the editors, and so on, may be factors which, more from an objective necessity than by subjective choice, determine the degree of attention given to a foreign item. But here we also wish to state that these quasi-objective data – e.g. the distribution of the available means – do imply a choice.

As *indicators of importance* we selected consecutively the number of items, the paging, the type of news, the size in square centimetres, the personality involved, dateline, source, the presence or absence of illustrations (photographs, graphics and/or cartoons), the headline of each story summarized in a maximum of 30 characters, and a general appreciation of the positive, negative or neutral position taken by the writer of each article. With these selections some modifying reflections are relevant. The layout of a newspaper can for instance be aimed at cutting up a certain subject, eventually approached from different viewpoints, in several articles. Measuring the total surface spent on a subject may not always be a solution. For the size of an article also depends on the chosen make-up and layout (size of the titles, blank spaces, framing, etc) of the newspaper. Also the pagination can cause difficulties for some newspapers that have their foreign news on fixed pages so that publication on the front page does not imply that the item under study comes into the picture. Another criterion to test the importance of an item could be to check which themes are emphasized by the editorial staff or editor-in-chief. But problems may arise here also since the coverage of an issue (news story) and the comment on it (opinion making) often overlap each other or may not be strictly divisible. Additional illustrating or emphasizing the subject by means of diagrams or pictures gives no uniform proof for the importance contributed to the subject either.

Findings

In what follows we will present both quantitative and qualitative findings separately as well as in an integrated fashion.

Quantitative findings

Armed with these critical notes we can start reviewing the figures. In the seven-month period from 1 April until 31 October 3 1998, *59 news items* about Thailand were found in the *IHT*. Seven articles appeared in April, seven in May, 18 in June, nine in July, eight in August, four in September, and six in October 1998.

Of the 59 articles published only three appeared on the front page, one on the second, six on the fourth and two articles on the fifth page. In other words, the majority of the articles got published in the *business/finance section* of the *IHT*. Of these 59 articles 13 can be considered as 'short' (less than 50 square cm); 36 as 'medium' (between 51 and 300 square cm); and 10 as 'long' (more than 301 cm).

Most *personalities* mentioned in the articles are international or Thai political and/or economic leaders and their advisors. The few exceptions include 'Mr Clean' (Seri Temiyavej), Chulalongkorn Professor Pasuk Pongpaichi, Rangsit University Professor Jaran Dithachai, and an anonymous Burmese student in Bangkok.

Forty-four articles were not illustrated, 13 articles carried one illustration each, and two articles carried two illustrations each.

Initially a list of 19 categories for types of news was drafted. However, all articles could be ranked under *7 types of news*:

- Economy/business/labour/finance: 42
- Political news stories: 6
- Social/human interest: 4
- International relations: 2
- Crime: 2
- Religion: 2
- Advertisement: 1

Total   59

None of the articles were coded as purely opinion making; 24 articles mix opinion with 'news stories'; whereas the bulk of the articles (36) give an account de facto of the events. The advertisement for the 'Amazing Thailand' tourism promotion campaign was not considered in this count.

What can be concluded from these figures? We already stated that it is difficult, within the frame of this study, to compare the attention which the *IHT* paid to Thailand with the interest in other international political events which occurred about the same time. However, it is obvious that 59 articles published in a period of seven months proves that *Thailand is not a priority country for the IHT.*

These figures support one of the common hypotheses in international comparative news studies, namely that one can still speak of a historically rooted *news dependency relationship* between the 'West' (the 'centre') and Thailand (the 'periphery') (see Golding & Harris, 1997).

We can also compare the *IHT* to the hypothesis that there is more interest in Thailand according to the (historical, economic, political or cultural) *proximity* to or degree of involvement with the country.

With its 42 news stories (71 percent of the total number of news stories on Thailand found in the sample period) on economic and financial issues, The *IHT* clearly shows its *economic self-interest* in Thailand.

Qualitative findings

So far, this mainly quantitative indicator study has, within the limits of the named constraints, given us an idea of the interest the *IHT* directed to Thailand.

Basing ourselves on the perceivable social, political, economic and cultural context, we may find out the reasons for this interest. To determine which ideological and irrational motives are underlying this interest, a more thorough qualitative study will be necessary.

Therefore, we first of all intend to analyze the most important themes and subjects in this coverage. Next we will dwell on the comments and opinions by the newspapers in view of these most striking news themes.

Major events reported in the *IHT* were:
- Financial and economic measures taken by Thai government to comply with IMF conditions (more than 50 percent of all the stories)
- 'Mr Clean' (Seri Temiyavej), a Thai policeman, leads fight against corrupt politics
- Changes within Thai political and banking system
- Thailand's unemployment figures on the increase
- Financial news on specific Thai companies
- Reshuffling of cabinet
- Religious leaders speak out
- Trafficking in children
- The fluctuations of the Thai baht
- The Thai crisis in the Asian economic context
- Thai international relations.

Worth mentioning is also the full-colour full-page advertisement for the 'Amazing Thailand' tourism promotion campaign.

Now that we have an idea of the themes which interested the *IHT*, we also want to find out in which way it has covered and interpreted these themes. In other words, *what is its opinion on Thailand?* This can be studied in several ways. The subjects covered can be quantitatively crossed with the size of the articles, the illustrations with photographs used, the location of articles on the front page, or the fact that the subjects are or are not featured by the newspaper. Although we did all these operations in the study, we will only present the results of the last-mentioned method because it presents the clearest research findings.

Our findings show that the Thai issues were covered by the *IHT* from a *US-nationalistic* and to some extend *also 'ethnocentric' perspective*. Though the coverage of Thai stories is rather biased toward financial and economic issues and the universal 'unusual' stories (in this case: crime and human interest), the tone of the coverage itself is 'ethnocentric'.

Most often the writers attempt to assess the impact of the Thai economic crisis from a US or international perspective. A clear-cut example can be found in the *IHT* of 9 October 1998 (p.15). The news story consists of a picture depicting a number of people getting a haircut. The commentary to the picture reads: 'CUTBACKS – An American tourist getting a free haircut alongside poor and unemployed Thais in Bangkok. The free trims are part of a programme to help those affected by the country's economic crisis.' Apart from the obvious linkage to a US citizen, this story at least implicitly portrays the image that assistance to individuals can solve structural problems.

Another example provides the article entitled 'Mr Clean, a Thai Policeman, leads fight on corrupt politics', published on pages 1 and 4 of the *IHT* of 27 April 1998. Lieutenant General Seri Temiyavej, as head of the Central Investigation Bureau, has become a national folk hero because he refuses to accept bribes and has dogged underworld bosses, pursued top bankers and bureaucrats once considered untouchable. The article portrays Seri Temiyavej as the lonely cowboy 'attacking Thailand's notoriously corrupt political system'. The article continues: 'Indeed, while many Thais and foreign investors expect that more open markets, better regulation and more competitive companies will emerge from today's financial morass, the most tangible changes may not be economic at all, but political and legal'. Thailand's 'corruption became extravagant to the point that some see it as a direct contributor to the melt-down'. In other words, Thailand's current economic crisis is mainly due to internal political problems, especially corruption.

A second general conclusion can be that the broad political framework in which the newspaper covered Thailand was the *dependency axis*. This dependency axis has two major components: on the one hand stories which assess the changes which may occur on a geo-strategic and political-economic level; on the other hand the domino effect of the Thai economic crisis on other neighbouring countries (especially ASEAN) or the world at large. Sixteen articles carried a dateline outside of Thailand (Paris, The Hague, Melbourne, Sydney, Adelaide, Seoul). Of the 43 articles with a dateline in Thailand, 41 originated from Bangkok, only two from other places in Thailand (Surin, Rangsit). Almost exclusively these stories were assessing the consequences of this dependency axis from a western (mainly US) perspective in general. Consequently, it is noteworthy that the *IHT* leaves the Thai perspective largely under-illuminated. Few or no examples of a comprehensive Asian perspective have been found.

For instance, a front-page article published on 23 July, entitled 'A shake-up looms for bankers in Thailand', reports on the poor performances and great losses of the 15 major Thai commercial banks. 'The losses raise new concerns about the viability of the financial system in Thailand and make further bank closures appear inevitable, analysts said.' Though the dateline of this story by the *IHT* staff correspondent Thomas Crampton is Bangkok, two foreigners are quoted as 'analysts': Mark Greenwood, head of sales at Paribas Asia Equity, and Masatsugu Nagato, general manager of the Industrial Bank of Japan. A Thai perspective is not presented.

The same observations can be made in other articles. For instance, the article by the same *IHT* correspondent Thomas Crampton, entitled '"Model" Thai Bond backed by World Bank is a hit' (7 October, p.17), quotes only Nina Shapiro, director of the project finance and guarantees department at the World Bank, Darayes Mehta, the World Bank's principal project manager in Thailand, and Brian Lawson, director of the global syndicate at ABN-AMRO. The thrust of the article is that 'the successful issue . . . of a Thai bond with unique guarantees from the World Bank has created a new tool to use against financial crises in emerging economies'.

A rare exception was the report on a study by the Asian Development Bank (published on 26-27 September, p.17, entitled 'Thais cope by cutting pay first, not jobs', author: Thomas Crampton), which found that per-capita income in Thailand had fallen more than 20 percent, but that most of the drop was due to a decline in average wages, with a much smaller proportion attributed to the fall in the number of wage earners as unemployment rose. Not only Sudipto Mundle, a senior economist at the Asian Development Bank, and Nanak Kakwani, professor at the University of New South Wales in Australia, get quoted, but also Ammar Siamwalla, a senior advisor at the Thailand Development Research Institute, and William McCleary, a professor at Thammasat University and a former World Bank economist. The article recognizes the importance of these findings for both Thailand and other Asian economies: '. . . these and other findings would have an impact on economic policy in Thailand while influencing the design of social assistance packages throughout the region . . . More people have been brought toward the level of impoverishment than headline unemployment statistics imply . . . This study makes it clear that there is no macroeconomic solution to the crisis.'

Up till now we have not been able to figure out whether the newspaper looks at Thailand through its own glasses or through borrowed ones. Therefore, the question here is whether the emphasis and theme selection emanates from its own editorial staff and collaborators or from other sources like news agencies? What differences in approach are perceptible according to the use of its own news communication or outside sources?

The number of special correspondents and editors at the Asia desk of newspapers who are acquainted with the local culture and speak the local languages is increasing. However, they often write the feature stories and leave the hard news stories to the news agencies. There is a preference for American and European agencies (especially Reuters) to the detriment of Thai or Asian news-makers.

Secondly, one may, generally speaking, state that newspapers prefer for their secondary information supply to use an agency with which they have some affinity. This can be on linguistic and journalistic ground, but certainly also on ideological grounds. Therefore one considers a great variety in the origin of 'outside' sources.

The above also applies to the *IHT*'s coverage on Thailand. Twenty articles originated from so-called *primary sources*; i.e. correspondents or journalists from its own editorial staff, or from *The New York Times* or *The Washington Post* exchange services. The other sources quoted are the major world news agencies, Reuters, Associated Press and Agence France Presse, as well as the agency Bloomberg for financial information.

In addition to the above observation a related question may be which themes and subjects were provided and emphasized by which sources. We tried to find an answer to these questions by crossing the source with the subject. Here we concentrated mainly on the differences in thematic interest between the regular contributors (staff and correspondents) and the news agencies. Scrutinizing the output of journalistic and news agencies' activities, however, we have to be aware of the fact that, due to the limitations of this study, we cannot make any statement upon the way foreign correspondents and agencies covered Thailand, since our focus is limited to those articles selected and edited by the Paris-based editorial staff. Thus we are not able to find out whether a low score for a certain subject by one agency can be interpreted as proof of a drop in attention for the theme by the agency or as the result of the selective interest of European gatekeepers. The European agencies paid less attention to specified Thai or Asian concerns and concentrated more on possible repercussions of the local Thai events on countries other than those directly involved. It is apparent that they have less obvious interest for themes in connection with Southeast Asia, but rather go further into the international dimension of the Thai economic crisis.

They also do not, except for three articles, cover typical Asian subjects. Also in the category of individual staff members/correspondents some noteworthy points can be raised. First of all one is more interested in the international complications of the Thai crisis. Secondly one also directs one's attention to a description of the events in economic and financial terms.

To conclude the source and subject analysis, there is little difference in the conduct and attention of individual staff members and agencies on one side and between agencies amongst themselves on the other side.

The so-called *news values*, which form the 'structure' of the news product, have also been confirmed in this analysis. Values of composition and continuity, of elite nations and personality treatment, of negative reporting and human interest stories, etc were identified. Basically the *IHT* follows the news values perspectives: most coverage is based upon economic, political or/and historical interpretations from the perspective of the 'home base' of the newspaper.

Conclusion

This study started from the assumption that the production of news is influenced generally by the political, economic and cultural system, as well as by the actual situation, in which the production and transmission of information takes place. Therefore we perceived news as the result of combined action based on unintentionally determined and collectively made choices under the prevailing societal interests.

After a careful examination of a 'quality newspaper', the *International Herald Tribune,* we may conclude that even quality papers operate on the basis of implicitly agreed news conceptions and modes of production.

References

Barthes, Roland (1973) *Mythologies*. Paris: Seuil.

Beardsworth, A. (1980) 'Analysing press content: some technical and methodological issues' in Christian, H. (ed.) *The sociology of journalism and the press*. Keele: University of Keele.

Booně, L. & Servaes, J. (1982) 'De structuur van het nieuws. Enige methodologische kanttekeningen by Galtung en Ruge's nieuwsfactoren-theorie', *Communicatie,* 12, 1, pp.1-8.

Brown, A. (1995) *Organisational culture*. London: Pitman Publishing.

Campbell, J. (1988) *The power of myths*. New York: Doubleday.

Dahlgren, P. (1984) *Beyond information: TV news as a cultural discourse*. Stockholm: School of Journalism.

Davis, H. & Walton, P. (eds) (1983) *Language, image, media*. Oxford: Blackwell.

Galtung, J. & Ruge, H. M. (1965) 'The structure of foreign news: The presentation of the Congo, Cuba and Cyprus crises in four foreign newspapers', *Journal of Peace Research,* 1, pp.64-90.

Glasgow University Media Group (1980) *More bad news.* London: Routledge & Kegan Paul.

Golding, P. & Middleton, S. (1982) *Images of welfare: Press and public attitudes to poverty.* Oxford: Martin Robertson.

Golding, P. & Harris, P. (eds) (1997) *Beyond cultural imperialism. Globalization, communication and the new international order.* London: Sage.

McQuail, D. (1994) *Mass communication theory.* London: Sage.

Mowlana, H. (1997) *Global information and world communication.* London: Sage.

Rachlin, A. (1988) *News as hegemonic reality: American political culture and the framing of news accounts.* New York: Praeger.

Ramanathan, S. & Servaes, J. (1997) 'Asia reporting Europe and Europe reporting Asia: A study of news coverage.' Final Report prepared for the Asia-Europe Foundation, Singapore, and Asian Media Information and Communication Centre (AMIC), Singapore.

Servaes, J. & Drijvers, J. (1986) *Grenada: Een kruidnagel in de Europese pers.* Louvain: CeCoWe.

Servaes, J. & Tonnaer, C. (1991) *De Nieuwsmarkt. Handel en wandel van de internationale berichtgeving.* Groningen: Wolters-Noordhoff.

Servaes, J. (1991) 'European press coverage of the Grenada crisis', *Journal of Communication*, 41, 4, Autumn, pp.28-41.

Servaes, J. & Malikhao, P. (1997) 'Europe reporting Asia. A study of news coverage'. Report prepared for the Asia-Europe Foundation, Singapore, October, Brussel: CSC-KU.

Tuchman, G. (1978) *Making news : A study in the construction of reality.* New York: Free Press.

van Dijk, T. (1984) *Structures of international news: A case study of the world's press.* Amsterdam: University of Amsterdam.

Weischenberg S. (1985) 'Die Unberechenbarkeit des Gatekeepers: Zur Zukunft professioneller Informationsvermittlung in Prozess technisch-ökonomischen Wandels', *Rundfunk und Fernsehen*, 33, 2.

White, R. (1985) 'The significance of recent developments in the field of mass communications'. Paper presented at Sommatie 1985, Veldhoven.

Thailand's economic crisis and its effects

Sripan Rattikalchalakorn

Introduction

Thailand is currently in the so-called 'Yook IMF' or 'IMF Age'. Ever since the Thai economic crisis struck in July 1997, the label has been applied to Thai society. What do the Thais mean by 'Yook IMF'? Does it mean something similar to what Kaewthep (1999, p.3) said, namely, '. . . IMF or I'm fine', or is it more like '[m]y country will go on with IMF loans' – a satire about a film soundtrack from the 'Titanic' which was a blockbuster of 1998?

This chapter does not intend to condemn the Thai government's economic management and the way Thai businessmen/women have managed the banking system, financial companies and private enterprises. Rather it looks at how local opinion leaders, who work closely with the Thai people, view the crisis. The chapter also examines the effects of the Thai economic crisis from the perspectives of local opinion leaders. The term 'opinion leaders' is used as shorthand in this chapter for influentials who are involved with information flows centring on three functional areas of international communication, viz. education, tourism and mass communication.

The chapter commences with a discussion of the backdrop to Thailand's economic crisis and how international news agency reportage of the crisis. It then reviews conceptual frameworks, derived from political economy, global cultural economy and international information flow, deemed useful for a discussion of this case study. Next, the methodology employed to conduct this study is described. Finally, the views of local opinion leaders in Thailand, in relation to the economic crisis and its effects, are presented and discussed.

Background of the Thai economic crisis

Over the past two decades, many development policies that have been promoted by the World Bank and the International Monetary Fund (IMF), have been implemented by Thailand's government. According to Chris Dixon, this trend was seen clearly when '. . . during the 1980s both the economic and political situation in Thailand changed radically and the Kingdom became regarded as politically and economically stable and an investment "hot-spot". . .' (Dixon 1996, p.42). The Five Year Plans focused on two main concepts: economic growth and development. They succeeded in expanding the Thai economy at the rate of about 7-9 percent since 1985 (Phongpaichit & Baker, 1996, pp.8-84, 235-238).

The magnitude of the figures was a result mostly of industrial specialization. Other growth areas were the extended Bangkok metropolitan region, industrial infrastructure and industrial municipalities located in main provinces in Thailand. An increase in importation of luxury products, from Japan, European countries and the United States, reflected growing prosperity. The popularity of real estate and the Stock Exchange of Thailand (SET) as investment avenues for major financial institutions were also considered as important factors of industrialization. Consequently, such specialization strategies accelerated economic growth rate with the creation of an over-supply in comparison with real demand (Wongsuphasawat, 1997, pp.206-219).

This economic bubble, however, burst when the Thai government suddenly devalued the Thai baht on 2 July 1997 (*Bangkok Post*, 3 July 1997). Devaluation led to a splash-down for the Thai economic balloon, which had risen steadily since the 1980s and 1990s. A new image emerged of Thailand, one of a nation floundering in a sea of financial difficulty. The economic crisis arose on one hand from flawed investment and loan applications by business people in Thailand and on the other through economic mismanagement by the Thai government. These ineptitudes provided an expensive lesson for the country as a whole.

Because of the crisis, Thailand became one of the subjects of international economic discussion. It was postulated that the crisis has various impacts on Thai society, the Asian economy and international markets (Chitty & Rattikalchalakorn, 1998). This can particularly be seen through exogenous perspectives portrayed by the main international news agencies such as the ABC (Australia), the BBC (UK) and CNN (USA). According to these news agencies, the so-called 'Thai economic crisis' was attributed to economic mismanagement by the Thai government (Pongwecharak, 1998). The concomitant obligations of the IMF in assisting the country to restore the Thai economic crisis and social stability with reconstruction of a new financial system and regulation were also regarded (Jordan, 1998, pp.2-5).

Why did the Thai economic crisis become a hot issue as portrayed by the news agencies around the world? There is no doubt, according to Peter F. Bell, that 'Thailand serves as an excellent case study of many of the contradictions of the current development policies which are being practised on a global level' (Bell, 1996, p.49). In support of this statement, it is also the nature of news agencies that they tend to focus much more on short-term benefits when covering and commenting on news. This is because the selected stories are usually involved with cultural factors, community norms, journalistic traditions and fashions, other media, news management by sources, commercial concerns, pressure from interest groups, journalistic and commercial competition, and forms of ownership (Jletcher 1981, pp.1-34). As Frederick Jletcher points out:

> . . . journalists make choices, that news is more often created than discovered.
> Although much news is 'discovered' as news workers perform their routine
> functions, these discoveries are determined in large part by where reporters
> choose to look. (Jletcher, 1981, p.35)

There is no exception in the case of Thailand's economic crisis. That is
why international news agencies selected to portray this case in the manner
they did by selecting both what they wished to and wished not to cover and
comment upon. How did the Thai economic crisis happen? This is a major
question posed by economists, journalists, businessmen and academics ever
since the crisis began in July 1997. Does this mean that the fetal Thai
economic crisis was undetected by experts and country specialists in
international financial organizations, such as the World Bank and the IMF,
that are now trying to assist Asian countries to resolve the economic crisis?

The answer to this question is 'No'. I am concerned as to why this
might be so. It was not on July 1997 that I personally started to worry
about the Thai economic eclipse. As a Thai, I was concerned about the
crisis since 1996, after reading a book titled *Uneven development in Thailand*
edited by Michael Parnwell (1996). An intriguing point made in a chapter
of the book by Peter Bell is that '[i]ndeed, the IMF pointed to Thailand as
one of several possible danger spots for capital flight following the collapse
of the Mexican economy in 1994' (Bell, 1996, p.55).

It is not the purpose of this chapter, nor is it necessary to that purpose,
to discuss at length the international news agencies' reportage on the Thai
economic crisis. My aim is to find out know how local opinion leaders
working with Thai people in Thailand view the crisis and its effects on
Thailand.

Conceptual frameworks

The Thai economic crisis attracts international interest because of the
magnitude of information flowing through global mass media agencies.
Because of the multi-dimensional nature of this issue, concepts drawn from
political economy (domestic and international), global cultural economy
and international flow of information are used as analytical tools in
discussing the Thai economic crisis and its effects as viewed by local opinion
leaders in Thailand.

International and domestic political economy
An important perspective of international political economy is an 'emphasis
on the impacts of the new turbulent international markets' (Cho, 1994,
p.334). It is not only new communications and telecommunication
technologies that influence international markets, but also the world
economic organizations such as the World Bank and the IMF. By virtue of
this perspective, international commercialization 'is a production of politics

and the market' (Stevenson, 1994, pp.170-171). To investigate the international market is, therefore, to observe the basic structure and development of mass media, which are largely dominated by English-speaking countries (Stevenson, 1994, pp.139-156).

Viewing through a perspective of domestic political economy, on the other hand, it is 'regarded as distinctive and significant, with particular attention being given to ideas about the role and the autonomy of a state, and to the degree of monopolization of interest representation' (Cho, 1994, p.335). Domestic political economy also includes concerns about nationalism and themes of self-management (Dyson, 1983, p.33), which are obvious in developing countries. Many developing countries may have *high levels of human development* (life expectancy, literacy, educational attainment, and adequacy of income or buying power). However, they have lower levels of popular participation in the exercise of *political rights* (enabling people to participate freely in the political process), civil liberties (the freedoms to develop views, institutions and personal autonomy apart from the state) and *levels of freedom rating* (free, partly free, and not free in developing countries, including Thailand) can be seen (Stevenson, 1994, pp.127-132).

In order to discern the connection between international and domestic political economies, a review of Chitty's P-matrix is applied. The political-economy matrix (P-matrix) has the environmental matrix (N-matrix), regional matrices (R-matrices), administrative matrices (A-matrices), ethno-historical matrices (E-matrices), and individual matrices (I-matrices) nested within it (Chitty, 1997a, pp.3-7). According to Chitty, however, the 'P-matrix influences and is influenced by human agency' (Chitty, 1997b, p.2). Initial relationships between systems of international and domestic political economy are connected when each of these matrices interacts with the others. For instance, Thailand, as a domestic political economy, interacts with ASEAN, which is a political and economic organization in the Southeast Asia region, and with the UN – the largest organization of the world political economy.

The international and domestic organisms of political economy will be accelerated in frequencies of information dissemination, if individuals, agencies and organizations interact with each other via telecommunication technologies. However, there is a concern in the use of new communication technologies that:

> . . . the new communication technologies are developing and disseminating in the world rapidly. As well known, the combination of computer and communications has brought about a revolutionary transformation in our media environment, to make possible the prompt transmission of a huge amount of multiplex. But some scholars cautioned that the new media might not be always beneficial to all the people, and that by the distribution and availability of them might be exacerbated the situation of politic and economic inequities, both domestic and international. (Kang, 1994, p.7).

Global cultural economy

Global cultural economy develops and increases the complexity of global economy through ethnoscapes, mediascapes, technoscapes, finanscapes and ideoscapes (Appadurai, 1990, pp.296-303). These scapes are summarized as follows:

1. Ethnoscapes are created by people who may have or want to move, such as tourists, immigrants, refugees, exiles, guest/inviting workers. Their movements within and between involved nations are politically affected.

2. Mediascapes are important scapes that electronic media produce and scatter information internationally. Electronic media create international interests and global images. Mediascapes, hence, affect global cultural phenomena.

3. Technoscapes (high and low, mechanical and informational) are moving without boundaries. Under technoscapes, countries are linked and become multinational through the use of technologies that have motivated multi-relationships between money exchange, political affairs and labour activities.

4. Finanscapes take into account global capital and are involved with currency markets, national stock exchanges, and commodity speculations which create international investments through the process of 'deterritorialization'.

5. Ideoscapes refer to concatenations of ideas, terms and images, including freedom, welfare, rights, sovereignty, representation and democracy. These concepts have globally been concerned since the 19th century. By adopting or adapting them, the transnational process is focused and may be interpreted differently.

Five scapes based on the global cultural economy create new patterns of international communication. International communication was traditionally focused on 'official transactions . . . when governments do communicate with each other . . . through representatives of their foreign offices . . . [such as] formal diplomatic channels' (Singer, 1987, pp.214-215). The global cultural economy, however, has affected relations between nations that are not necessary restricted within the boundaries. With the extension of global cultural economy, individuals, private sections and non-governmental organizations have more chances to communicate internationally. In other words, the global cultural economy has created complex patterns and a new means of international communication.

Information flow in international communication

International communication has become an essential part of the conceptualization of global politics and economics with the facilitation of an understanding what is happening in the world (Mowlana, 1994, p.133). In this study, two concepts of international communication – international and individual levels – are focused on. At the international level:

[i]nternational communication, simply defined, is communication that occurs
across international borders, that is, over the nation-states. It is sometimes
referred to as transborder or transnational communication, particularly among
economists who study transborder data flow . . . (Fortner, 1993, p.6)

Individuals are regarded importantly as factors of international
communication. This can be viewed as follows:

Individuals as media for international communication become most important
in the light of the view that feedback is more instant, and communication is
perhaps more complete and lasting, when it is executed on an interpersonal
level. While this realization may appear elementary, it is a benchmark of what
may heretofore be the most important effects in research on the global flow of
information. (Mowlana, 1986, pp.123-124)

Both levels in international communication bring about the consequences
of international flow of information 'that consists of the transfer of messages
in the form of information and data through individuals, groups,
governments, and technologies' (Mowlana, 1986, p.4). To view this
transformation more precisely, human and technological dimensions are
engaged (Mowlana, 1986, p.2). Human orientation includes: 1) educational,
artistic and cultural exchanges, including conferences and sports events; 2)
diplomatic and political channels, including military and related conferences
and organizations; 3) tourism, travel and migration, including religious
and other personal contacts; and 4) mail, telephone, telegraph, telex and
related telecommunication channels.

Technological orientation consists of: 1) satellite and planetary resources
including transborder data flow, computers and related technologies; 2)
newspapers, magazines, books, technical and scientific journals and news
agencies; 3) radio, television and direct broadcast satellite; and 4) films,
recordings and video, marketing, advertising and public opinion polls.

The interaction between humans and technologies in different areas is
significant in most states. In this study, in the present Thai context,
education, tourism and mass communication are areas of focus in relation
to international flow of information. They are briefly addressed as follows:

1. International flow of information in Thailand has gone hand in hand
    with the international education system ever since the reign of King
    Chulalongkorn (Rama V) when the modern Thai educational system
    was constructed on the basis of western principles. This is in support
    of an assumption that exposure of elite Asian youth to international
    education has provided a portal for American culture (an important
    part of western culture with its two main pillars of politics and
    economics) into Asian countries (Mowlana, 1994, p.135). When
    increasing numbers of Thai students choose, every year since the
    beginning of the economic boom in the 1980s, to study abroad, this

trend is seen clearly (Mulder, 1992). It is Thai lecturers, successful people and elites in general who mainly hold an MA and/or PhD degree(s) awarded by universities or institutions from western countries. These people are seen as models of modernity for less fortunate Thais. These elites therefore continue as important channels through which transnational information is moved from the west into Thailand.

2. The tourism industry has become an outstanding industry in Thailand, bringing a major income to the country (TAT, 1996, p.186). Thailand has been viewed, since the 1990s, as one of the world's most popular destinations. In order to deal with this trend in international tourism, the Thai government pays more attention to the promotion of the industry through the use of telecommunication technologies and international public relations. As a result, the attraction of the Thai tourism industry seems to flow from the national policy level to every Thai villager. The impact of this industry is enormous. Mowlana argues that:

> . . . international tourism – viewed as a distributive communication process converging telecommunications, transnational banking, and international relations – provides a seminal example of the increasing utility of international communication to contemporary global strategies of regional optimization. (Mowlana, 1994, p.138)

Hence, business people involved with Thailand's tourism industry have become a powerful group within the Thai economy, a group that behaves as a portal for the international flow of information leading to the Thai people.

3. Mass media and telecommunication development in Thailand are prioritized and often used to develop and increase international relationships and understanding. Also 'the fragile economic and political structures of most third-world countries need the support of mass media to assist the process of nation-building' (Stevenson, 1994, p.13). In order to assist in national development, on 17 December 1993, Thaicom I, the first Thai satellite, was launched, followed by Thaicom II (7 October 1994) and Thaicom III (16 April 1997). These satellites have been used as networks between Thailand and other regions: East Asia (e.g. Eastern China, Korea and Japan), Southeast Asia (e.g. Philippines, Malaysia, Burma and Indochina), Europe, Australia and Africa (www.Thaicom.net).

It is hoped that mass media and telecommunication technologies will help solve problems in Thailand: the Eighth National Economic and Social Development Plan (1997-2001), IT 2000 policy, and a plan of information technologies and telecommunication for human and social development (1999-2008) propose the development of media and telecommunication with this end in mind. These national policies, determined during the last phase of the economic boom and the 1999-2008 Plan, drawn up after the economic crisis began, concur in framing guidelines for the use of mass media and telecommunication technologies for development.

Thus, people who work with mass media and telecommunication companies in Thailand become important agents of international flow of information. Through their communication networks, they can increase the delivery of international political economy and socio-cultural information to Thai people.

Methodology

The research sites
In-depth interviews of 24 local opinion leaders were used in this study. The local opinion leaders were involved with the following functional areas: education, tourism and mass communication. The opinion leaders were selected randomly from four provinces: Chiang Mai, Khon Kean, Songkhla and Bangkok, which are regarded in Thailand as the regional centres of the North, Northeast, South and Centre respectively. These four provinces were selected as research sites because they are comparable in regards to six criteria: socio-cultural history, educational sites, tourist destinations, transportation, mass communication, and economic importance. To be selected as sites for this research regions must have the following characteristics:

1. Significant socio-cultural history based on ethno-historical background.
2. Significant state university/ies.
3. Significant tourist destination promoted internationally by the Tourist Authority of Thailand (TAT).
4. Significant infrastructure such as five-star hotels, highways, train stations and regional airports, providing good accessibility to and from other regions.
5. Significant mass communication and telecommunication infrastructure in the form of radio and television stations.
6. Significance economic centres, particularly in relation to the first five characteristics.

Data resource
Opinion leaders working in the three functional areas (lecturers, tourist business people and mass media practitioners) were selected at random. In Thailand, these people are seen as opinion leaders who work closely with people in their community. They are also seen as cosmopolitans who have contacts across cultures with people from international organizations such as NGOs, universities, private companies and foreigners. In this study local opinion leaders are:

1. 25-50 years old.
2. Accepted as the community's key persons or leaders.
3. In higher statuses/positions in comparison with most people in their community, seen in their membership of important organizations and/or associations in the community and/or Thailand.
4. Often involved with both international and domestic media. They often receive new information and knowledge through various channels, both traditional/local and modern media. It is likely that their exposure to the media makes their social criticisms interesting.
5. Key persons who usually share and transmit the information they have received with other people in the community. And they may employ this information to direct and interact with other individuals and/or organizations.
6. Key persons who often play an active role to make important decisions in response to the community's problems because people in the community believe in their outlook and capability.
7. Privileged people, as considered by the community, who can influence and negotiate with individuals and/or organizations.

Instrument and data collection
To conduct 24 in-depth interviews with the local opinion leaders in the four provinces, open-ended questions were designed as the study's instrument. The 24 in-depth interviews were conducted between November 1998 and January 1999 by the present researcher. Most of the interviewees were appointed in advance through the project's research coordinators because the researcher was in Sydney before data collection began. In Thai society, men are likely to be local opinion leaders. As a result, there are 15 male and 9 female interviewees.

Research findings

The research findings consist of perspectives of lecturers, tourism businessmen and mass media practitioners on Thailand's economic crisis and its effects. They are respectively presented as follows.

Perspectives of lecturers
The economic crisis reveals that the easy Thai lifestyle and simple practices are still useful and practical for Thai society, if people know how to apply these. Simple practices such as having dinner together with family could protect social problems because everybody in a family has a chance to talk and share or find out what she/he has been doing each day. Through discussions over the dinner table, people could learn their roles and ways of solving problems. More Thai people now prefer to eat outside. Also, current social issues such as recycling and environmental protection are similar to what our grandparents have taught us. 'Our parents taught us

how to use and save natural resources effectively. They taught us how to live with nature but we do not believe them. We believe in materialism and finally we found the collapse of our economy. The economic crisis has shown that . . . things that are grown fast are likely to die fast' (Respondent 1, 28 November 1998).

People voted for bad politicians to govern the country and the politicians brought about the economic crisis. As a result, 'people have to sacrifice their jobs and financial security. Many Thai people are suffering from mental illness which is the negative impact of the economic crisis. So, the Buddha's principle that "nothing is permanent" remains to be seen' (Respondent 3, 2 December 1998).

The economic crisis has shown that Thailand has not achieved NIC status. 'We put too much emphasis to develop economy and industries particularly in big cities. Thailand is still an agricultural society, and the country should be developed on this basis' (Respondent 2, 28 November 1998). 'What we did about economic development is wrong. Making money is not an easy task any more, however, we now learn to save for the future. This may be a positive effect of the crisis' (Respondent 4, 3 December 1998).

The economic crisis reveals that 'our society and Thai families are not strong enough to cope with this situation. More problems, such as crime, drug addiction, prostitution and divorce, are now increasing. The crisis destroys our dignity because Thailand is named as a collapsed country and the IMF restricts us to do something we never want e.g. our economic system is reconstructed and we lose control of foreign trade and financial management. It is a historical record that Thailand has lost its economic sovereignty to the IMF since 1997. And Thailand has to be a good student of the IMF' (Respondent 5, 15 December 1998).

The economic crisis has some positive effects on Thailand. It makes Thai people concerned about what would happen to their country. 'We never thought seriously like this before because everyone seemed to be happy about what they gained from the economic boom. So, the crisis creates a new condition to learn about what we are confronted with. We always followed foreigners in and never felt like they took advantage over our country. Now we realize that it is difficult to survive' (Respondent 6, 15 December 1998).

The economic crisis is an unfortunate situation experiencing by all Thais. 'However, it makes us realize what we should do in the future. We are now learning to work hard and to be realistic when making decision' (Respondent 7, 29 December 1998). As a whole the economic crisis has shown that 'Thailand lacks . . . clear goals and good policies. People are crazy about nonsensical values and materialism that are not necessary for their lives. The economic crisis is a result of these facts and is a tragedy of our country' (Respondent 8, 29 December 1998).

Perspectives of tourism business people

The economic crisis actually helps to increase the number of foreign tourists because of the devaluation of the Thai baht. Another direct effect of the crisis on Thai people is that they spend their money more carefully and many Thai people have to stop travelling abroad (Respondent 9, 28 November 1998). People have to be careful about their living expenses and are under stress (Respondent 10, 28 November 1998). Because of the economic crisis, more people become more selfish (Respondent 11, 2 December 1998).

'Thai government lacks a realistic vision for economic management and this has brought about the economic crisis. There is no plan, no warning and no solution from our government in regards to the economic crisis. Real estate, for example, was so expensive during the economic boom. How come the government did not develop a policy for real estate. There is no real investigation of wrong doing by politicians and their cronies. Economic development was only a political game and purpose which was concerned and used by Thai politicians to increase and maintain their power' (Respondent 12, 3 December 1998).

'Obviously, the economic crisis has affected the Thai tourism industry, because hotel bookings were cancelled. It seems that the crisis stops everything. After the announcement of the devaluation of the Thai currency, many small businesses, which were connected to the tourism industry, were collapsed within a month' (Respondent 13, 16 December 1998). 'It was a big mistake of Thai government and businessmen because they created too much supply in comparison to real demand of the markets' (Respondent 14, 16 December 1998). However, the crisis prompts tourism businessmen to look at or create new and different market niches such as 'Kanchanaburi province [which] is now being promoted to Japanese tourists who want to visit one of the World War II's historical sites. This may be seen as a positive effect that the Thais have seen resulting from the economic crisis. Before the economic crisis began, this province was only seen as a destination for domestic and western tourists who love bush walking' (Respondent 13, 16 December 1998).

The education system is an important factor that destroys Thailand's economy because 'it increases capitalists who care for nothing but money' (Respondent 15, 25 December 1998). The educated capitalists exploited poor people who do not know how to manage their finance. Rural people, who have never studied in a university, become a target of educated (but selfish) capitalists who use their knowledge to take advantage over poor people. 'Farmers, for example, are convinced to sell their lands and buy new cars. They never have a lot of money and have no idea how to save and invest their money in business. Hence they have lost the money they gained from selling their lands to buy unnecessary products that were produced by the capitalists. Finally they have lost everything: money, land and job. In the city, poor people were persuaded to get involved with the

Stock Exchange of Thailand (SET) which was manipulated by small groups of people. The end, for both rural and urban poor, is indebtedness and homelessness. The economic crisis reveals how bad our leaders are. Don't believe in politicians and their promises' (Respondent 15, 25 December 1998).

'Unlike Western people who have their future plans, most Thais never have both short-term and long-term plans. Western people will prepare for what, when, where, how and why to do something. And this makes them achieve their goals and develop what they want more effectively. Planning is an important step. Thai people try to follow every pattern of developed countries, but we fail to follow the first step: planning. In terms of economic planning, Western people learn to save first and buy what they want later. This is opposite to most Thais who buy first and pay by installments. So people are in debt and have to pay out interest' (Respondent 16, 26 December 1998). The economic crisis makes millions of Thai people jobless because they never prepare for this. As a result when the economic crisis took place, most Thais, 'lost everything, such as house, car, television and so on, because they had not yet owned these things completely. Our government, schools and education institutions teach our people how to consume and get rich, but they forget to teach them to be humane and responsible' (Respondent 16, 26 December 1998).

People are selfish and concerned about how to get rich and benefit from each other. This crisis, however, makes many people learn to plan and to be realistic. 'People have learned to buy things because they are necessary and not because they are brand names. Many people start to be concerned about their organizations as well, because they can survive if the organizations survive. This is an important concept that Japanese people take into their consideration and this helps them to be successful' (Respondent 16, 26 December 1998).

Perspectives of mass media practitioners

In regards to the economic crisis, more Thai people are concerned about the future of their country, whether or not Thailand will survive the crisis. In contrast to a view expressed by a tourism businessman, Thai people seem to care for and sympathize with each other. Many people realize that 'we made a wrong decision when we voted for *bad politicians* and let them corrupted our country' (Respondent 17, 28 November 1998). 'The economic crisis forces us to be tough and simplistic. Things went wrong because we behaved and consumed improperly and we should accept the results' (Respondent 18, 29 November 1998).

'Thailand has collapsed because of politicians. Bad politicians know that people in rural areas are honest and do what they have promised. So, bad politicians always convince the people to vote for them. How come a politician paid 20 million baht in order to be an MP who earns only 100,000 baht per month for the 10-18 month life of a Parliament. Parliaments never last their four-year term. People in rural areas are also crazy to use products from Bangkok and other countries. They have adopted wrong values. They are convinced to do and to buy things easily. This is bad for them and our country' (Respondent 19, 2 December 1998).

'Thai government always supports free trade, but most investors are foreigners. While more foreign investors owned factories, companies and business in Thailand during the economic boom, Thai government informed people that Thailand was going to be a NIC' (Respondent 20, 3 December 1998). It is not fair for local Thai businessmen, who have to pay tax and supply Bangkok, because they have to manage and deal with the problems themselves. 'Big cities have consumed rural materials and products. Whatsoever belonged to and is produced by rural people is consumed by or developed for people in Bangkok and big cities. Our economic system does not distribute fairly, just a few percents of the economic outcomes returned to rural people. So it is difficult for rural people to develop themselves and their communities. This is why Bangkok is growing faster and faster, while rural areas are declining. If, most of the rural products and tax were fairly allocated to rural areas, Thailand should not be like this. Thailand has provincial governments, but the provincial governments are used to support the Bangkok's administration and decentralization' (Respondent 20, 3 December 1998).

'The economic crisis reduces the number of shoppers who like to buy imported products. This is good for our country. Many people look back and reconsider the importance of local and traditional ways of life that may help them to deal with the crisis. For example, many kinds of jobs based in the agricultural sector have increased since the economic crisis began in 1997' (Respondent 21, 16 December 1998). 'People never expected that they have to live in this crisis, but they are now experiencing it . . . The economic crisis unites people in trying to improve their economic system' (Respondent 22, 16 December 1998).

'It is good for us to rethink who we are and to learn how we should manage our economy and money, particularly for young people who used to spend lots money on luxuries and unnecessary things. They were spoiled as children, but they now have to work hard and save for themselves because their parents are jobless' (Respondent 23, 28 December 1998). 'The crisis is the most expensive lesson that we have ever learned. Naturally, everything is connected. In the case of the economic crisis, rich people take advantage over poor people. Finally everybody has to share the pain because the whole system has collapsed' (Respondent 24, 24 January 1998).

Discussion

Taking an international political economic perspective one might argue that Thailand's economic crisis and its effects as viewed by opinion leaders is 'a production of politics and the market' (Stevenson, 1994, pp.170-171). The opinion leaders were likely to believe that Thai politicians brought about the economic crisis, while Thai people became victims of the crisis. The crisis revealed that Thailand was not a NIC. However, the opinion leaders agreed and hoped that Thai people would consider and learn what should be done for the country, organizations and themselves. This can be described in domestic political economic terms (Dyson, 1983, p.33) as the economic crisis having generated nationalist concerns and a desire to emphasize self-management.

Chitty's P-matrix (Chitty, 1997b, p.2) is another conceptual framework that can be applied for a discussion of Thailand's economic crisis. Thailand's P-matrix (A-matrix or domestic political economy) has interacted with the international political economy through international markets and the IMF. The significance of the economic crisis in relation to the P-matrix is an unequal interaction between the domestic and international political economic systems, particularly when individual matrices in a domestic political economic system over-consume products from the international political economic system. This unequal interaction brings about negative effects to the domestic political economy, spilling into domestic 'individual matrices' in Thailand that (led by the opinion leaders and organizations in the Thai A-matrix) had previously consumed more and more products imported from the West and had become vulnerable through their indebtedness in a credit-based society.

Global cultural economy (Appadurai, 1990, pp.296-303) develops and increases the complexity of the Thai economic system. Through ethnoscapes, technoscapes and mediascapes, Thai people who respectively travel, acquire new technologies and communicate with international markets, have learned and transmitted new values based upon political and economic information flows. As a result, this information influences Thai people to imitate the western lifestyle. Within finanscapes, rural people are persuaded to consume urban and international products, whilst people in Bangkok are preoccupied with stock exchanges. Increased international investment in the Thai finance system has affected Thailand by making it vulnerable when foreign companies repatriate investment. The economic crisis has resulted in contributions to the Thai ideoscape that prescribe political improvements, social responsibility, future planning, and socio-economic security based on working hard, saving money and spending reasonably.

The economic crisis in Thailand demonstrates that opinion leaders or an 'individual orientation' in international communication (Mowlana, 1986, pp.123-124) are a crucial factor in providing a clear picture of what is happening in Thai politics and economics. The perspectives of Thai lecturers, tourism businessmen and mass media practitioners describe the magnitude of international flow of information, reflecting an unequal interaction and orientation between humans and technology.

Conclusion

This case study has revealed that Thailand's political economy is influenced by the international political economy symbolized by the IMF. International news agencies viewed the Thai economic crisis negatively; however, according to perspectives of opinion leaders in Thailand, it is hoped that Thai people would find ways to cope with the crisis and really learn to be independent. 'Yook IMF' is seen as a new 'dark age' in Thai political economic history; it may make Thai people fashion a new approach to development that discards the old concept of materialism and creates a desire for self-empowerment. If this becomes the case, the economic crisis may help Thailand to reconstruct its political, economic and socio-cultural values in a robust manner for the 21st century.

References

Appadurai, (1990) 'Disjuncture and difference in the global cultural economy', *Theory, culture and society: Public Culture,* Vol. 2, No. 2.

Bell, Peter F. (1996) 'Development or maldevelopment? The contradictions of Thailand's economic growth' in Parnwell, Michael J. G. (ed.) *Uneven development in Thailand.* Aldershot: Avebury.

Chitty, Naren (1997a) 'A tale of two cities: Contiguous moments of reported political and cultural reality in Sydney and Singapore.' Paper presented at the IAMCR Conference, Oaxaca, Mexico, July, 1997.

Chitty, Naren (1997b) 'Telecommunication & world order: Terra cyborg.' Paper presented at the AMIC Conference, Kuala Lumpur, June, 1997.

Chitty, Naren & Rattikalchalakorn, Sripan, (1998) 'Headings of state: A study of the *Sydney Morning Herald*'s coverage of international news events in January 1998.' Paper presented at the International Communication Section, Biennial Scientific Conference of the International Association for Media & Communication Research (IAMCR), Glasgow, Scotland.

Cho, Paek-je (1994) 'New media policy in Korea: Issues and policy suggestions' in Hyeon-Dew Kang (ed.) *International communication in North-East Asia,* Seoul: Nanam.

Dixon, Chris (1996) 'Thailand's rapid economic growth: Causes, sustainability and lessens' in Parnwell, Michael J. G. (ed.) *Uneven development in Thailand.* Aldershot: Avebury.

Dyson, Kenneth (1983) 'West European states and the communications revolution'. *Politics of communications revolution in Western Europe*. London: Frank Cass Company.

Fortner, Robert S. (1993) 'Introduction to international communication'. *International communication: History, conflict, and control of the global metropolis*. California: Wadsworth.

Jletcher, Frederick J. (1981) 'Concepts and perspectives' and 'Influences on press coverage of public affairs', *Newspapers and public affairs*. Ottawa: Canadian Government Publishing Centre.

Jordan, Bill (1998) 'Globalisation on trial'. *Annual meeting of the Board of Governors* (6-8 October 1998) (International Monetary Fund and World Bank) Washington: International Confederation of Free Trade Unions.

Kang, Hyeon-Dew (ed.) (1994) 'Editor's note' in *International communications in North-East Asia*. Seoul: Nanam.

Kaewthep, Kanjana (1999) A paper in response to Dr Glen Lewis's paper on 'The role of media in Thailand's economic crisis' and Dr Ubolwas Pitipatanacozit's paper on 'Another decade of women magazines (1988-1998): An attempt to change'. Papers presented at an International Conference on Thailand's Communication and Culture under the Current Economic Crisis, Bangkok, Thailand (6-9 January 1999).

Mowlana, Hamid (1986) 'International flow of information: A framework of analysis' and 'International interaction: Implications of tourism', *Global information and world communication: New frontiers in international relations*. New York/London: Longman.

Mowlana, Hamid (1994) 'Communication ecology and the changing international order' in Hyeon-Dew Kang (ed.) *International communications in North-East Asia*. Seoul: Nanam.

Mulder, Niels (1992) 'The Thai opening to the world'. *Inside Southeast Asia: Thai-Javanese interpretations of everyday life*. Bangkok: Duang Kamol.

Parnwell, Michael J.G. (ed.) (1996) *Uneven development in Thailand*. Aldershot: Avebury.

Phongpaichit, Pasuk & Baker, Chris (1996) *Thailand boom!* New South Wales: Allen & Unwin.

Pongwecharak, Chakrapong (1998) 'Introduction' in 'The coverage of the Thai financial crisis in 1997 in *The Bangkok Post* and *The Australian*'. MA Thesis. Centre for International Communication, Division of Society, Culture, Media and Philosophy (SCMP), Macquarie University.

Singer, Marshall R. (1987) 'Intra-and international communication', *Intercultural communication: A perceptual approach*. New Jersey: Prentice-Hall.

Stevenson, Robert L. (1994) 'The context of global communication', *Global communication in the twenty-first century*. New York: Longman.

SMMIHD (Sub-committee of Mass Media and Information for Human and Social Development) (1998) 'Draft Development Plan of Mass Media, Information Technology and Telecommunication for Human and Social Development (1999-2008)'. A Practical Conference held at Prince Palace Hotel, Bangkok, Thailand on December 21, 1998, (in Thai).

Tourism Authority of Thailand (TAT) (1996) *Annual report*.

Wongsuphasawat, Luxmon (1997). 'The extended Bangkok metropolitan region and uneven industrial development in Thailand' in Dixon, Chris & Smith, David W. (eds) *Uneven development in South East Asia*. Aldershot: Ashgate.

www.Thaicom.net.

Covering the 'New World Order': Challenges for news dissemination

Bruce C. Allen

As a consumer of media messages from a variety of sources each day, and as a person who has travelled widely, I find the media coverage of international conflicts enormously confusing and not at all helpful in my understanding of the underlying causes of these conflicts. This is particularly true of television where I feel at times as if I am on a roller coaster, sometimes led gently into an impending war such as the two Gulf Wars or, as is more often the case, tipped headlong into a war I had no idea was imminent, for instance those in Rwanda and Angola.

The media in close-up

My first problem is that early television reports of a typical crisis usually focus on the action, that is, close-ups of the military or civil strife, which is considered to have strong news value. However these reports fail to accurately establish the geographical setting and I have no real idea exactly where the conflict is taking place, a problem I note was shared by President Clinton when he first was briefed on the Kosovo crisis. Locating *where* the crisis is occurring within a news story seems to me to be a fundamental first step in the process of understanding a media report.

My second concern is that the social, political and economic issues which lie at the heart of reported conflicts are either not covered, are covered in a reporter's narration which is read over footage of dramatic action, or is delivered by a reporter as a stand-up piece to camera. The result is that it is difficult to find out from television news reports *why* the war has started.

A third concern is that this situation does not improve as the crisis develops, and if anything the focus on action as news increases and there is less, not more, information about the geographic *where* or the social, political and economic *why*. Of course experience shows that with patience and an acquired skill of reading television messages it is possible to piece the more complex and vital elements of the story together. This assumes a high level of interest in the subject and I argue that this is not possible in practice if one is to rely on television news services alone. It is only possible by reading in-depth analyses in newspapers and magazines and, to a far lesser extent, by listening to radio current affairs programmes such as the *AM* and *PM* programmes on the Australian Broadcasting Corporation (ABC). But even this is not enough, and non-media-based independent research is needed.

Great expectations

So why does television fail to deliver, particularly since its promoters promised so much compared to contemporary newspapers and radio broadcasters when it was in the early stages of development in the United States? Writing in 1930, Sheldon and Grisewood observed:

> The modern newspaper is, after all, nothing more than an instrument to enable
> us to see and hear more, and further. We can visualise from its printed pages
> what has happened; but would we read the account as written in the newspaper,
> had we the time and facilities to be present at the event? Television brings us
> somewhat nearer to a perfect realisation of an event.

In the same general context, in 1936 David Sarnoff, President of the Radio Corporation of America, told the Advertising Federation of America:

> Sound broadcasting will remain the basic service for the programmes
> particularly adapted to its purposes. On the other hand, television will bring
> into the home much visual material – news events, drama, paintings,
> personalities – which sound can bring only partially or not at all.

More than 60 years later, not only does television deliver a wide range of entertainment and information programming on a national and international basis in most parts of the world but the industry also has the capacity to collect and disseminate live news reports from most parts of the world, at short notice. This achievement has helped elevate the status of international news within daily news bulletins and has established it as a programme type in its own right, which has allowed the creation of international worldwide television news channels such as CNN and BBC World. But with all of this valuable technical and logistical capacity there remains the difficulty of interpreting news events in a way which will be readily understandable to viewers in another country. The recent conflict in the Balkans provides an opportunity to examine the problem from a viewer's perspective. It also provides an opportunity to recommend improvements to the coverage of the conflict and to analyze the professional practices of television journalists, which I argue would limit the implementation of these improvements.

The media in action

The social, political and economic background to NATO's attack on Serbia is at least as complex as is its geography. Setting aside for a moment the image of Slobodan Milosevic as the architect of ethnic cleansing and genocide, there is the issue of just where all this activity was taking place. The main focus of stories has been on Kosovo but, in an attempt to locate it, the most commonly used description of the neighbouring region was either the Balkans, Yugoslavia, the Former Yugoslavia or Serbia. The interrelationships between Kosovo, Montenegro, Albania, Macedonia and most importantly Bosnia Hertzegovina were rarely clarified.

As well, at least one of the maps used was inaccurate. *Media watch*, a weekly ABC television programme featuring critical analysis of the media, drew attention to a map used by the commercial television network, Channel Ten, in its prime-time news bulletin. The map clearly showed Belgrade within the borders of Kosovo.[1]

For the most part, however, the relatively few television news programmes which used maps did not attempt to use them to help viewers locate Kosovo in its relationship to neighbouring countries such as Germany, Austria, Italy and Greece, let alone Russia. Maps were used more frequently in newspapers but these also failed to show the region as a whole.[2] One exception was the weekly American news magazine *Newsweek,* which is published in Australia within *The Bulletin* magazine. In addition to showing Kosovo in relation to Yugoslavia, the magazine prepared a far larger map which showed much of Western Europe.[3]

Within the first two weeks of NATO's military action, a common thread emerged in the use of maps to illustrate newspaper stories or television news bulletins. Most maps showed details of aircraft movements, bombing targets and the routes taken by refugees, and whilst the use of maps for this

---

1. Ackland, Richard – Excerpt from *Media watch,* Australian Broadcasting Corporation, 5 April 1999.

2. Newspaper cuttings:
The Australian, 26 March 1999, p.3.
The Sydney Morning Herald, 26 March 1999, p.11.
The Australian, 30 March 1999, p.1.
The Australian, 6 April 1999, p.11.
The Sydney Morning Herald, 6 April 1999, p.1.
The Daily Telegraph, 7 April 1999, p.29.
The Sydney Morning Herald, 7 April 1999, p.8.
The Australian, 8 April 1999, p.1.

3. *Newsweek* in *The Bulletin,* 6 April 1999, pp.26-27.

purpose was useful, it did not help the better understanding of the background to the conflict. Maps, especially designed for use on television, together with concise summaries of the social, political and economic issues underlying the reasons for the conflict, would, in my view, not only have solved the problem of *where* the conflict was taking place but also allowed effective communication of *why* it was occurring. These maps would be computer driven and be programmed to show the immediate area of conflict. Importantly the computer programme would be capable of widening the field of view in a visually dramatic way to include neighbouring countries and those more distant.

In addition to allowing viewers to quickly identify where the action is taking place, the computer programme would generate easy-to-understand graphic representations illustrating relevant social, political and economic factors. Concise backgrounders would match the selected graphic sequences.

Professional practices of journalists

Media organizations, however, rely on the professional practices of journalists to compile and present news stories, a practice which has led to an internationally accepted way to present news programmes and which rarely includes maps. A typical segment of a news programme begins with an introduction from a news presenter followed by video-taped coverage of the news event with a narration read by the reporter and video-tape of the reporter speaking to camera, often known as a 'stand-up piece'. The whole news story must fit within this format and within a preset time-frame to allow for other stories, produced in the same fashion, during the remainder of the news programme. However this format has serious limitations. It is an axiom of audiovisual story-telling that sound and vision must complement each other and yet basic geopolitical information, vital to understanding where and why the action is taking place, is routinely included with narration describing the action. As a result television news reports are produced with narration and images which do not complement each other and, typically, the strength of the visual action, either in close-up or in the background to a reporter's stand-up piece to camera, almost completely removes a viewer's capacity to hear, let alone understand, what is being said by the reporter, except that narration which relates to the action on the screen at the time. Where news reports are produced with complementing narration and images, there is nowhere within the report to include information which does not relate to the action.

If geopolitical or more complex social, political and economic information is needed to understand the background to the story, it is my contention that the way to do so is to use the kind of computer-generated maps I have suggested, either within the reporter's story or during the studio-based introduction by the news presenter.

However, in addition to the limitations imposed by the accepted approach to the presentation of television news, there are, in my view, three main reasons for the reluctance amongst television news journalists to use maps. Firstly, there is an emphasis on the perceived need to select only those images which contain action. Secondly, there is a belief that spelling out the geopolitical background to a story is like being a teacher with a white board, the use and repetition of which in future bulletins would lose, not attract, audiences. In any event this is not the role of a news journalist. Thirdly, and most importantly, providing backgrounders would take up valuable air time.

The television journalists have a strong case, which is supported by Postman (1986), who argues:

> The single most important fact about television is that people watch it, which is why it is called television. And what they watch, and like to watch, are moving pictures – millions of them, of short duration and dynamic variety. It is in the nature of the medium that it must suppress the content of ideas in order to accommodate the requirements of visual interest; that is to say, to accommodate the values of show business.

This view is also held by Robert MacNeil (1983), former executive editor and co-anchor of the *MacNeil-Lehrer Newshour* broadcast each weeknight on the American Public Broadcasting System (PBS), who wrote: 'The idea . . . is to keep everything brief, not to strain the attention of anyone but instead to provide constant stimulation through variety, novelty, action and movement. You are required . . . to pay attention to no concept, no character and no problem for more than a few seconds at a time.'

Each day, BBC World and CNN broadcast NATO briefings on the progress of the attacks on Yugoslavia. These briefings were orchestrated by the military establishment – white boards, coloured maps, media monitors and finally curtains which open and close on cue. The war as entertainment format of these news conferences by the generals and media managers concentrated on visuals with computer graphics and video toys such as 'bombcams' to zero in on the target with no human perspective or reality. The rhetoric and propaganda in the political speeches, such as British Foreign Secretary Robin Cook's prepared monologue on 13 April 1999, are reminiscent of the narrator of supposed war footage in the futuristic film of George Orwell's novel *1984*.

I argue that the professional practices of journalists should be reviewed and the development of visually stimulating computer graphics programmes encouraged and adopted as part of the armoury of a modern television newsroom. Nightly television coverage of the Balkans war did not include adequate visual depictions of the geopolitical landscape, did not provide a comprehensive social and economic background to the conflict, and did not relate it to the most recent problems in Bosnia-Hertzegovina. What it did was focus on military strikes, the plight of the refugees, and Slobodan Milosevic as the anti-Christ who, like Saddam Hussain, was personally responsible for the alleged human rights violations in Kosovo. Preparation of a series of backgrounder segments incorporating visually dramatic computer graphics, written and produced to avoid the appearance of repetition, would have overcome much of the concerns of television journalists and editors and meet the expectations of viewers, who, as Postman (1986) argues, expect television to deliver moving pictures – millions of them, of short duration and dynamic variety.

References

MacNeil, Robert (1983) 'Is television shortening our attention span?' *New York University Education Quarterly*, 14:2, Winter 1983, quoted in Postman, Neil (1986) *Amusing ourselves to death, public discourse in the age of show business*. New York: Penguin.

Postman, Neil (1986) *Amusing ourselves to death, public discourse in the age of show business*. New York: Penguin.

Sheldon, H. H. & Grisewood, E. N. (1930) *The future of television*. New York: D. Van Nostrand Company Inc.

Sarnoff, David (1936) 'Television in advertising', excerpts from 'The message of radio', an address delivered before the Advertising Federation of America, Boston.

About the authors

Bruce Allen lectures at the Macquarie University Centre for International Communication, Sydney, Australia (www.mucic.mq.edu.au) and is a Media Consultant specialising in media regulation. He is a former Member of the Australian Broadcasting Tribunal and has produced television programmes in Australia, Canada and the United Kingdom. His Master of Journalism is from Carleton University, Ottawa, Canada. E-mail: ballen@laurel.ocs.mq.edu.au

Belinda Barnet is eCommerce Producer for NRMA Insurance Limited, a member company of NRMA Insurance Group. She is doing her PhD in Hypermedia at the University of New South Wales, and was a Visiting Scholar at the University of Baltimore in late 2000. Her work has appeared in journals such as *Continuum, Metro, Convergence, M/C* and (soon!) the *American Book Review*. E-mail: belinda@senet.com.au

Melissa Butcher completed the chapter in this book on the basis of research undertaken for her Ph D thesis, completed at the Macquarie University Centre for International Communication, Sydney, Australia. Currently she is Project Manager/Researcher at the Institute of Cultural Research, University of Western Sydney, Australia. E-mail: m.butcher@uws.edu.au

Naren Chitty is Director of the Macquarie University Centre for International Communication (www.mucic.mq.edu.au), Editor-in-Chief of *The Journal of International Communication*, Convenor of the Under-Represented Areas Network for Media and Communication Research (www.mucic.mq.edu.au), and a former Secretary General of the International Association for Media & Communication Research. His PhD in International Relations is from American University, Washington DC, USA. E-mail: nchitty@ocs1.ocs.mq.edu.au

Hart Cohen is a Senior Lecturer in media in the School of Communication, Design and Media at the University of Western Sydney, Australia. He coordinates media production in the Bachelor of Communication (Media) and the MA in Communication and Cultural Studies. He is currently Editor of the journal *Australian-Canadian Studies* and recently guest edited a special supplement on the work of Marshall McLuhan for *Media International Australia* (No. 94, February 2000). In 2001, Dr Cohen wrote and directed a one-hour documentary film on the life and work of T. G. H. Strehlow titled *Mr Strehlow's films* for SBS TV. E-mail: h.cohen@uws.edu.au

Stephen McElhinney lectures at the Macquarie University Centre for International Communication, Sydney, Australia. He has worked previously in policy research for the Australian Department of Communications, the Communications Law Centre and the Privacy Commission. He received his PhD from Macquarie University. E-mail: skmcelhinney@yahoo.com.au

Anura Goonasekera is Deputy Director General of the Asian Media Information and Communication Centre (AMIC) Singapore and is an Adjunct Professor in the School of Communication Studies of the Nanyang Technological University, Singapore. He is a former Director General of National Television and a Permanent Secretary in Sri Lanka. E-mail: amicline@singnet.com.sg

Suda Ishida is a graduate of the Macquarie University Centre for International Communication, Sydney, Australia. She is a candidate for a PhD at the University of Iowa. E-mail: suda-ishida@uiowa.edu

Adam Knee, Assistant Professor in the Department of English at Mansfield University of Pennsylvania, holds a doctorate in cinema studies from New York University. He has previously taught at universities in Australia, Taiwan and Thailand. E-mail: adamknee@hotmail.com

Sripan Rattikalchalakorn lectures at the Macquarie University Centre for International Communication, Sydney, Australia. She is a graduate of Chulalongkorn University. She is a candidate for a PhD at Macquarie University. E-mail: srattika@ocs1.ocs.mq.edu.au

Jan Servaes and Patchanee Malikhao are members of the Macquarie University Centre for International Communication, Sydney, Australia. A former Dean of the Faculty of Social Science of the Free University in Brussels, Belgium, Jan Servaes is President of the European Consortium for Communication Research and a Vice President of the International Association for Media & Communication Research. E-mail: freenet002@pi.be

Scott Shaner lectures at the Macquarie University Centre for International Communication, Sydney, Australia. He is a graduate of State University of New York. E-mail: S.shaner@unsw.edu.com

Momoyo Shibuya completed her chapter in this book on the basis of research being undertaken currently for her PhD thesis, at Macquarie University Centre for International Communication, Sydney, Australia. E-mail: mshibuya@laurel.ocs.mq.edu.au

McKenzie Wark is Associate Director of the Macquarie University Centre for International Communication, Sydney, Australia and author of *Virtual geography*. E-mail: mwark@ocs1.ocs.mq.edu.au

Yong Zhong completed his chapter in this book on the basis of research undertaken for his PhD thesis, completed at the Macquarie University Centre for International Communication, Sydney, Australia. Currently he is a Senior Lecturer at the University of New South Wales, Sydney, Australia. E-mail: Y.zhong@unsw.edu.au